P9-EAI-515

DATE DUE

MY 19'98		
DE 2 0'00		
SE 9'04		
JE 6'05		
MY 23'10		

DEMCO 38-296

THE CULT FILM EXPERIENCE

Texas Film Studies Series
Thomas Schatz, Editor

The Cult Film Experience

Beyond All Reason

Edited by J. P. Telotte

UNIVERSITY OF TEXAS PRESS, AUSTIN

Riverside Community College
Library
4800 Magnolia Avenue
MAY '93   Riverside, California 92506

Copyright © 1991 by the University of Texas Press
All rights reserved
Printed in the United States of America

First Edition, 1991

Requests for permission to reproduce material from this
work should be sent to Permissions, University of Texas
Press, Box 7819, Austin, Texas 78713-7819.

⊗ The paper used in this publication meets the mini-
mum requirements of American National Standard for
Information Sciences—Permanence of Paper for Printed
Library Materials, ANSI Z39.48-1984.

Library of Congress Cataloging-in-Publication Data

The Cult film experience : beyond all reason / edited by
J. P. Telotte. — 1st ed.
     p.   cm. — (Texas film studies series.)
     Includes bibliographical references, (p.
     Includes index.
     ISBN 0-292-71135-2 (alk. paper)
     1. Motion pictures. 2. Motion picture audiences—
United States. 3. United States—Popular culture—
History—20th century. I. Telotte, J. P., 1949–
II. Series.
PN1995.C78   1991
791.43—dc20   90-12965
                                   CIP

Contents

Photos following pages **3, 41,** and **105**

Acknowledgments

Many people have been involved in the production of this volume, and much patience was sorely tried in its journey to press. I here want to thank those numerous individuals for their help, encouragement, and forbearance. My contributors especially deserve plaudits for their calm endurance and unflagging interest, as I revised their work, revisioned the entire project, and far too often neglected my correspondence with them.

More particularly, I need to acknowledge several special debts: first, to Larry Vonalt and Jim Card, who put together the original seminar from which this volume grew; second, to Marshall Deutelbaum of Purdue University for his advice, encouragement, and early participation in this project; and finally to Jim Welsh and Tom Schatz, whose insightful readings of the essays and suggestions for reorganization gave final shape to this volume and helped make it a highly readable and coherent collection.

Finally, I want to thank Frankie Westbrook, my editor at the University of Texas Press, for her patience with and encouragement of this volume; my colleagues at Georgia Tech for contributing to an environment in which my strange interests can be pursued; and my family, especially my wife, Leigh, for the understanding and support that ultimately made this book possible.

PART I

Introduction:
Mapping the Cult

The various articles grouped here sketch the broad outlines of the cult film experience. While they clearly share certain basic assumptions, though, these perspectives just as obviously do not represent a single methodology, ideology, or critical agenda. Thus, even as they commonly recognize in the cult film experience a near kinship to other sorts of cult activity, particularly religious cults, in terms of group dynamics, privileged texts, and esoteric knowledge, in other ways these pieces should seem quite uncultish, perhaps even heretical. They freely disagree, for instance, as to what a cult film is, how we should go about defining it, and especially whether a work might be designed from the start as a cult piece. However, this disagreement seems a healthy, perhaps even a necessary characteristic for a volume such as this if it intends to suggest the scope of both the cult phenomenon and the diverse discussions it has already engendered.

Where these essays are clearly alike is in their mutual assumption that there are certain dominant sorts of cult films. Thus these pieces, as well as those that follow in the volume, commonly describe the broad field of cult films by locating two poles: the classical cult film and the midnight movie. Of course, these are not the only films that we might label "cult." The "art film," for example, particularly as it was constituted in the late 1950s and early 1960s, generally involved a specific set of narrative practices different from those of the Hollywood cinema, addressed a different audience, and played in a pointedly different venue, the now nearly defunct "art house." In today's market, though, the small art film has itself almost disappeared, and films that might once have fit this almost generic category often end up playing at midnight showings or in repertory theaters. While the classical and the midnight cult films are not the sole types, therefore, they are used here simply to mark off a field of cult activity—of film types and film viewing practices that are themselves constantly changing.

There are, we might note, a few other constants here, reminders that the various speakers are neither talking in a vacuum nor addressing wildly different cultures than our own. While some effort has been made to eliminate unnecessary duplication, for instance, a certain number of critical sources and theories repeatedly surface, reminding us that the essays here speak within a particular critical community. The movies themselves also provide a useful constant; titles like *Casablanca, The Women, The Rocky Horror Picture Show, Pink Flamingos,* and *Repo Man* recur, serving as both regular points of reference for an ever-expanding canon (if we can use that term a bit loosely in this context) and as yardsticks for different sorts of cult-audience response. In fact, all of the essays included in this introductory section approach the cult film from a generally similar angle, as they explore the relationship these works establish with their audience and the sorts of responses they typically evoke.

Within that broad similarity of approach, though, there remains much room for disagreement about just what constitutes the cult film. My own essay offers overview of the territory to be traversed in this volume. It does not so much try to map this territory as to suggest its dimensions, first by sketching its general boundaries, and then by describing a kind of activity that occurs within its precincts. While the tendency of critics is to think of these films generically, the bounds of the cult clearly seem to be drawn a bit differently from those of more traditional film genres. What my essay describes, therefore, is the sort of "supertext" that the cult constitutes. Given that broad, or "super," field that it operates within, this piece then tries to explain its appeal through a pattern of boundary crossings or territorial "violations" that the cult film permits its audience to enjoy.

In his essay Bruce Kawin sets out to define the cult film in a far more personal and dynamic way, describing it as a kind of individual encounter that speaks in very different ways to diverse viewers. Drawing on the midnight movie as his primary model, he explores the nature of that after-dark encounter and metaphorically extends it to suggest a common need we have for such "dark" experiences. As he ranges over a variety of these films, Kawin synthesizes what might almost be described as a *personality* for the cult work—a dark personality that reflects and appeals to some equally dark, repressed, or "other" aspect of our own selves. What he finds valuable in the cult film experience, then, is this nearly personal encounter, what he describes as a shock of mutual recognition that ministers to a deep-felt desire for self-affirmation.

Timothy Corrigan similarly focuses on a kind of need satisfaction to which the cult film caters. However, he finds the real lure of these works not so much in their unexpected familiarity, but in their very strangeness. In part, he echoes the geographical trope of the first essay by describing the cult moviegoer as a kind of "accidental tourist," who finds great pleasure in this casual encounter with a cultural terra incognita, that is, with the images of our world that these films frame and present to us in a decidedly different, almost "foreign" context. This encounter, Corrigan suggests, typically results in a special sort of appropriation, a kind of souvenir gathering, as the viewer takes something from this public encounter back to his or her private life and thereby enriches it. In a telling shift of tropes, he then suggests that in this act of appropriation the work becomes much like an "adopted child"—almost alive and, while not really our own, still embraced, *loved* as if it were.

Together, these introductory essays should begin to suggest the protean nature of the cult film, as well as the challenge it poses to the ways we commonly think about film. This first section should therefore seem by turns quite conservative and a bit unconventional, as it attempts to relate this phenomenon to more traditional patterns of film criticism and to demonstrate some rather different ways of approaching this rather different film experience.

The classical cult film—*Casablanca*. (Warner Bros.)

The defining image of the midnight movie, Frank-N-Furter of *The Rocky Horror Picture Show*. (Twentieth Century–Fox)

James Dean—the archetypal
cult figure of the movies.
(Warner Bros.)

Rita Hayworth as icon of
feminine allure in *Gilda*.
(Columbia/Museum of
Modern Art)

The idealized romantic couple—Bogart and Bacall in *Dark Passage*. (Warner Bros.)

The Marx Brothers and their brand of anarchic comedy have developed a large cult following. (Paramount)

CHAPTER 1

Beyond All Reason: The Nature of the Cult

J. P. Telotte

I stopped lowering my head at the epithet "cultist" as soon as I realized that the quasi-religious connotation of the term was somewhat justified for those of us who loved movies beyond all reason.

—Andrew Sarris, *Confessions of a Cultist*

It is likely that transgression has its entire space in the line it crosses. The play of limits and transgression seems to be regulated by a simple obstinacy: transgression incessantly crosses and recrosses a line which closes up behind it in a wave of extremely short duration, and thus it is made to return once more to the horizon of the uncrossable.

—Michel Foucault, *Language, Counter-Memory, Practice*

W e do not usually think of the film cultist, of the often bizarrely costumed patron queued up outside a theater showing *The Rocky Horror Picture Show*, for example, in Andrew Sarris's terms, as someone who just loves movies. But Sarris's qualifier, that the cultist loves films "beyond all reason," *is* a point worth considering, for there is indeed something strange, even beyond reason in the relation between the cult film in its various manifestations and its nearly worshipful audience. In that movement beyond reason, beyond the usual ways of seeing, caring about, and identifying with a film or its characters, the cultist embraces a comfortable difference: from those who find film a brief diversion or pleasure, but of little lasting interest; from those who give scant attention to film, seeing little of themselves in its admittedly alluring imagery; even from those who take film quite seriously, but bridle at the excessive attachment or identification that marks some moviegoers. Cultists might well be said to *love* such differences, for to them they suggest something unusual, noteworthy, and valuable not just about the movies, but about their own character, too.

What the film cultist embraces is a form that, in its very difference, transgresses, violates our sense of the reasonable. It crosses boundaries of time, custom, form, and—many might add—good taste. And this is the case whether we are talking about classical films that have been resurrected by a special audience or the popular "midnight movies." In fact, the popularity of both draws on their challenge to certain norms usually associated with the movie experience. And that challenge masks another sort of unreason, for as Foucault implies, the act of transgression may be little more than a gesture; it might only signal a kind of cook's tour of various formal and cultural borders that, in the end, simply returns us "to the horizon of the uncrossable," to a world of reason where we can relish the *feeling* of transgression. Still, that tour has proved quite popular, a transgression many love, and one that, I would suggest, speaks of the seemingly *unreasonable* way popular films often appear to work.

In using the term "cult" to mark off a group of films for study, I may already be suggesting another sort of transgression. For such an approach implies a kind of routine genre criticism, rooted in the idea that "cult" marks off a reasonably distinguishable film genre. That is a notion that many would quickly and justifiably challenge, for what we commonly label "cult" has come to embrace a very broad narrative territory. And even if we accept the notion of cult as genre, it clearly differs from others. As John Cawelti notes, "The essence of genre criticism is the construction of what . . . might be called a macro- or supertext. The supertext (genre) claims to be an abstract of the most significant characteristics or family resemblances among many particular texts, which can accordingly be analyzed, evaluated, and otherwise related to each other by virtue of their connection with the supertext" (56). So even if we conveniently describe the cult film as a genre and trace out characteristic markings or "family resemblances," those markings will never quite produce the sort of relationships that genre usually implies. The reason is that with the cult film we are hardpressed to find a clear "supertext" or storehouse for the form's varied stylistic and thematic elements. The cult film simply transgresses even the boundaries we usually associate with the very notion of genre.

In fact, many of the elements that link such disparate films as *Casablanca* (1942), *Rebel without a Cause* (1955), *The Rocky Horror Picture Show* (1975), and *Liquid Sky* (1983) fall outside genre study's normal focus on plot, setting, character type, and theme. Instead, we find ourselves examining such often overlooked concerns as strategies of presentation and audience response.[1] The point is that an aesthetic of the cult film, as well as models for thinking about it, is still evolving; and one goal of this collection is to help in that evolution. Faced with the sort of difficulties noted above, then, I want to begin by suggesting that we simply alter our usual notion of "supertext," drawing the generic circle more broadly, extending its bounds beyond the purely textual to include the audience and its seemingly unreasonable "love" for these films.

Let us consider a simple initial definition of the cult film that includes these elements: it is a type marked by both its highly specified and limited audience as well as a singular pleasure that this audience finds in the film's transgressions. Of course, it may well be that a particular cult film, *Casablanca,* for example, at one time appealed to a large and varied moviegoing public, and for quite conventional reasons, just as it is equally possible, as *Rocky Horror* suggests, that the cult work has at some point had great difficulty locating *any* audience prior to its successful cult incarnation. But in that life—or second life, if you will—it seems to speak meaningfully (or *lovingly*) to a select group.

While this distinction is a simple one, it reflects tellingly on our normal film marketing and viewing practices. In the United States, after all, feature films are generally targeted at and marketed for the broadest possible audience, as production companies, distributors, and theater owners all try to capture as great a share of the viewing dollar as possible. As a result, most films still take the most conservative path, following a classical narrative pattern that reiterates far from disturbing truisms about the moviegoers' culture. Controversial topics tend to disappear—or to dissolve in the most simplistic imaginary formulations. So there is nothing to truly offend, nothing to hate, but by the same token often little *to love*. At its extreme, this practice leads to the current sequel mania, as almost every film that demonstrates a certain earning power quickly generates a slightly modified sequel, prequel, or third cousin—so we get, and perhaps as a culture well deserve, a *Friday the 13th, Part*[n].

Against this backdrop, the conjunction of a *limited* audience and a limited, even unconventionally measured *success* becomes significant. For it underscores how that "love" aspect of the cult film functions: it works in a realm of *difference*—from normal film viewing practices and from marketing customs. And this realm of difference, the space beyond the "line" Foucault describes, derives from a number of factors that contribute to the cult supertext, ranging from elements of the film narrative, to its exhibition practices, to the audience's needs, and to a spirit of the times (which effectively constructs that audience).

It might be argued, as film historian Gerald Mast does, that some variations of the cult film work otherwise. He sees several briefly popular groups of films as signaling the emergence of a new, deliberate marketing strategy by the American film industry. Influenced by the unanticipated popularity of the so-called "underground" films of the late 1960s and early 1970s,[2] especially the work of filmmakers like Robert Downey, Brian De Palma, and the Andy Warhol–Paul Morrissey team, and impelled by the increasing difficulty of competing with television for the larger entertainment market, the industry, according to Mast, embraced "elitism"; that is, it adopted a practice of segmenting and targeting potential film audiences, much as other American industries—the automobile and soft drink industries especially—have segmented and targeted particular consumer groups. Rather than trying "to make all of the films for all of the people, producers and exhibitors realized that they must appeal to very special tastes" (423). As evidence, he points to the appearance in the late 1960s of such special-audience forms as the "blaxploitation" film, the new "art" films of directors like Arthur Penn, Mike Nichols, and Robert Altman, and "sexploitation" films aimed at a variety of sexual orientations and tastes.

However, this targeting explanation cannot bear too much weight, since many films that gain a cult label and following are never successful through normal patterns of film distribution. In fact, many seem to become cult works largely because their audience—their potential lovers—*cannot* be accurately assessed through conventional wisdom, much less segmented and targeted. Indeed, many works initially gain a cult aura more because of anticanonical and extraindustrial forces, although distribution practices invariably try to follow the lure of new audience dollars. For example, a rising gay awareness, coupled with the new feminist consciousness, clearly has much to do with the resurrection and cult embrace of an old and conventional Hollywood hit like *The Women* (1939). And a more recent film like *The Rocky Horror Picture Show*—which inspired its own unsuccessful sequel, *Shock Treatment* (1981)—seems to owe much of its phenomenal success to its unique blurring of genre forms, which attests to both an appreciation and violation of certain classical narrative formulas. What Mast helps us see, though, is how much the cult relies for its very existence on what we normally think of as extratextual matters, in effect, how much the cult film's nature depends on both its own amorphous shape and a set of industrial practices divorced from a specific film's creation.

These matters that challenge our usual notion of a supertext also help account for a major difficulty we have in explaining the appearance or popularity of the cult film. All of our explanations, after all, must consider two very different sorts of films that together tend to be lumped into the cult category. On the one hand, we typically label as "cult" a number of conventionally successful films, usually resurrected from Hollywood's past, the period of classical film narrative. The list of works that fall into this category is long and subject to change, but it almost invariably includes films like *Gone with the Wind* (1939), *The Women, Fantasia* (1940), *Citizen Kane* (1941), *Rebel without a Cause,* and most obviously *Casablanca.* These films generally appeal to a heterogeneous audience, albeit one apparently united by a certain fondness for the conventions and appeals of classical narrative, and by an almost worshipful—and thus truly cultish—attitude toward particular figures from Hollywood's so-called "golden age"—Humphrey Bogart, Joan Crawford, James Cagney, Judy Garland.

Our love of such films turns partially upon their previous success: their prior ability to evoke a desirable or soothing response, particularly through their stars' numinous quality, and our desire to repeat that earlier experience or even to enjoy it for the first time. In effect, they evoke a kind of nostalgic thrill, even if it is only the pleasure of a parvenue. But we would be mistaken to see that as the sole reason for their cult status and success, since the ways in which they speak and the themes they develop are equally important. For example, it almost goes without saying that the Bogart and Dean personas, bearing their burdens of existential angst or youthful frustration, are mainly responsible for the continuing appeal of films like *Casablanca* and *Rebel without a Cause,* while Joan Crawford's spirit and emotional strength in a work like *Mildred Pierce* (1945) clearly strike a responsive chord in modern audiences attuned to feminist issues.

Yet such iconic figures also work so powerfully upon us *because of* their placement in time. For despite their rootedness in an era, they display a remarkable ability to live on through and, in effect, outside of history. Like one of modern fiction's cult figures, Kurt Vonnegut's Billy Pilgrim, they are "unstuck in time" and, in that transgression of temporal bounds, win a kind of victory over it. Our nostalgic attachment to such figures thus carries a double weight. On the one hand, those human icons evoke all the more keenly a modern sense of estrangement and alienation that we commonly feel, as we increasingly seem bound to an unsatisfying time, an era that somehow feels not quite right. But on the other, they suggest a hope of overcoming the present, or at least breaking free of the stifling mundanity that seems to mark it. Such cult figures essentially represent what Christopher Lasch terms "ego-ideals": "admired, idealized images," in a most fundamental sense, *loved ones.* In their ability to capture "the contradictory quality of unconscious mental life" (178–180), he argues, such images prove "indispensable" for our well-being. For by speaking simultaneously of our place in "the natural world" and of our "capacity to transcend it," they offer a soothing, imaginary release from the various tensions that impinge on the modern psyche.

Initially, we might see a somewhat different appeal, due partly to its different audience, in that other type of movie we often term "cult." In fact, the small, far more homogeneous audience—usually identified by age and social situation—and the special viewing circumstances they prefer quickly distinguish the midnight movie from the classical cult film. The former's audience is usually the middle-class teenager and young adult, the 17- to 24-year-old group that often—as a sort of rite of passage—sees itself as separate from the cultural mainstream. This subculture's interests and concerns—drugs, rock music, sexual experience, alienation from their parents and established society—clearly surface in such films as *Night of the Living Dead* (1968), *The Fantastic Planet* (1973), *The Harder They Come* (1973), *The Texas Chain Saw Massacre* (1974), *Eraserhead* (1978), *Liquid Sky,* and the most popular of midnight films—indeed, the one that has prescribed so much of the behavior that helps define them—*The Rocky Horror Picture Show.*

The typical venue for these films is the midnight showing, usually at suburban mall theaters rather than art or rerun houses. And this alternate viewing practice seems essential, a defining characteristic of the midnight movie, as we have come to call it; in fact, it is part of its true supertext. For the midnight film, like a kind of forbidden love, apparently loses much of its appeal in a conventional or culturally sanctioned context; it is simply no longer *sub*cultural and other. Even the traditional art house—the few that remain—cannot quite sustain this context, since it bears a burden of intellectual pretension and acceptance, by virtue of being a home for *recognized* art, a *sanctioned* venue for difference (nonmainstream viewing practices). For the same reason, it is nearly unthinkable for the midnight circuit's films to appear on television as well and still retain their full cult appeal, since it is precisely their alterity that we love in them. Originally, they may have seen little or no main-line distribution, and hence slight or no box office success. They have only been properly mated to an audience—and found profit—on this special late-night circuit.

Another obvious distinction between the classical cult film and its midnight movie alter ego lies in their respective conditions of production. Sourced in the Hollywood studio system, the classical work is typically marked by a large budget, a big-name cast, technical expertise, and a measure of original and conventional success—all of which signal a cinematic status quo and quickly mark it off from the "outsider" cinema of a *Putney Swope* (1969), *Pink Flamingos* (1970), or *Eraserhead.* The stories of George Romero's use of friends and neighbors to flesh out his cast of zombies and of his simple but effective "special effects"—such as raw meat from the local butcher—for *Night of the Living Dead* are well known, and they suggest just the sort of *bricolage* that characterizes these films, a catch-as-catch-can approach toward production that seems more their rule than an exception. Perhaps the forthrightly "crude" look that often results not only underscores their difference from mainstream cinema, but also hints at their basic appeal, specifically, their ability to play effectively at the very margins of cinematic illusion. By turns, they seem to make us aware of that illusion—of what we term the "cinematic imaginary"[3]—and, by the persistence of its power, to draw us into that realm, allowing us to relish our awareness of the illusion, and to willfully abandon ourselves to its lure. *Rocky Horror,* for example, repeatedly calls attention to the iconography and patterns of the classical cinema, including the RKO logo in one scene, even as it deploys various genre conventions that help cue our responses to and ensure our participation in its narrative. This dual pull might also explain the "camp" attraction we find in such pointedly *bad* cult films as *Reefer Madness* (1936) or *Plan 9 from Outer Space* (1959). But more important, it recalls the complex nature of the "love"—its "contradictory quality"—we noted in the classical cult film and its iconic personalities.

Despite some obvious differences, then, the two broad categories of cult film identified here have much in common that justifies grouping them generically. For example, they seem to respond to audience needs— and thus *define* their audiences—in a fundamentally similar way. That is, they evoke a kind of subcultural desire, a desire not simply for difference, but for an identifiable and even *common* difference, in effect, for a *safe* difference that is, ultimately, nearly not difference at all. While classical cult films project appealing images that speak to the contradictions in our present lives, midnight movies fashion a context of difference—of rebellion, independence, sexual freedom, gender shifting—that helps us cope with real-world conformity. In common, they offer a kind of loving understanding that acknowledges our own sense of difference or alienation, even as it mates us to other, similarly "different" types in the audience or the films themselves.

Of course, the forces of modern mass culture always seem to pull us in very different directions. On the one hand, all the forces of mass culture typically urge us to conform, to be like everyone else. Indeed, television, radio, film, and the other voices of culture address us as if we are one, and the lure of answering that voice, of identifying oneself as the subject of that direct address, is great. So we wear the same jeans, buy the proper running shoes, eat at the fast-food chains of current choice. But we also comply partly because of other voices we hear, those that admonish us to assert *our* individuality; in many cases, we even hear that wearing those jeans, buying those running shoes, or eating at certain places is the surest mark of such individuality. We might well see the cult film, then, with its highly ritualistic conditions of presentation, as a kind of mass (i.e., "religious" service) of cultural contradiction, calling us to worship simultaneously gods of difference and sameness, or at least permitting us to feel better about those unresolved cultural contradictions in which we instinctively feel ourselves enmeshed.[4]

In light of this impulse, it is most fitting that the very term "cult" bears a curiously double implication that harkens back to Sarris's original notion of "love"—a term I may already have stretched beyond common recognition. Most often, we use that term to signal a feared or ominous difference, such as when newspaper headlines speculate on the role of cult religions or satanic groups in the latest crime. Fundamentally, though, used in this way, "cult" could refer to any organized minority beliefs that threaten the status quo. When so deployed, it intellectually exiles the group, thing, or theology so designated beyond the pale of the normal or accepted, certainly outside the circle of our "love." The thing so designated seems potentially dangerous in a vague *variety* of ways; the subcultural has simply become subversion itself. The term "cult," consequently, often becomes a kind of warning sign, a psychic surgeon general's report, denoting taboo intellectual, emotional, and even spiritual territory.

And yet the cult is also desire itself, a longing to *express* the self, to express difference. The cult film, after all, is a way we have of crossing boundaries, even if we let others share in that brief, satisfying transgression. Such sharing still expresses our yearning for distinction; we at least want to *feel* different from the norm and from the conventional self we are supposed to become. So the cult film, whether in the reggae rhythms of *The Harder They Come* or the new-wave sensibility of a *Liquid Sky*, becomes for a time—or perhaps, as with the multiple viewings of *Rocky Horror*, for time after time—our voice, our vantage, an expressive mask we don to speak in ways we ordinarily cannot.

The act of differentiation is thus fundamentally linked to the sort of love we feel for/through these films. If the imagery and themes of some of these films seem to have something of the aura of "forbidden fruit," it is because they embody a most basic desire. For the cult audience implicitly desires something unavailable in the undifferentiated world; and the cult promises a meaning different from that handed down or sanctioned by society and its privileged institutions. It thus holds the implicit appeal of the secret, the cabalistic, and that appeal gains in potency by suggesting a lack of real meaning, significance, or relevance in the everyday world—even the sort of slipping away of the real that Jean Baudrillard has so persuasively described.[5] At the same time, this privileged knowledge promises a freedom, since its very alterity suggests a release: temporarily from reality itself, as Baudrillard would suggest, or simply from the dominant culture, as cultists assert their special character—as when *Rocky Horror* devotees dress up like their favorite characters and, in so doing, temporarily discard their normal, culturally determined identities. In this way, the cult fills a human need—or desire—one made all the more pressing by the routine, repetitive, and impersonal nature of modern technological societies such as ours.

Of course, we also *need* society *for* our identity; every subculture implicitly constitutes itself as an alternative to the establishment. For this reason, we should note that "cult" is also clearly linked to "culture," and thus to the body of human society and all that we imply when we label someone or something *acculturated*—that is, made one with the group in its most fundamental beliefs or practices. From this vantage, we might better understand the body of practices that clusters around every cult film, whether a midnight movie or classical narrative. Memorizing dialogue, practicing gestures, wearing costumes, and attending repeatedly are required. In effect, a body of ritual, of the sort that marks both the religious and theatrical experiences, attends the cult film experience and, in the process, gives it, almost in spite of itself, a clearly social dimension. It effectively constructs a culture in small, and thus an island of meaning for an audience that senses an absence of meaningful social structures or coherence in the life outside the theater.

In essence, therefore, every cult constitutes a community, a group that "worships" similarly and regularly, and finds a strength in that shared experience. The true *Rocky Horror* experience, for example, depends on more than just a time slot that differentiates the film and its viewers, the cult object and its worshippers, from a world of daylight and conventional viewing habits. It relies on a set of practices or conventions shared by the devotees. And the demonstrated knowledge of those things certifies the initiates, binds them in their privileged knowledge to others—and even to another side of the self, a repressed self that longs to be known *other*wise and to find expression. Knowing and even reciting lines of dialogue are part of this bonding ritual—a "wisdom" of the other—but as *Rocky Horror* again dramatically demonstrates, such a practice goes beyond sheer rote. For one thing, it can involve a participatory action, as audiences anticipate lines and furnish answers to rhetorical questions, or as those who come costumed as screen characters prance around the auditorium at set times in the narrative (doing "The Time Warp," for instance), as if affirming, if only briefly, that their usually prosaic world is coextensive with another, admired, and exciting one. For another, it invokes a kind of transubstantiation as well, a transformation of the cinematic event into something totally outside the diegesis, such as when, on a specific cue and as a demonstration of their initiate status, viewers hurl rice or slices of bread toward the screen. The glory of successfully negotiating these tests of understanding—reciting dialogue, answering questions *in unison*, knowing what to hold up or throw into the audience and *when*, situates viewers in a new community. They know their catechism. And that acceptance is reaffirmed by the repeat experience.

It is only natural, then, that both "cult" and "culture" come from the same root, although one with its own varied implications. For the original Latin term *cultus* signifies both "worship" and "cultivation," an act of adherence and mastery, submission and domination. Perhaps we might even say, with an eye to traditional use of the terms, that it hints of both the feminine and masculine, and thus always of an opposite side of the self that we might, deep down, desire. The etymological underpinnings of "cult," then, point to a dual impulse. These films let us join in common worship, acknowledge common allegiance to a god of sorts, and admit our common possession *by* that god. But they also let us cultivate our own gardens, grow individually beyond the rules and roles laid out by society. In effect, they let us possess and be possessed, as in a real love relationship, surrendering the self in a most satisfying *self*-expression.

At the same time, the films participate in the ongoing ideological project of the mass media. They contribute to the constructing of a cultural cinematic imaginary, for example, by building upon the pantheon of gods and mythic actions already established in Hollywood legend, or by contributing new images for commercialization and exploitation. The song "Don't Dream It, Be It," one of *Rocky Horror*'s paeans to difference, for example, has recently provided the melody for a cotton fabrics commercial on television. But even as they work in these conventional, even co-opted ways, cult films also manage to assert their own difference, cultivating a new, separate life that continues to grow outside of the normal nurturing conditions of conventional production and exhibition practices. Thus certain figures of difference, spawned by cults, haunt our movies and our psyches: the Bogart persona codified in *Casablanca;* Leatherface, the killer in *The Texas Chain Saw Massacre* and model for the unending *Friday the 13th* series; or the late Divine, John Waters' 300-pound transvestite star.

While we seem to talk about two different types of films, then, I want to emphasize that we are also talking about two common thrusts that mark and link these films. Whether it is the classical narrative redivivus or the midnight movie, our subject has two thrusts. Part—the most visible part— of its appeal is the way it transgresses the normal to fashion a statement of difference. In going to a cult film, we embrace the other in us—the com-

mitted hero in the uninvolved cynic (*Casablanca*), the rebel in every ma-
turing teenager (*Rebel without a Cause*), the gay in the straight (*Rocky Horror*). But because of the insecurity that embrace implies, we also need a
stable ground from which to make that assertion, a ground *within* the very
boundaries we seem to transgress. Thus these films also express a fundamental *need* for culture, for a society that will let us, from time to time,
acknowledge our difference. And that necessary society is not just one of
similar transgressors, of other *different* types—as in *King of Hearts'* alternate world of the insane or *Liquid Sky's* punk subculture—but the social
world we daily inhabit. Acknowledging that world as ultimately inescapable, our cult films, in their minor subversions and assertions of individuality, finally help us love it, too.

I am already hinting at why this phenomenon of the cult film has
emerged, as well as why the lure—and life span—of some cult films seems
so weak. While many films aim at a very specific market—the youth market, black moviegoers, a rural audience—it is clearly difficult to *design* a
film for cult status. Arranged marriages seldom work, and trying to dictate
desire seems almost inimical to the cult spirit, as the failure of *Rocky Horror's* sequel, *Shock Treatment,* attests. As Sam Kitt of Libra Films, dis-
tributor of many successful cult movies, notes, the cult experience usually
involves a "discovery on the part of the audience," assuring them "that
they're part of an inner circle. *Rocky Horror* is the best example of this. It is
a need to identify with something, to have something that is emblematic of
their feelings" (Strout 74). As is the case with most successful films, the
cult work touches some deep-felt and perhaps unacknowledged desire; yet
in its most successful instances, it seems to do so almost accidentally, off-
handedly, letting the audience find that pleasure in the film as if by themselves. So while the cult plays upon transgression, it tends to disguise it as
an act of *discovery*—or rediscovery, as when one age resurrects and finds
anew the pleasures of an old film like *Casablanca*.

What we discover varies with the particular cult text. Whether it is our
need for and embracing of a specific persona like Bogart or Dean, or our
longing for the social and sexual transgressions of a *Repo Man* or *Rocky
Horror,* we face a form that transgresses the limits of time and custom,
and that implicitly speaks a dissatisfaction with the status quo. We might
do well, therefore, to return to Foucault's vantage as he speaks of the very
nature of transgression: "It does not transform the other side of the mirror, beyond an invisible and uncrossable line, into a glittering expanse.
Transgression is neither violence in a divided world . . . nor a victory over
limits . . . and exactly for this reason, its role is to measure the excessive

distance that it opens at the heart of the limit and to trace the flashing line that causes the limit to arise" (35).

"At the heart of the limit"—in this phrase Foucault strikes to the very core of that strange link between transgression and love that defines the cult film experience. For despite the midnight movie's counterculture trappings and the classical film's nostalgic retreat from the present, these films are finally not about violence or violation. Rather, their experience of limits marks a longing to measure our longings, not a desire for some*thing,* but a yearning that humanly identifies us and differentiates us one from the other. While it lets us experience limits, it does so without ever vanquishing those limits or wielding any sort of truly radical power. In fact, no really radical films have ever become cult favorites, since the "tracing of limits" in these films proceeds from within the violated border, from this side of limits that stay in effect. But the cult film's transgressive thrust helps us see beyond, trace our own limits, and even feel a momentary power over them. Of course, eventually the film ends, and then we return to that world and its boundaries. However, that return is bolstered by the fleeting affair we have there had—truly an affair of the heart—that leaves us feeling better about ourselves and our world, better because we have seen and spoken our desires.

For this reason, it is very difficult to think of the cult film outside of the cult film *experience.* It does, after all, represent a "supertext" that can be described only in terms of a boundary crossing—including the boundary that often divides viewers and critics from the text. If that crossing evokes a kind of loving experience, it is because we thereby sense something special in the cult film: that we are part of this text, our embrace necessary for its very identity. In this experience, we celebrate a most pleasurable transgression, as we vicariously cross over into taboo territory—the self's *terra incognita*—and then emerge to tell of it. There we do not simply trace out a foreign shape. On that other side of the mirror, there beyond the usual boundaries of common reason, we discover another, different self, and gain a brief, interrogatory power over the limits that seem to shape our lives. This simultaneously dangerous and safe trip is what we so love about the cult film.

NOTES

1. Cawelti points in this direction, as he notes that Aristotle also approached genre from two complementary directions, focusing on both "the object of imitation"—the common form of genre studies today—and the "manner or form of representation" (55).

2. We should note that underground films anticipated and helped establish a common viewing practice for today's cult and midnight films. The late 1960s saw the development of a nationally circulating program of underground, camp, and experimental films entitled "Underground Cinema 12." These programs, which changed weekly, usually played at midnight in local "art" houses in the major film markets around the country.

3. The cinematic imaginary refers to the artificial sense of self and the self's relations to its culture that a film's images fashion. Bill Nichols, in his study of cinematic ideology, *Ideology and the Image,* offers probably the clearest explanation of this concept: "How we see ourselves and the world around us is often how we believe ourselves and the world to be. Images generally present views; films present particular kinds of views . . . and how we see them has everything to do with how we see ourselves" (5).

4. In this regard, the cult film seems to operate almost in the sort of mythic pattern outlined by Claude Levi-Strauss in his famous essay "The Structural Study of Myth," wherein he suggests that the basic function of any myth "is to provide a logical model capable of overcoming contradiction" (226). When viewed in this context, the cult film more clearly reveals its status as a kind of cultural myth, one characterized by certain constants despite its widely varied manifestations.

5. As Baudrillard has noted, in the modern world we increasingly seem to inhabit a realm of simulacra, of *versions* of the real, and that environment has had the effect of essentially squeezing out the real. Thus Baudrillard concludes that today what we are seeing is nothing less than "the murderous capacity of images: murderers of the real; murderers of their own model as . . . Byzantine icons could murder the divine identity" (168).

WORKS CITED

Baudrillard, Jean. "Simulacra and Simulations." In *Jean Baudrillard: Selected Writings,* ed. Mark Poster, 166–184. Stanford: Stanford Univ. Press, 1988.

Cawelti, John. "The Question of Popular Genres." *Journal of Popular Film and Television* 13, no. 2 (1985): 55–60.

Foucault, Michel. *Language, Counter-Memory, Practice.* Ed. Donald F. Bouchard. Ithaca: Cornell Univ. Press, 1977.

Lasch, Christopher. *The Minimal Self: Psychic Survival in Troubled Times.* New York: Norton, 1984.

Levi-Strauss, Claude. "The Structural Study of Myth." In *Structural Anthropology,* trans. Claire Jacobson and Brooke Grundfest Schoepf, 202–228. Garden City: Doubleday, 1967.

Mast, Gerald. *A Short History of the Movies.* 4th ed. New York: Macmillan, 1986.

Nichols, Bill. *Ideology and the Image.* Bloomington: Indiana Univ. Press, 1981.

Sarris, Andrew. *Confessions of a Cultist: On the Cinema, 1955–1969.* New York: Simon & Schuster, 1970.

Strout, Andrea. "In the Midnight Hour." *American Film* 6, no. 4 (1981): 34–37, 72, 74.

CHAPTER 2

After Midnight

Bruce Kawin

In his/her activity, the interlocutor displays not only a great promptitude, but also an authentic desire of adhesion, an availability to involvement, a willingness for co-responsibility. . . . Such a description brings us back, undoubtedly, to a circular model, since it emphasizes the viewer's contribution to the construction of the sense of the discourse, without forgetting the contribution of the discourse to the construction of the viewer. . . . A text is never given *per se*, but always directed toward others (in search of a mirror wherein to fix its own image); . . . a text is never given once and for all, but always bound to be reformulated.
—Francesco Casetti, "Looking for the Spectator"

I go walkin' / After midnight / Out in the moonlight / Just hoping you may be / Somewhere a-walkin' / After midnight / Searching for me.
—Don Hecht and Alan Block (performed by Patsy Cline)

The cult film has most often been defined in two ways: as any picture that is seen repeatedly by a devoted audience, and as a deviant or radically different picture, embraced by a deviant audience. A film like *Casablanca* fits the first definition just fine, although a film as different as *High Sierra* would fit it just as well, while *The Rocky Horror Picture Show* clearly fits the second. Either way, the cult film can be defined primarily in terms of its acceptance: it is a movie with a following.

The property of being a cult film, whatever that turns out to be, is not necessarily inherent in *Casablanca*, which is basically a romantic political melodrama that happens to have been elevated to cult status. But it *is* an inherent property of a film like *Evil Dead II*, which has been designed to please a cult audience, ignoring the Milquetoasts who would never enjoy or understand it anyway, and which has been identified in the journal

Cinefantastique (June 1987) specifically as a "cult horror film . . . obviously made by and for fans of the genre" (114).

There are, then, at least two broad categories of the cult film, both of which invite us to go out walking after midnight. The first might be called inadvertent, the second programmatic. An inadvertent cult film, like *Casablanca*, may well be a straightforward, conservative, unself-conscious studio picture that appeals to an audience without threatening or redefining its values in the slightest. There is nothing in *Casablanca* that would offend the mainstream. It is dead-center, gung-ho mainstream, and no one has ever been able to imitate it. But a programmatic cult film, such as *The Texas Chain Saw Massacre 2*, sets out to be a cult film and often makes its appeal in terms of (or in terms of violating) shared values. It is, more often than not, well outside the mainstream ideology and represents a disruptive rather than a conservative force.

The basis of its disruptive strategy is exuberance. Rather than a lecture, the programmatic cult film gives intense pleasure (which may, of course, be a postmodern lecture tactic, a self-conscious deconstruction of the playground of signification). When these films have a political subject, they may use style to transfigure it or genre to rethink it, but theirs will usually be the direct, unyielding statements, the ones with power. We might compare, for example, the "best" American film on the psychological problems of the Vietnam veteran, the muddled and sophomoric *The Deer Hunter*, with the cult horror film *Death Dream*, in which the vet comes home to mother, even though he's dead (perhaps this is his dream as he dies in Vietnam, haunted by his promise to return). Cult films offer and glory in such otherness—in extreme spectacles of rebellion (*Rock 'n' Roll High School*), wacko power (*Rocky Horror*), wacko banality (*Glen or Glenda, True Stories*), melancholy (*Eraserhead*), difference (*Freaks, Chained for Life*), nostalgia for symbolism (*Black Orpheus, The Seventh Seal, Phantom of the Paradise*), nostalgia for simplicity (*King of Hearts, The Gods Must Be Crazy*), relentless satire (*Putney Swope, The King of Comedy*), the power of style (*The Road Warrior*), unglamorized violence (*The Last House on the Left*), ghoul art (both of the *Texas Chain Saw* films), bourgeois apocalypse (*The Hills Have Eyes, Dawn of the Dead, A Nightmare on Elm Street*). Such films offer unifying visions for an alienated audience, uncompromised celebrations of an other integrity.

The *High Sierra* audience is clearly not the same kind of community as the *Rocky Horror* crowd, even if members of both might get a kick out of *Repo Man*. And neither group quite evokes the darker connotations of the word "cult" as do those who line up for the latest satanic horror film. Yet what all of these audiences share is the satisfaction of appreciating an unusually rewarding picture, a certain degree of group identification, and, I believe, a sense of being somehow validated by the film, as if it acknowledged their values, knew they were out there watching and listening, and had somehow especially invited them to its party.

Taking my cue from the Italian narratologist Francesco Casetti—who has eloquently investigated the ways that movies make room for, chart a path for, and intimately address their audience, an "I and Thou" relationship that guides us through the inferno, the labyrinth, the joyride, the game plan of the movie—I should like to suggest that the cult film offers the most radical example, within the context of the commercial/narrative cinema, of both the commercial potential and the rhetoric of direct address. These are films with which we, as solitary or united members of the audience, feel we have a relationship. In the case of oldies like *Casablanca*, it is because we have enjoyed and allowed ourselves to feel open to them for so long; in the case of oddities like *Eraserhead* or *Liquid Sky*, it is perhaps because *we* made them hits, or perhaps because we found there the mirrors for which we were searching, the mirrorings of our buried concerns, our true self-images, and the outrageous projections of nightmare, of rebellion, or of style: a vision that, if not literally ours, still clicked with or spoke to ours. If the normal audience—and, even more so, the cult audience—feels "an authentic desire of adhesion, an availability to involvement" (28), as Casetti puts it, surely a film like *Rocky Horror*, built to fulfill those desires, must be considered a privileged text, a gold mine for the study of the rhetoric of second-person film, the film that says "you" when it means "us."

Most such direct-address or second-person films have been of two types: propaganda and follow-the-bouncing-ball. There is a lot of the bouncing ball in *Rocky Horror*, but there is also a great deal more. It shows not only how a film may be "directed toward others (in search of a mirror wherein to fix its own image)" (Casetti 28), but also—through its costumed and participatory following, for example—how a film might literally construct an audience after its own likeness. *How* the films are open, how they, more than others, are liable to be read by their audiences as actually addressing them, are rhetorical and semiotic questions that would take rather too long to probe here. But there is such a rhetoric, and there is room to observe here that it has been developed by films that have, like the self-styled cult horror films of the 1980s, deliberately set out to engage, address, and patronize a cult audience. Such films have built on and in a way imitated the successful strategies of *Rocky Horror* and the other pioneering mutations of the 1980s in a virtually Darwinian manner.

The Texas Chain Saw Massacre was made as a horror film. Eventually, it became a cult film. To reach the audience that deserved and awaited a successor to the original, *The Texas Chain Saw Massacre 2* was conceived and marketed as a no-holds-barred *cult* horror film; in a manner of speaking, it hung itself in the Hall of Fame it had helped to create. Those who cared witnessed the birth of a genre, almost a species. Between *The Texas Chain Saw Massacre* and *The Texas Chain Saw Massacre 2*, a lungfish turned to a lizard before our eyes.

Such films survived the box office's version of natural selection because they were found by the untargetable audiences who had, perhaps without knowing it, been waiting for their address: fans who saw more in them than in what by comparison seemed lay or secular pictures, fans who found in them meanings they had not found elsewhere and recognitions not only of especially interesting and valuable spectacles, but also of themselves; such films, they gratefully thought, knew they were there. Even as they selected each work as one of special value, they felt selected by it.

Because of such effects, the cult film should be recognized as an extreme of spectator pleasure and as a site of audience power. The patronage of cult films demonstrates, in box office terms that producers understand, that what gets people into the movie theater is not novelty but quality. Repetition is a pleasure.[1] With the same degree of power, and making just the sort of decision that advertisers would die to be able to control—a consumer choice as definite as the decision to switch toothpastes—the cult viewer makes his or her product preference known. Not *Blue Thunder* but *Blue Velvet*, not *Parenthood* but *Parents*, not *Cocktail* but *The Cocoanuts*. One of the messages the cult audience is sending, then—along with the blatant demand for more "risky" new movies—is that the studios are wrong not to keep "old" movies in theatrical circulation, where the group could gather (forcing a further consumer move toward 16mm and video, laserdisc and late-night TV, and away from the theaters with their first or last runs of the same old—sorry—*new* thing), since the great works beloved by a culture should always be available for a people to see in their original form, which in this case is the theatrical release print, the real thing, the 35mm, the *movie*—not panned and scanned, not cropped, not abridged, not interrupted, and certainly not colorized.

Another message is that misfits and weirdos and film freaks do, sooner or later, buy a lot of tickets. Now, producers and distributors are not fools. It has not escaped them that pictures with small but devoted followings of *repeat viewers* have made good money. Where marketing considerations and film history intersect, the cult film has set up a fruit stand. Its financial viability has established, within the industry, a haven for the offbeat picture. The lure of achieving cult status and long-term revenue has often tipped the balance, so that even if the producer considers a project to be terminally weird, it may still be approved for production on the grounds that it might well address and wildly appeal to a cult film audience. This may be the producers' rationalization for putting their own unacknowledged fetishes into production, or it may be genuinely intuitive marketing. What makes a difference is that it acknowledges the existence of a diverse audience and attests to the wisdom of catering to—which is to say, including and culturally addressing—minority and outsider tastes and perspectives. Because the cult film does not need to please or reach the mainstream, it may be uniquely free of the mainstream's terms, its dominant discourse, its way of insisting how things should be phrased and done. It can be off the wall—or blow up the wall—and still make money; it has license to be subversive, to be avant-garde, and above all to be tasteless. This is not true of just any independent or low-budget production, for the average independent feature is clearly targeted to as much of the mainstream audience as it can hope to attract.

As a business decision, the production of the cult film might be said to validate the financing of the obscure. It upholds the value of putting money into something that is down the alley, not on the main boulevard; something that not everybody knows about; something you have to get into and perhaps give some of yourself to; something that, despite being far into itself (like *Eraserhead*), can reach out and speak intimately to a vast number of outsiders; something so private that it's public, so systematically or antisystematically artistic that it has a chance to be popular—and so cheap that it has a good chance of turning a profit. Again because it is targeted to a small, repeat audience, the distribution of the cult film validates the sort of reliable commitment between an artist and a patron or publisher that is so utterly foreign to the film business: one that involves keeping the work in print and in circulation, even if it takes a long time to find its audience and make back the costs of production, rather than pushing the work for a short time and then remaindering or shredding it. So the cult film has, among other things, allowed more "special interest" pictures to be financed and to remain in distribution for relatively long periods of time, even if we must also acknowledge that some of the filmmakers have been ripped off down the line by unscrupulous distributors and bad contracts.

Still, the cult film succeeds, and it may prove a viable radical form, largely because it happily writes off mainstream audiences. It doesn't need them, though, and is free to laugh at them; it can make them squirm. If this counterideology has its own dark and guilty secret, it might be the desire (hidden under mockery) to have Ozzie and Harriet for parents.

As the cult film is free to express unconventional perspectives, the cult audience is free to find its pleasures where it will. Maria Montez, Humphrey Bogart, Tim Curry . . . the scrambled eggs of vision in the deserts of *El Topo*, the Blob-meets–Dairy Queen brilliance of the fast food/health food/ Bug-Eyed Monster nexus in the best science fiction satire of the 1980s, *The Stuff* . . . the heartless gross-outs of *The Texas Chain Saw Massacre*, the sexual horror movies of David Cronenberg, the Family According to Wes Craven . . . or the Marx Brothers, who went from four musketeers to three, Ma and Pa Kettle, the maligned Ed Wood, anything from Monogram and Republic studios, especially the serials . . . the movie queen in her bath—and what all this is, at the root, is the pleasure of the movies. It's an insult to call it "camp." We don't go back to these films to say how silly they were; what we keep discovering is how terrific and even necessary they are to us. This deep appreciation is a serious province of value, almost a matter of devotion.

The pleasure of the movies, revealed to us through the unabashed enthusiasm of the devotees of cult films or stars, is the incense in the temple. And it is in the temple, of course, that one reads again and again the sacred text, the story that defines the tribe. The cult film creates a ritual space, and the repeated movie is the center of the service. It is the cult object, the epic, the familiar scroll that unwinds to the devoted attention of the following that feels defined by it—and by following it.

Those who fail to understand, or who are closed to the beauties and revelations of these pictures, may well be dismissed as closed to the values of the subculture as well as to the full range of art. To a devotee, whether you are able to appreciate these films—that is, respect the sacred mysteries and recognize the sun when you are staring at it—may indicate what kind of person you are, whether you can be trusted. Such an attitude has, of course, popped up once or twice in the history of the politics of religion. And it is just as prone to show up in the political underground or among punk rockers or gay activists or golfing Republicans or polarized clumps or poets, take your pick.

Without conferring (because this is still in essence a private act, an intimate gesture of selection), without even declaring itself as a group, a self-selected elect founds a minor religion around the repeatable text. It is a work that they particularly understand and appreciate, but also one that appreciates, understands, and addresses them. They may be outsiders galvanized by something well outside the mainstream, or they may feel that there is something special about them because they appreciate this particular mainstream film. They may even feel that it calls to them, or that it presents itself as a calling. The ritual viewing may include a responsive reading, even the imitation of interaction. Respect and affection are part of this viewing experience, and homage, too—perhaps even in the form of a code of dress that acknowledges the power and special nature of their icon, as is easy to see in the case of *Rocky Horror.*

What this sacred text gives its worshippers, and what they are grateful for, is a mirror. It tells them something they realize as the truth, something they have been waiting to hear and to have validated. It does not flinch; indeed, it seems to take a certain glee, like the capricious Goya, in setting nightmares loose. Or it may, like the sappy *King of Hearts,* unabashedly express a sentimental worldview and make it stick. *Evil Dead II,* addressed to the fans of the horror magazine *Fangoria,* thumbs its nose at the values of the country club that runs America, absolutely confident that its inventiveness and nonstop creativity will be appreciated by that target audience it *knows* is out there, and becomes so gory that it's funny. A film like that, or *They Came from Within,* honestly provokes from me a rich, deep laughter; "They got it!" is how I feel in those moments, and I'm grateful to them for going all the way, for getting it right. I can be shuddering at the pain and still feel that way about the sawed-off face mask in *The Texas Chain Saw Massacre 2,* or that earlier moment when a grossly excited Leatherface touches an erect chainsaw to the crotch of a screaming woman who must attempt to please him—one of the most uncompromisingly tasteless images of phallic aggression in any movie. Like the brother's habit of burning his scalp with a hanger and eating the broiled scabs, it just doesn't stop. It goes on to the end, as true horror is prone to do. It gets down to my sense of the dark side of the truth, and I am finally grateful to it for that—grateful enough to join a fan club, start up a cult. As I used to line up outside Cinema I for films like *Red Desert* and *Stavisky,* about which I now could care less, today you can find me at the mall for the opening of *Day of the Dead.* I know when the horror films are not made for me or those who share my tastes: when they are timid and stupid, like *Friday the 13th, Part VI;* or empty and unbelieving, like *The Guardian;* or unable to rise to the challenge of the material (in this case, Lovecraft), like *From Beyond.* I know, and I wait for the ones that *are* for me, aware that it can be a long wait.

But it is a joy to discover a work or an image that is (all right, *relatively*) free from compromise, as perhaps only the programmatic cult film and the avant-garde film can be, especially in a culture that eats and breathes and oils itself with compromise, from the script conferences of megaHollywood to the arms conferences of our leaders. If the images I find uncompromisingly true, or disgustingly on target, or genre-perfect, prove a lonesome pleasure, too intense for most people to watch, too extreme to enjoy, and too insane to agree with, and if the only way to see *Salo* or *Motel Hell* or *Peeping Tom* is after midnight, then that is when I shall go out to meet them, alone or in company: searching for the films that are searching for me.

NOTES

1. For a historical discussion of repetition in film narrative and its relationship to the pleasure principle, see my *Telling It Again and Again*.

WORKS CITED

Casetti, Francesco. "Looking for the Spectator." *IRIS* 1, no. 2 (1983): 15–29.
Fischer, Dennis K. "*Evil Dead II*." *Cinefantastique* 17, no. 4 (1987): 114.
Kawin, Bruce F. *Telling It Again and Again: Repetition in Literature and Film.* Niwot: Univ. Press of Colorado, 1972, 1989.

CHAPTER 3

Film and the Culture of Cult

Timothy Corrigan

Cult films are usually identified and valorized in far too vague a manner, precisely because they seem marginalized or eccentric in some way. Yet they are what they are—and they are valuable—*because* they are peculiar. As Umberto Eco notes, these films create, by definition, a private world whose furnishings can be acted upon "as if they were part of the beliefs of a sect," and they are postmodern in the sense that "the quotation of the topos is recognized as the only way to cope with the burden of our encyclopedic filmic competence" (3). Linking these movies even more to that postmodern impulse, I would argue that this private filmic space is *especially* a product of an audience's historical burden and that it has as much to do with how these movies are historically acted on as it does with any strictly textual features. Unlike B-movies, the public precursor of the cult, cult films become part of an audience's private space, and in this embracing of public images as private space, they become much like furnishings or material acquisitions. On this point I differ from Eco, who argues that these films "are born in order to become cult objects" (11). No film, I would say, is naturally a cult film; all cult films are adopted children.

With cult movies, as opposed to most other films, audiences seek out not only the unfamiliar in character and story, but the unfamiliar style, frame, and imagistic texture. But once discovered and identified, the cult film and its strange images are then brought home, appropriated by viewers, who make these images privately and personally meaningful (just as Jean-Paul Belmondo and Woody Allen each take home parts of Bogart to suit their own fantasies in *Breathless* and *Play It Again, Sam*). Both classic and modern film theory usually describe these viewers as urban natives, individuals who, for better or worse, find themselves at home in the vast architecture of images before them: the factory worker of Eisenstein, who lives the environment of *Strike* (1925); the city flaneur of Stanley Cavell, who wanders wide-eyed but comfortable, like Chaplin in *City Lights* (1931); the courtyard voyeur of Christian Metz, who watches the city from his own *Rear Window* (1954); and even Teresa de Lauretis's female spectator, who remains unhappily trapped at home in one of Calvino's invisible cities.[1] Yet my cult spectator is a tourist whose relationship with the city of images begins from outside and who inhabits that city only by taking parts of it over. He or she stands in this city like a visitor in a photograph before the Eiffel Tower. For cult audiences, films are all stranger than paradise, and it is the ability of these audiences to make a paradise out of that strangeness that marks them as cinematic tourists, so different from the urban natives.

For all of us on this tour there are some easily identifiable landmarks. In low-budget films, from *Night of the Living Dead* (1968) to John Sayles's more elevated efforts, the economics of production and distribution become a means of distinguishing these films from a typical Hollywood production, yet also a way of claiming a kind of common or secret ground for audiences who might feel closer to Pittsburgh and grainy stock than to the glamor of Hollywood. These are cult films as home movies. Similarly, there are the technological peculiarities that, for modern audiences, define a cult territory: as in 3-D films, silent movies, or the special-effects wizardry of science fiction films like *2001* (1968)—all of which take an opposite route to a similar cult position. Here audiences establish a relationship with technology itself, and even when that rapport is only metaphoric (as with early science fiction films), cult spectators are allowed the mastery of their own position as technological participants. These are cult films as video arcades.

Whether the audience focus for these films is economics, technology, or some other material dimension of the text, cult movies are always after a fashion foreign films: the images are especially exotic; the viewer uniquely touristic; and within that relationship viewers get to go places, see things, and manipulate customs in a way that no indigenous member of that culture or mainstream filmgoer normally could. Why Jerry Lewis is so loved in France follows from the same reason that Lina Wertmuller, despite her mediocre reception at home, became so popular in the United States. Cultural distance allows for the textual transformation of cult audiences. As Susan Stewart in *On Longing* suggests, such films "allow one to be a tourist in one's own life, or allow the tourist to appropriate, consume, and thereby 'tame' the cultural other." Often displaying their text's mobility through the quotations, tee-shirts, or posters worn or claimed by their audience, these films "speak to the possessor's capacity for otherness: It is the possessor, not the film, who is ultimately the curiosity" (146, 148).

Cults of any kind, especially those made up of film audiences, are cultural revisionists. What they do is to wrench representations from their naturalized and centralized positions and create what Eco terms "glorious incoherence" (4): crucifixes with motorcycles, lace over leather, Maoists in America, Woody Allen as Bogart. Here any sense of a legitimacy or true place for the original representations becomes exactly what is under attack: for film audiences and other cult groups, cult action is radical *bricolage,* the play with and reassembly of signifiers from strikingly different cultures and contexts. With these films, the thematics—no more than any notion of spiritual essence found within a religious cult—are only slightly relevant.[2] Of course, these are often films about outsiders, yet they differ vastly from the many mainstream films wherein the rebels always have a cause. Then, too, these movies commonly dramatize a clash between different cultures or subcultures, yet they share little with movies like *Moscow on the Hudson* (1984), where the clash is, in fact, a thinly disguised assimilation into American society and, more important, Hollywood conventions. If one wants to privilege thematics, the most important motif in these movies is the debris and excess that define characters and environments, which never quite fit or relate to each other as natural or "useful." Yet this excess is important mainly as a signpost to the real action in the film, the audience's use of the film text as material debris in and of itself.

Far more than thematics, what defines cult films are two related ways in which the text is materialized. Through the transformation of the film into a kind of physical fabric (most clearly dramatized, in one instance, through the repeated viewings that VCRs allow), the textual materiality of the images largely replaces a sense of visual presence and textual transcendence, whereby the viewer simply accepts the movie. In a more theoretical sense, this dislocation represents a perverse swerve from the Oedipal trajectory that some see as underlying the cinema. According to that model, the spectator is positioned by the play of and desire for images whose absence makes their illusory presence all the more mesmerizing. However, with cult films—where fathers and mothers might also be children and incestuous lovers—this notion of a presiding, determining, or patriarchal relationship comes apart between audience and screen. The acquisition of images as a material and moveable substance in their own right becomes the chief significance for the cult spectator, and the audience's physical presence comes to override any other absence. Whether through the redefinition of cinema as an adult toy (a domestic game rather than a public ritual) or through the perverse materialization of an Oedipal imaginary, cult movies are the product of a viewer who acts out simultaneously the vision of child and adult. Rather than making the audience's perspective the figurative child of an imaginary world that dominates it, that perspective becomes a shifting dominant that claims the movie images as its own adopted child.

What this unique audience-screen relation testifies to and why I believe it is so significant (significant enough to pass over the dubious quality of the films themselves) is its unusual disregard for textual authority and systemic coherence. It pinpoints, in short, a relatively rare instance of dominant viewing and a semiotic practice that refuses to play by the rules of the traditional film game. These interpretive disruptions cannot, moreover, be simply dismissed as the "subjectivist madness" of a poststructuralist angst, since this action is not only collective but often the very terms of the texts it engages.[3] Certainly, one of the most obvious and crudely exemplary cult films of recent years, *The Rocky Horror Picture Show* (1975), is a low-budget mish-mash of genres from musical to science fiction. Centered on a sexually random family of media outsiders, it presents a chaotically intertextual range of subcultural clichés as social debris. Yet its true, if unsubtle, mark as a cult film is how, in the first years of its cult attraction, it generated a variety of representational distortions (squirt guns, toilet paper, etc.) from different urban viewers who, in appropriating the film, nonetheless established a shared set of responses that quite materially dispersed the movie in the clutter that surrounded it. (In contrast, one might argue, the standardization of these responses as a type of mythology today has pretty much redefined this film as subculture, not as cult.)

If this kind of viewer response works not just as a series of textual disjunctions but as particular sorts of disjunctions, ones that turn the text into a tourist's souvenir, I would now like to map and specify a few varieties of this historical tour. That is, I want to suggest both how cult films have evolved in different ways and how the dynamics of cult viewing have recently been adapted to achieve sometimes more complicated and serious aims.

One of the most prominent of these types is the historical cult film, which locates itself precisely along that edge where temporal and historical distance initiates audience reaction. *Casablanca* (1942) may be the most familiar choice, though we could list many similar ones that might appear as a ten-best list and that, depending on a catholicity of taste, might serve as a cult catalogue of revival films. These too are always and ironically marginalized products, if only through the label "best"; and as these lists change according to the groups making them, the entire notion of a canon begins to waiver through the instability of its cult status. To be most polemical, one might say that the historical valuation of films is frequently no less fetishistic about deep focus or auteurs than a teenage audience might be about rock music or kinky sex. Indeed, even when our relation to certain films is supposedly based on intellectual rigor, this relation is made across historical disjunctions that force these films to be recuperated and reconstructed through the mobility of our perspective. In these films particularly, the debris and waste always at the heart of cult activity is, most apparently, a materialization of history itself, whether in the form of film stock, lack of color, ancient props, or even the presence of a dead actor. The 1985 rebirth of Fritz Lang's *Metropolis* (1926) suggests the sort of archetypal adopted child that cult is: a historical souvenir dramatically materialized in tinted film stock and reconstructed through the fabric of contemporary rock video.

Orson Welles's *The Magnificent Ambersons* (1942) might be a more subtle example, for its regular appearance as part of the canon might not be despite its clearly truncated and even butchered look, but because of that look. Appropriately, this is a film about the ravages and losses of history, marked with nostalgic references to an even older cinema—like the long iris—that signals the end of George's innocence. It is a film in which the soft-focused edges of the first shots look intentionally like old photographs or, as Manny Farber complained, like a succession of postcards (McBride 56). While images such as these may point the way for a contemporary viewer, the harsh cuts and breaks which resulted from the studio's taking the film's editing out of Welles's hands provide the crucial openings for its success as a kind of cult movie: these are the material scars which, in only a partly metaphoric sense, let the viewer remake the film as what it might have been under the guidance of its auteur-father. From the perspective of the present, historical films of this kind always lack the continuity and verisimilitude needed to represent history authentically for the viewer, and through these representational discontinuities the audience constructs its own history. History is, essentially, torn from its original context and then reconstructed, sometimes recklessly, through the historical present of the viewer. Thus the historical cultist in Scorsese's recent *After Hours* (1987) does both: pretentiously referring to "the film" *The Wizard of Oz* (1939), she tells of the lover who was able to have an orgasm only by shouting "Surrender, Dorothy." Where the lover performs a piece of the film as his own private movie, the teller of this tale casually exhibits the film itself as a valorized fragment of film history—the twin action of historical cult.

This quiet violence implicit in a contemporary audience's rapport with historical cult films becomes much more explicitly a part of the image in what we have come to call "midnight movies." These are similarly a somewhat arbitrary and constantly shifting group. Anything from the quirky surface play of *Harold and Maude* (1978) to the bizarre nightmare of *Eraser-head* (1978) might figure into this group. But, as a *USA Today* list indicates, the most cultish of this group tends toward what that writer calls "outrageous trash": *Attack of the Killer Tomatoes* (1978) and *Blood Sucking Freaks* appear alongside such classics as *The Texas Chain Saw Massacre* (1974), *Pink Flamingos* (1971), and *Liquid Sky* (1985) (Gundersen 3E).

What all of these films have in common is, unmistakably, that they are after-hours films in every sense, and usually appear rough-cut even in the final cut. It is hardly necessary to detail the violence and very real trash to be found here, often even in mainstream films like *Blade Runner* (1982) and the *Mad Max* movies, as indications of how history "has already" or "will have" laid history to waste. More telling, perhaps, is the proleptic rock-video form of some of these movies and, even more than historical cult, the potentially infinite repetition of their social reception. Anticipated by older musicals and anticipating television shows like "Miami Vice," these narratives often seem to undermine their own narrative structures through loosely connected nonnarrative events whose excessive display either of the visuals or the music becomes a perceptual or aural format for the audience's own performance. Whether these nonnarrative, often musical scenes announce the preparation for or the acting out of love or violence, they afford the viewer an exhibitionist's space, not a voyeur's. If there is identification here, it is the *mise-en-abyme* identification with exhibition itself, with the material of the eyes and the skin of David Bowie in *The Man Who Fell to Earth* (1976), not with his perspective or character. The star performers in these films are, after all, realizable, like the music, off the screen and beyond the fiction, and that, in large part, makes for a cult attraction: concretely and erotically in excess of the narrative fiction and frame.

If these performances become vacuously repeated both in the films and at their midnight receptions, this repetitious pattern and its referential insignificance—both corollaries for the meaningless violence that often occurs in these films—comprise the formula which allows an audience to master and perform the film as an exhibitionist's stage. Here an encounter with an Other, a "foreign image," is contained like a postcard sent again and again with the viewer's personal signature: David Bowie is a cult figure only because he repeatedly falls to earth, an avatar made through the desires and imitations of his audience. If the process of recreation and mixing of archetypes becomes itself a central signifying practice in cult films, it is certainly not in the traditional sense of archetypes but only as they are reified, made material, and offered up to their audience for mechanical reproduction. *Road Warrior* (1981), for example, might employ a conventional flashback technique to tell the story of a classical hero from another time, but what distinguishes that film and describes this hero is his special identification with and performance of the scattered waste and debris of some other, lost culture—ours to take hold of because that culture was and is ours, again and again in this film or in its repetition from the previous *Mad Max* (1980) to the sequel *Mad Max: Beyond Thunderdome* (1985).

To speak of conventionally "reading" either of these two types of cult films is to misunderstand them, just as to talk about "camp," cult's first cousin, is, according to Susan Sontag, already a kind of betrayal of its spirit. Cult films, whether by nature or choice, invariably subvert and run contrary to the immobility and passivity which regulate standard viewing and reading practices.[4] If they initiate a kind of identification, it is quite unlike the usual internalized identification of fantasy, but rather an identification with the materiality of the image, an externalizing of imaginary signifiers as marks of the image's significance: single lines of dialogue, a gesture, a piece of clothing. These images and markers thus do not have any essential stability or balance in themselves, and without this essential stability, they lack the binary structure that has supported most notions of reading (reader-text, viewer-identification, sign-interpretation relationships). Instead, there are always, at best, "rereadings," for in these cases the audience invariably comes armed and overprepared with a text of its own that makes the film text almost secondary. There are, for cult films, no first-time viewings, since these movies by definition offer themselves for endless reappropriation: their entirely worn-out tropes become the vehicles not of original connotation but for the potentially constant regeneration of connotation, through which the audience reads and rereads itself rather than the film. In a more complicated sense than most critics recognize, these films are indeed trash, but trash as it refuses the domesticated place of cultural reading. This is historical junk like repossessed cars (hence the subject of a cult film like *Repo Man* [1985]), which the spectator experiences as an exotic monument to his or her own present; consumer art like generic food that accommodates not just an artist's name but all names; touristic texts like a videotape memoir of Paris, which even when it is first shot is already a "misreading" of that city as a memory and souvenir.

What these films are about, though, is more than the distortion of memory. Today, a historical spiraling and cultural marginalizing that these first two categories map have already become culturally and politically central. In a day when a president comments on his own assassination attempt with quips from W. C. Fields and video stores are rapidly replacing bookstores, these historically and socially marginalized films seem to move more to the center of culture as a third category of cult, a commercial cult that reflects the confusing collapse of public and private space. In this commercial cult, films aim to manipulate an audience through the very terms that audience itself created in its prior assaults on history, but that play with the material of the image has moved its source at least partially back into the text as a way of eliciting the kind of reckless and self-conscious audience response that I have associated with more recognizable cult films. When these contemporary films work as cult, their seams, gaps, and shiftings often look slicker and more aesthetic than their prototypes, yet imagistically and narratively they remain materially overdetermined and ultimately about the performance of the spectator. This is why, despite all the right signals, a film like *Raiders of the Lost Ark* (1981) is not of this type but a film that makes cultish references only within the Hollywood model of passive fascination.

More specific examples of this contemporary sort of cult movie are works like Fassbinder's *Veronika Voss* (1982), Scorsese's *After Hours,* or Alan Rudolph's *Choose Me* (1984). To indulge in a bit of cultish *bricolage,* we might see *Choose Me,* for instance, on a direct line from *Casablanca,* with its Hollywood counterpart in *Play It Again, Sam* (1972). While *Casablanca* achieves its cult status through the influence of history and the creation of an audience which, in many ways, liberates it from history, the Woody Allen film simply absorbs that cult status and audience to refocus them on the intellectual and dramatic irony that is the character of Allen himself. *Choose Me,* on the other hand, eschews that stability. The mobile center of this film (which is, in effect, no center) is the media cult that develops around Dr. Nancy Love (played by Genevieve Bujold), a radio talk-show host who seems to affect everyone's romantic and sexual life. As long as her encounters are limited to phone conversations, she is the emblem of conservative stability; but when she enters the visually excessive world of Eve's Place, that stability begins to give way and she, like the characters around her, starts to live out the random obsessiveness that characterizes a truly contemporary cult. Indeed, Micki, the protagonist who first initiates her, crystallizes this odd obsessiveness when he asks everyone he kisses to marry him and then points out that he only kisses women he wants to marry. For Micki, a kiss is not just a kiss in any sense.

But still, Micki clearly aligns himself with the Bogart archetype. He is a spy, jet pilot, tough guy—and a Yale professor. But if Eve is his Ilsa and her place his cabaret, all those types within Micki become merely a kind of material evidence (magazine covers, blurred signatures, etc.) which may or may not be fraudulent. This world is as far from Casablanca as it is from the real Los Angeles: here the touristic intrigue and exoticism revolve around not mystery but the material instability of the place itself and the exhibitionism which is the only way the characters can relate. Eve owns the cabaret and bar only because Eve's Place was for sale and her name happened to be Eve; she meets Micki only because he comes looking for the original Eve, but is just as happy with the new version he found "under the blinking sign"; finally, the two marry only because of their mutual willingness to act out what coincidence offers them and to accept marriage as both sacred and sordid. If the Nancy Love–Eve relationship focuses this film in still another direction, as a remake of *All About Eve,* this Eve and her companions exist and communicate only in the terms of that 1950 movie, as it appears as a poster in a character's apartment—that is, as cult material.

The last scene in this film, consequently, is removed by far more than forty years from Rick and Ilsa's farewell in *Casablanca.* However, this distance is not because the final choice in *Choose Me* is so much less noble or idealistic, or because this Rick stays with his Ilsa. Rather, it is because these characters realize that truth, love, and idealism are only cult gestures today, and, if one is to commit to them, it is only so long as his passion remains aware of its material instability. In the medium close-up of the final shot, there is no "looking at you" for these characters, as they sit side by side, eyes shifting askance. Yet there is still commitment and passion, if ever so tentatively. In *Choose Me,* the Oedipal trajectory of the narrative is not, in the end, rejected or even interrupted, but rather split in a way central to what can best be described as a cult logic: in the nervous eye-lines of this last shot, *Choose Me* describes a state of having it both ways, of participating without confinement, of active commitment without a central presence.[5]

In the same way, the film audience remains oddly inscribed as the adopted child of a perspective that never anchors itself in any secure or authentic reality. This unusual position partly reflects the film's unconventional production and distribution strategies, and helps account for the consistently different and uncertain reactions the film has generated. Made for just $800,000, *Choose Me* was produced and distributed through the semi-independent channels of Island/Alive Pictures and consciously aimed at the more "private" audiences of commercial cult who, in Rudolph's own words, want "to work a little bit" (Siegel 38). Specifically, this "work" involves dealing with the spectacularly artificial sets and carnivalesque narrative of *Choose Me,* which dislocate the audience both from Hollywood's public fantasies and from the ironic play of an auteur director. The style of this film might be termed cult realism, or what Jean Baudrillard calls the "hyperrealism of simulation" (126–134). Its false depths and dense surfaces at once attracting and arresting vision, *Choose Me* engages its audience through a billboard perspective that aims to collapse the distinction between public and private space, the illusory and the real, the imaginary and the symbolic, the reader and the text. Toward the end of the film, Micki and Eve fittingly act out their reconciliation in front of a rooftop billboard while an audience of prostitutes watches from below. At the same time, the entire film works to inscribe us, their second audience, between the no-point-of-view of the advertising image and the exhibitionistic stance of those onlookers. Just as this romantic union is materialized in all its "obscenity" (Baudrillard 129–130), the perspective of *Choose Me* forces its touristic audience to treat its public images as property for private consumption: like a rock video where an imaginary materializes in the viewer's endlessly repeated and theatrical performance of it. In *Choose Me,* an audience indeed finds a temporary cultural home, but it is one that defines itself as a constantly mobile, private scene.

Whether we describe this sort of geography and situation as a response to film history, as the repressed activism of the "me" generation, or as the effect of videocassette recorders with their constant promise of replaying the same scenes, this home away from home in film has been built of an excess of images that is rapidly becoming a debris of images. Today we live the downtown art of *After Hours,* where we all seem like postmodern tourists in our own cities, wandering from attraction to attraction. Today's culture has become the cult of *After Hours,* a film whose title should have a very silent *H* in its second word, testifying to the disappearance of a cultural screen that once could have collected all those separate exhibitionists.[6]

Whether through revivals, midnight movies, or commercial forms of cult, all that this cult of culture may have to offer us is the rare and suspect coincidence of meeting glances. Night people, we are audiences desperately and comically locked in our shared singularity, freed from a burden of truth or authenticity, and performing ourselves again and again in order to give a certain cultural significance not to images but to ourselves. At the beginning of *After Hours,* we might recall, the camera drifts away from a central conversation and focuses, as if aimlessly, on various irrelevant objects. For Andrew Sarris this camera action was perversely inexplicable in the way it commandeers the point of view, and the concomitant tittering of the audience was equally annoying and inexplicable (54). Yet this kind of irrelevancy, this cutting loose from a central perspective, is exactly what this film is about and why it might be described as an allegory of the contemporary cult audience: as the film's protagonist eventually learns, today's audiences must learn to embrace and even revel in the connections and meanings that may be there or which may only be generated by their own performance of those images.

Appropriately, there seem to be two general responses to this film. If one is not from New York, it seems a paranoid fantasy; if one lives in New York, it is documentary. Either way, of course, it is a tourist's view of a city that represents every modern city and a view in which our own marginal and temporary places, as the city's adopted children, are its only center. Recognizing what we have in common as tourists moving through this city of images and understanding what the politics of this terrain are may be more critical today than attempting to make an accurate map of it—let alone feeling at home there.

NOTES

A version of this essay appeared in *Wide Angle* 8, nos. 3–4 (1986): 91–99, and another will appear in my forthcoming book *A Cinema without Walls*, to be published by Rutgers University Press.

1. See the perspectives taken by Eisenstein in *Film Sense*, Cavell in *The World Viewed*, Metz in *The Imaginary Signifier*, and de Lauretis in *Alice Doesn't*.
2. A focus on thematics is the usual approach to cult films. See, for example, Hoberman and Rosenbaum's *Midnight Movies*.
3. I would add that this kind of audience activity is probably too socially random to fit within most reception aesthetics.
4. I argue this complicated point more fully in "Illegible Films: Texts without Secrets," in *A Cinema without Walls* (forthcoming).
5. Rudolph's more recent film *Trouble in Mind* is an equally striking variation on this splitting of the Oedipal trajectory.
6. Thanks to William Galperin for this observation.

WORKS CITED

Baudrillard, Jean. "The Ecstasy of Communication." In *The Anti-Aesthetic: Essays in Postmodern Culture*, ed. Hal Foster, 126–134. Port Townsend, Wash.: Bay Press, 1983.

Cavell, Stanley. *The World Viewed: Reflections on the Ontology of Film*. New York: Viking, 1971.

de Lauretis, Teresa. *Alice Doesn't: Feminism, Semiotics, Cinema*. Bloomington: Indiana Univ. Press, 1984.

Eco, Umberto. "*Casablanca:* Cult Movies and Intertextual Collage." *SubStance* 14, no. 2 (1985): 3–12.

Eisenstein, Sergei. *The Film Sense*. Trans. Jay Leyda. New York: Harcourt, Brace, 1975.

Gundersen, Edna. "Cult Films." *USA Today,* Oct. 21, 1985.

Hoberman, J., and Jonathan Rosenbaum. *Midnight Movies.* New York: Harper, 1983.

McBride, Joseph. *Orson Welles.* New York: Viking, 1972.

Metz, Christian. *The Imaginary Signifier: Psychoanalysis and the Cinema.* Trans. Celia Britton, Annwyl Williams, Ben Brewster, and Alfred Guzzetti. Bloomington: Indiana Univ. Press, 1982.

Sarris, Andrew. "Stranded in Soho's Mean Streets." *Village Voice,* Sept. 17, 1985.

Siegel, Joel E. "Alan Rudolph's Urban Fables." *L.A. Weekly* 8, no. 16 (1986): 38.

Sontag, Susan. "Notes on 'Camp.'" In *Against Interpretation,* 277–293. New York: Dell, 1966.

Stewart, Susan. *On Longing: Narratives of the Miniature, the Gigantic, the Souvenir, the Collection.* Baltimore: Johns Hopkins Univ. Press, 1983.

PART II

The Classical Cult Film

I should introduce this section with something of a warning. For I recognize that terming a particular version or group of cult films "classical" might prove a bit misleading. As this term is most often employed, it denotes a certain set of storytelling practices, various conventions of shot arrangement, editing, and character development that are associated with traditional Hollywood filmmaking. My intent here, though, is not simply to suggest that a body of cult films strictly adheres to this narrative style, but rather to indicate a broad linkage to classical cinema, in terms of both its narrative and its exhibition practices, that helps account for the appeal of a number of cult works.

Of course, the classical cult film is usually a rather conventional sort of narrative, although we might find its appeal rooted in the enduring *power* of that narrative, as seen in a film like *Gone with the Wind*, or in its *fragility*, that is, its tendency to stretch at the bounds of classical narrative and our acceptance of its world, as do a great many films that have been embraced for their "camp" appeal. Thanks to either of those appeals, this sort of cult film has managed to overcome many of the restraints that usually limit the distribution and exhibition practices of classical cinema. While a particular film may have been carefully tailored to work within one set of cultural circumstances—representing a particular studio, playing at its theaters, for a certain audience—in its cult incarnation it continues to exercise a hold in other times and conditions. Thus its plot and characterizations, easily embraced by one era's audience, remain accepted, if often nostalgically, by another's. And its stars, who effectively embodied one generation's aspirations and anxieties, still fascinate us or satisfy our desires for identification and vicarious expression. It is, in sum, a form that has found extra life outside the old patterns of presentation—as in the cases of repertory cinemas and, more recently, specialized cable channels—and that can continue to live on, partly because of the very conditions that often seem to limit the appeal—and life span—of other films.

Most of the essays that follow focus on what many see as the paradigmatic classical cult work, *Casablanca*. That perception follows in part from the American cultural landscape, which has tended to idealize a romantic, highly glamorous, and heroic past—one often located in the period surrounding World War II and visually fixed for us by the classical Hollywood cinema that reached its peak in both production and influence in that era. It follows as well, though, from prior critical commentary and particularly from what is probably the seminal analysis of the cult film phenomenon, Umberto Eco's discussion of *Casablanca*. Indeed, Eco's essay clearly haunts much of this volume—much like the mythic Echo, whose voice mockingly spoke even in her absence.

Precisely because it is so often reprinted, Eco's essay is not included here, although its approach to *Casablanca* and the cult sensibility serves as a springboard for discussion and disagreement in many of those pieces that follow. While my contribution to this section accepts *Casablanca* as a useful paradigm, it takes issue with Eco's description of the film as a "hodgepodge," a notion he then extends to describe the heterogeneous nature of every cult film. What I find most interesting about *Casablanca* is a suggestive consistency, particularly a concern with a pattern of "larcenous" behavior that I believe also typifies the cult film in general. This behavior, as *Casablanca* models it, involves violating the normal world, defying its everyday laws, liberating something. In essence, that "something" is another identity, an outlaw persona that, for a time—the duration of the film experience—an otherwise law-abiding, even a normally conservative self might adopt. In that pattern, I feel, we can more clearly see *Casablanca*'s position as a paradigm for all classical cult films.

The next two essays look at particular dimensions of this model text, one by examining a revealing image pattern, the other by placing *Casablanca* in the context of its cult history. Larry Vonalt looks at the influence of style on our experience of the film and, particularly, a strange conflation of visual styles in *Casablanca* that combines what he terms "the artfully glamorous" tradition with the emerging *film noir* look. As the film shifts from one to the other, and thus plays off of our conventionalized readings of these different looks, he suggests, it compels us to view the characters and events of the film in a curiously double way—one that generates a constant play of alternate possible readings that helps account for its quite varied appeal. James Card takes that appeal as his primary focus, as he looks at the variety of reasons for *Casablanca*'s cult status. In a subjective assessment that ranges over the complex background to its creation and reception, he explores how he and so many others have become devoted, nearly "beyond all reason," to this classical cult film.

The last two essays in this section extend Card's focus on audience reception to other cult films and figures. T. J. Ross sees a film like *Beat the Devil* as symptomatic of a number of offbeat works that appeared in the 1950s and 1960s, all of which, despite their seemingly conventional narrative lines, have a strangely reflexive, almost "camp" twist. That mix, he offers, points to one of the preconditions of their success: such films require—and play off of—the audience's mindfulness of earlier cult works. In this way, they hint of a kind of spiraling trajectory for the cult that might be traced out in a later generation of cult works, the midnight movies. In his essay on Judy Garland, Wade Jennings looks at another way in which audience reception comes into play in cult formations, in this case, as it lends its own shaping hand to the star persona. Along with Humphrey Bogart, James Dean, and Marilyn Monroe, Garland most epitomizes the film cult figure, and Jennings examines how the growth of the myth surrounding her life and career increasingly powered the audience response to both the person and her films. What he thereby demonstrates is the almost irrational, loving relationship between the cult audience and its varied objects of attention.

Sam plays, while Rick and Ferrari bargain for his services. (Warner Bros./Museum of Modern Art)

The *film noir* look of *Casablanca*. (Warner Bros.)

Rick "negotiates" in his own way for the Letters of Transit. (Warner Bros./Museum of Modern Art)

The older, self-aware romantic couple—Bogart and Jennifer Jones in *Beat the Devil*. (United Artists)

Judy Garland as child star in *The Wizard of Oz*. (MGM)

Garland as romantic lead—paired with child alter ego Margaret O'Brien—in *Meet Me in St. Louis*. (MGM/Museum of Modern Art)

CHAPTER 4

Casablanca *and the Larcenous Cult Film*

J. P. Telotte

[*Casablanca*] is a hodgepodge of sensational scenes strung together implausibly; its characters are psychologically incredible, its actors act in a manneristic way. Nevertheless, it is a great example of cinematic discourse, a palimpsest for the future students of twentieth-century religiosity, a paramount laboratory for semiotic research in textual strategies. Moreover, it has become a cult movie.

—Umberto Eco, "*Casablanca:* Cult Movies and Intertextual Collage"

Casablanca is undoubtedly one of the most popular films of the American cinema. In 1943 it won Academy Awards for Best Film, Best Director, and Best Screenplay, and in 1977, when the American Film Institute asked its members to select the ten best American films of all time, *Casablanca* finished third, behind only those two popular and artistic institutions, *Gone with the Wind* and *Citizen Kane.* As Umberto Eco notes, it is also what we commonly call a cult movie (3), a film with a devoted audience that seems to know every line of dialogue and to anticipate with great relish every plot twist. In that very status, however, we also get a hint of its problematic position among film historians and critics; for we typically associate the "cult," whether in film, literature, or music, with something less than high art and consign its examples to a netherworld of popular culture.

Despite all of its mesmerizing connections, Eco's discussion of *Casablanca* is firmly rooted in this attitude, as he describes the random pattern of signification that occurs in this film, a pattern that, he suggests, demonstrates its ties to other cult works. A cult movie, as he explains, is one that lacks "a coherent philosophy of composition. It must live on in and because of its glorious incoherence" (4). Of course, as a student of semiotics, Eco naturally finds *Casablanca*'s rich variety of signs—Bogart as existential emblem, the patterns of melodramatic formula, conventions of good and evil character portrayals, the elements of classical Hollywood narrative—a most fertile ground for investigation. At the same time, the legend of *Casablanca*'s filming, that it was shot in sequence as the script was daily being written and finalized, only encourages this approach. Despite his efforts to avoid judging the film itself, though, Eco's analysis inevitably seems to trivialize what the public perceives to be a classic of the American screen, as he suggests that it continues to find an audience only because it has "something for everyone" and little of coherence, depth, or unified focus to appeal to more discriminating moviegoers.

Focusing on the film's "organic imperfections" in this way obscures one of any cult film's most important characteristics, namely, its ability to take on a life of its own and thus to "live on," appealing across time periods and generational lines. Certainly, there are enough instances in the film industry today of a work trying to attract a large audience share by shrewdly reading our culture's current and varied enthusiasms, and then incorporating "tested" elements calculated to play on those immediate enthusiasms. But that same random and current appeal would, in turn, almost assuredly work against a film historically, as our attitudes, values, and appeals go through their normal evolution. Viewed against a broad historical backdrop, a film might well seem like a mishmash, a piece of "camp" art, or worse, meaningless to an era in which none of those original attractions works for audiences any longer.

Casablanca's appeal, however, is hardly "camp," and while there is much going on in the film, it is also surprisingly unified in a number of ways that Eco's semiotic perspective overlooks. One such source of unity shows up in the film's overarching mythic structure. As David Middleton has convincingly demonstrated, *Casablanca*'s narrative closely follows a familiar, even timeless pattern, that of the monomyth which describes "the journey of the hero figure through his physical and psychic life" (11). Joseph Campbell, particularly in his *The Hero with a Thousand Faces*, has provided the classic analysis of this universal narrative formula, which we find graphically modeled in a wide variety of Western culture's masterworks, including *The Iliad*, the New Testament, and *The Divine Comedy*.

Two phases of this mythic formula in particular, its "retreat" and "quest" phases, help to structure *Casablanca*. In the retreat phase, a hero withdraws from the world of action and stubbornly resists all efforts to draw him back into this realm. Eventually, though, the hero emerges from his retreat and embarks on a quest, through which he proves himself and gains a new understanding of his being. In this vein, as the action of *Casablanca* begins, we find the American expatriate Richard Blaine withdrawn into a private world, his own cafe in Casablanca, but by the time the narrative concludes, he has abandoned his isolation—sold his cafe—and fully committed himself to a world of action, even embarking on a personal quest of sorts, as he joins in the worldwide fight against the Nazis. In following these fundamental patterns, Middleton argues, *Casablanca* "manages to achieve a kind of universality" that accounts for its broad and enduring appeal.[1] In effect, it works out a mythic story that viewers will always find fundamentally coherent and attractive.

Still, I do not want to place too much emphasis on this notion of a mythic unity. Neither the key to any cult film's appeal nor the specific lure of *Casablanca* seems to lie precisely in this direction. However, one of the basic functions of myth is to shape the variety of human experience into a meaningful form. Even as we recognize that *Casablanca* operates within a broad mythic pattern, then, we should also acknowledge that it does pursue multiple themes and develop the various levels of coherence Eco suggests. On its broadest level, for instance, the film talks about the desire for freedom and the individual's ability to overcome any cultural limitations; the frequent images of airplanes, the airport, and talk of "the clipper to America" effectively evoke this motif. At the same time, it analyzes the lure and fallacy of isolationism as a personal and national policy. To this end, Rick repeatedly avows that "The problems of the world are not in my department. I'm a saloon keeper," even as he reflects on "what they're doing in America" on December 7, 1941, when these events are supposedly taking place. But what such nearly opposite concerns argue for is not so much the "hodgepodge" Eco observes, but a richness to the film's overarching mythic structure: a variety worked into unity and a depth that may well prove central to the way this and other cult films work.

What I wish to do here is to investigate one such structuring theme in *Casablanca* that helps unify its variety, while also shedding further light on its cult status. I am interested in the film's normally overlooked concern with thievery—a concern which, in many ways, proves metaphoric of the cult phenomenon itself. But first we should note that what Eco finds both amusing and intriguing in the film is not the presence of various themes, but the randomness with which they seem to operate, the fact that the connection of any one to the narrative whole appears so terribly elusive and arbitrary. A motif like thievery is instructive in this regard precisely because of its seeming slightness. It is the sort of motif that might have been worked into the film to provide what we vaguely label "atmosphere" or texture by helping to suggest a pattern of corruption in the world of *Casablanca*. Yet, fortuitously, it is also a pattern that sharpens the focus of themes like those cited above and eventually lends a quite different sort of unity to the entire film—the unity of cult activity.

This pattern operates so subtly, though, that one might well ask, "What thievery?" The film's opening establishes various settings, all of them linked by a significant pattern of thefts. As *Casablanca* begins, we see a turning globe, then a map of Europe and North Africa, while a voice-over sums up the current world situation—describing a world at war. Shifting from this global perspective, the narrative next introduces the city of Casablanca, which has become the focus of much of the refugee traffic caused by the war. Finally, we view various groups of individuals within the city, most of them anxiously seeking a way out to freedom. Accompanying each of these levels is a tale of theft that serves a monitory function, warning us of a need to be vigilant, not only at the individual level, but on the social and international levels too, and justifying the initial image of the turning globe by pointing to a worldwide problem. First, the people of Europe have been dispossessed, their countries forcefully taken from them by the Nazi war machine. Second, several important documents, "Letters of Transit" that effectively control the refugee flow, have been stolen from German couriers in the desert and are now on their way to Casablanca and its flourishing black market. And, third, a pickpocket lifts a wallet from an unsuspecting couple, even as he warns them about the "scum of Europe" who have migrated to Casablanca. From the international down to the individual level, then, a pattern of thievery is immediately established, and with it a sense of this world as a fluid, unpredictable, and threatening place, requiring constant vigilance.

The narrative is effectively motivated by the second of these acts, the theft of the Letters of Transit or official travel permits. The announcement of their disappearance starts a montage of search scenes, as the local police begin rounding up "all the usual suspects," and it introduces the major characters in the drama that will follow. This theft brings the Czech patriot Victor Laszlo, who is fleeing a German concentration camp, into contact with the American expatriate Rick Blaine, who operates a popular Casablanca nightclub; it involves the German officer Major Strasser in a contest of guile and strength to prevent Laszlo from obtaining those papers and return him to imprisonment in Europe; and it reunites Rick with his lost love, Ilsa Lund, who tries to get the papers from him, first by persuasion, and then by taking them at gunpoint—in effect, repeating the original theft. The initial theft thus establishes a relationship for all of the major characters here and even precipitates other thefts. It becomes their focal point, just as a similar purloined letter in Edgar Allan Poe's tale of that title forms a kind of hub for an interplay of deception and detection, guile and insight, and theft matched by theft in that classic story.

In fact, Poe's tale has much in common with and offers a revealing gloss on this film. In both instances, a letter or letters have been stolen; in both the person who possesses the stolen documents is known or suspected; in both a shift in political power seems to hinge on their possession; and in both the documents are "hidden" in relatively plain sight—in Poe's story, the letter sits unnoticed in a prominently placed letter holder, while in the film the letters are in Sam's piano, which occupies a central spot in Rick's nightclub. What may be most significant about these similar situations for our discussion is that both represent a fundamental challenge to the prevailing political order. For each narrative presents its motivating action as not just a theft but a defiant act. In one case, the thief is "the Minister D—, who dares all things" (227), as Poe notes, and even seems to delight in stumping the police who so thoroughly search his quarters. He "dares" because of the power to be gained, for through his theft of a personal letter, he wins control over the Queen and, through her, over the government itself. In the other case, the theft represents a significant strike at Nazi power—two German couriers were murdered to gain the letters—and an effort to usurp some of that conquering power's authority, since the Letters of Transit open up the lanes of free travel that the Nazis have sought to close. Subsequently, it promises to reveal weaknesses in the Nazi system by permitting the escape of "a subject of the German Reich," the resistance leader Laszlo.

While Poe's story seems to emphasize on one level the powers of reason, or "ratiocination," as the detective protagonist Dupin puts it, and on another, as Barbara Johnson sees it, the problematic nature of the signifier (238), *Casablanca* takes a more emotional focus. Through its romantic triangle of Rick, Ilsa, and Laszlo, it turns our attention mainly to the human feelings of possession and loss that are brought out by this motivating theft. Thus while the Poe tale works entirely through a distancing frame, as the letter's original theft and even the manner in which Dupin recovers it are *related* after the fact, *Casablanca* quickly drops its introductory voice-of-god narration[2] in favor of an individual focus that is consistent with traditional Hollywood narrative. The missing Letters of Transit shift into the background—are effectively replaced—as Rick Blaine's missing love, his *stolen* girl, comes to the fore. As we learn, just before they were to leave Paris and be married, Ilsa was called away and spirited to her husband, Laszlo, who had been presumed dead in a Nazi concentration camp. The aftermath of that loss shows up here as Rick by turns spurns his former love and considers stealing her back from Laszlo. In fact, the film's conclusion turns on this linking of the girl and the letters, with Rick contemplating using them to take the girl away with him to America, or keeping her in Casablanca while sending Laszlo off, the letters effectively taking Ilsa's place. That he does neither represents a significant turn in the narrative away from the personal, a turn again measurable in terms of the theft motif.

The primary love relationship, wherein Ilsa disappears, reappears, and effectively challenges Rick to steal her from her husband or lose her forever, plays against a broad pattern of theft at work in this world, and in the process points toward *Casablanca*'s larger significance. For the warring world around Casablanca is, after all, one where possession seems determined by strength or guile, by the ability to dispossess others of what is rightfully theirs. While the Nazis and their conquest of Europe and North Africa are the primary example, that model of action has clearly filtered down to the rest of this world, too. Our introduction to Casablanca, as we have already noted, is marked by a visiting British couple's being victimized by a pickpocket, who, even as he lifts the man's wallet, politely if ironically warns him to be on his guard because the "place is full of vultures, vultures everywhere." Shortly after, we see the same pickpocket at work in Rick's Cafe Americain, the film's main setting, where we encounter various "parasites," even "cut-rate" ones like the thief and murderer Ugarte, and Germans who, the waiter Carl notes, receive the best table in the club because "they would take it anyway." A flourishing black market adds to this cultural portrait, as does the information that not even Rick is immune from this atmosphere. His supply shipments, we learn, always come "a little bit short," with something stolen—a condition which the black market leader Ferrari passes off as the inevitable "carrying charges," but in recompense Rick's own club seems to rely heavily for its business on the various illegal activities that transpire inside and on its rigged roulette wheel, with which it takes back what is lost from its customers.

What this general climate of larceny and corruption helps sketch out is a world that is disturbingly fluid, readily open to dispossession and appropriation, in part because too many of its inhabitants are like the dotty British couple who, by their own admission, "hear very little and . . . understand even less." In such a context, people are constantly prey to being dispossessed and often seem little more than objects themselves, or as Ferrari notes, "Casablanca's leading commodity." Moreover, the authority that holds this culture together, as embodied in Captain Renault's Vichy French government, is itself little more than a kind of institutionalized corruption, permitted by that larger embodiment of social evil, the Nazis. The result of this pervasive atmosphere is a pointedly antisocial climate, an antisocial society, if you will. Thus Renault praises Rick's avowal that he would not help Laszlo escape Casablanca, because "I stick my neck out for nobody," as "a wise foreign policy." In such an unmoored, insecure world, the film warns, a cynical selfishness can quickly become the model for human behavior.

Just as the climate of thievery here reflects the larger Nazi model, so does this cynical selfishness mirror the German attitude and, in fact, even contribute to its power. In fact, the film repeatedly attacks the preeminent concern with self—a self that finds its own profit in this climate of larceny—as fueling the Nazi criminality. To this end, Rick's isolationist, self-serving code is repeatedly underscored, as when he refuses to help Ugarte; when he turns a deaf ear to Laszlo's pleas and tells him to "ask your wife" why he will not help; when he initially counsels the Bulgarian girl Annina, who asks for his help, to "go back" to her occupied homeland; or when he tells Ilsa, "I'm not fighting for anything anymore except myself. I'm the only cause I'm interested in." The larger implications of this stance become explicit, though, when Rick speaks of an America that, in December 1941, when these events take place, was still safely uninvolved and distant from the war: "I'll bet they're asleep in New York; I'll bet they're asleep all over America." It is the sort of retreat from involvement that only thinly masks a wish for oblivion to which the Nazis willingly cater. Thus when Laszlo argues that "if we stop fighting our enemies, the world will die," Rick simply sidesteps his argument, saying "What of it? Then it'll be out of its misery," and notes that he intends "to die in Casablanca. It's a good place for it."

Of course, that stance was meant to work ironically, challenging *Casablanca*'s viewers to adopt an opposite posture of action and commitment to a cause. As Robert Ray argues, though, posing such a challenge was difficult, since it evoked the very tensions implicit in the narrative. With their respective commitments to isolation and group action or rugged individualism and dedicated idealism, Rick and Laszlo represented "two divergent strains of American mythology" (103) that had never been satisfactorily reconciled. The motif of thievery, however, helps to effect that reconciliation by shaping an individualistic action that ultimately serves the group, a kind of outlawry that implicitly acknowledges the real need of law in this unstable world. Moreover, it is precisely the sort of paradoxical pattern that would ultimately contribute to its cult lure.

Again, Poe's story affords an interesting parallel. We never really know what the contents of the purloined letter are; our concern is solely with the power it conveys to the possessor, its effect. Similarly, the film's Letters of Transit signify nothing in a conventional "letter" sense; that is, they carry no message. They are pure signs that, as the thief Ugarte explains, "cannot be rescinded, not even questioned." Thus they are significant—they function as signs—solely in terms of their effect, their allowance of movement despite the Nazi effort to control all movement. As a result, the film's focus becomes largely on *effects*, not meaning, on what shifts in power their possession might produce, in how they too might upset the status quo. What those letters ultimately *say*, consequently, is just how unstable power and authority are here—on the one hand, how easily they might be wrested from their rightful possessors but, on the other, how available they also are to being retaken from the thieves. And this latter message would have been as comforting to audiences in the early war years as it is today for viewers who might see themselves as dispossessed or repressed by a monolithic system or status quo.

Poe's story, free from *Casablanca*'s historical constraints, manages a simpler visitation of justice through a narrative repetition; the theft of the letter is redressed by Dupin's stealing it back from Minister D—, which results in political power being restored to its rightful wielder. While the film moves toward a similar narrative repetition, its task is complicated by the fact that, unlike Poe's tale, we here shift over to the side of thieves and thievery—at least insofar as that thievery is directed against the global thieves, the Nazis. The film does set up a potential for such a turn, as Ilsa comes to Rick's room, asks him for the Letters of Transit, and, when he refuses to surrender them, tries to take them at gunpoint. Her theft fails, however, and appropriately so for the narrative's sake, since, as we have noted, the letters themselves are less important than their effect, in this case permitting Laszlo's escape. While Ilsa's effort to steal the letters from Rick, motivated as it is by a concern with "something more important" than her own feelings, seems a properly revolutionary theft, an action we might embrace, we have already been led to believe that it might ultimately accomplish little. It would neither change this world nor, in all probability, result in Laszlo's escape; as Rick notes, with his more realistic sense of how fluid and unpredictable this world has become, "People have been held in Casablanca in spite of their legal rights."

For this reason, it is important that Rick retain and dispose of the letters himself. For he represents a hope of difference or change, as his past history—running guns to Ethiopia to combat the Italian invaders, fighting on the loyalist side in Spain, or being on the Germans' "black list" in Europe—and his deep knowledge of this world attest. Then too, Rick, after the fashion of the heroic gunslinger of the Old West, shares this world's coloring; as we have noted, he too, in his small fashion, is a thief and thus able to deal with this world on its own terms in a way that neither Ilsa nor Laszlo can. Of course, he could not steal the letters from himself, but he can make off with what the Germans really want, which is Laszlo. And in the process he can affirm and make acceptable our previously uncomfortable placement in the narrative. Pulled alternately toward Rick's self-focused independence by the sheer weight of the Bogart persona and toward Laszlo's selfless idealism by the wartime situation, we finally locate a narrative identity we can embrace. It is that of the underdog thief who hopes to turn the tables on the authorities; for where evil is law, its defiance becomes the common good and the defier a proper hero. There can be no simple repetition of the prime or motivating theft here, then, because it is not a theft that we want set right. To the contrary, it must remain an open violation for best effect, since that very openness promises a difference or alternative to the Nazi status quo.

What is taken away—or "stolen"—at the film's end, though, is especially fitting given the notion that people are the "leading commodity" in this fallen world. Laszlo has all along been connected with the letters and pursued with even more vigor, as if he were what the Letters of Transit were really all about, their "meaning." And in effect he is, for his is the voice of freedom—or "transit"; he speaks a message made possible by the messageless letters that simply carry out an effect of freedom—or "transit." Thus, the initial theft here opens the way for another, more telling spiriting away from the Germans and their power, as Rick puts Laszlo and Ilsa—who is, as he says, "a part of his work, the thing that keeps him going"—on the plane to Lisbon and freedom.

With this conclusion the film looks toward an eventual reversal of the Nazis' criminal power, even the possibility of "stealing" back all that has previously been taken from Western culture by their rapacious march of conquest, summarized by the film's narrating voice at the beginning. In his famous seminar on Poe's "Purloined Letter," Jacques Lacan suggested that the tale is essentially about how "a letter always arrives at its destination" (72). What *Casablanca's* letters imply, particularly through their connection to Laszlo, is rather similar. It is the comforting notion that the stolen can eventually be stolen back, that theft—corruption, injustice, or simply repression—sets up the very conditions of its own undoing and thus will, in time, be redressed. In this way, the film speaks a hope felt throughout much of the world at the time of the film's appearance and a message which seems to have a universal and timeless appeal, that property—or people, even an ideal—will always return to its rightful place or destination, in effect, that what we have is naturally given, inalienable, and should be safe from theft.

A shift within the film's narrative structure reinforces this point. As we have noted, the film begins with a framing voice-over and documentarylike presentation that recalls the Movietone newsreels of the period; however, that framing device disappears and is forgotten as the narrative's romantic thrust comes to the fore. With this shift the film carries out a movement from the real or factual to the imaginary; that is, to that realm of our desires which the movies have always catered to. Simply put, *Casablanca* moves from the world of real experience—the harsh reality of unchecked German conquest in 1941—to the realm of the movies themselves and the wish fulfillment they have always offered viewers, marked most conspicuously here by Major Strasser's sudden death, Louis's improbably sudden conversion to the Free French cause, Rick's own enlistment in "the fight," and the escape of an effective leader, Victor Laszlo.

Eco's conclusion, that *Casablanca* finally represents "the movies" as a whole, already points in this direction. As he sees it, the factor that makes *Casablanca* a cult film is its naive use of so many conventions of classical film narrative: "it is not *one* movie. It is 'the movies.' And this is the reason it works, in spite of any aesthetic theory. For it stages the powers of Narrativity in its natural state, before art intervenes to tame it" (10). Of course, what most American films typically do, through their "powers of Narrativity," is imaginatively reframe our lives, providing us with the sort of appealing images or representations that will place us in an imaginary relationship to the real conditions in which we live. Like so many other narratives in this period, though, and especially those that had an implicitly propagandistic aim, *Casablanca* sought to link the imaginary to the real, thereby acting out or naively narratizing our wishes. In the transformation that its conclusion displayed, with Laszlo and Ilsa flying to safety and Rick and Louis heading off to continue the struggle, viewers were thus allowed to tap the very power of the movies in opposition to the Axis.

Even today, *Casablanca* exercises, as the most effective films always do, this imaginative power. Through its own successfully "purloined letters" and whole context of thievery, it not only manages to work its varied elements into a unity of concern, but it also models a kind of outlaw justice that seems a key to both the film's enduring appeal and its cult status. The thieves here, after all, are the true heroes, their transgressions actually a blow for law and justice. Since the ultimate effect of their action is all that matters, we are thereby allowed to embrace an identity that is at once dangerous and safe, revolutionary and conservative, outlawed and law-abiding. As is the case in so many of our "midnight movies," we can here transgress the status quo while remaining safely within our culture's generally sanctioned patterns of behavior. Perhaps it is in this sense that the film, after the imaginary pattern of most classical narratives, might be said to offer "something for everyone."

It is in this way too that *Casablanca* speaks of the very nature of the cult film and thereby validates Eco's fascination with if not his valuation of it. For the cult object ultimately works in a kind of thieving way. Perhaps its salient characteristic is an attractive difference—determined by its subject or its approach to the subject—that seems to place it (and, through our fascination with, immersion in, or dedication to it, us too) outside or at the margins of the mainstream, much like Rick himself, or the Bogart persona for that matter. Almost by definition, it stands apart from the cinematic norm, while providing us with our own temporary illusion of separateness. But with that privileged position, it gains a power of articulation. It can thereby speak of the movies' power, suggesting how, through them, we might swipe back the various hopes and dreams that the real world so often and easily takes away from the imaginary one we long to inhabit, and indeed come to the movies for. It is in this respect that the cult film surely comes to seem a kind of thief. Through its proscribed status, its own difference, it lets us feel comfortably and temporarily different, like thieves ourselves, as it postures at stealing our varied desires, as well as our freedom to express them, back from the restrictive world outside the movie theater.

NOTES

A version of this essay appeared in *Michigan Quarterly Review* 26, no. 2 (1987): 357–368.

1. Middleton argues that the changes made to the original play on which the film was based, *Everybody Comes to Rick's,* and to the film script suggest that the screenwriters took a mythic approach to their work. "What the screenwriters did," he offers, was "to strengthen the quality of universality in the material, to extend its likeness to mythic patterns" (15).

2. The "voice-of-god" narrator, a staple of the newsreels and semidocumentary narratives, was so-called because of the detached, omniscient, and authoritative voice-over it provided. For a discussion of the nature of this narrative device, see Kozloff.

WORKS CITED

Eco, Umberto. "*Casablanca:* Cult Movies and Intertextual Collage." *SubStance* 14, no. 2 (1985): 3–12.

Johnson, Barbara. "The Frame of Reference: Poe, Lacan, Derrida." In *Untying the Text: A Post-Structuralist Reader,* ed. Robert Young, 225–243. Boston: Routledge, 1981.

Kozloff, Sarah. "Humanizing 'The Voice of God': Narration in *The Naked City*." *Cinema Journal* 23, no. 4 (1984): 41–53.

Lacan, Jacques. "Seminar on 'The Purloined Letter.'" *Yale French Studies* 48 (1973): 38–72.

Middleton, David. "*Casablanca:* The Function of Myth in a Popular Classic." *New Orleans Review* 13, no. 1 (1986): 11–18.

Poe, Edgar Allan. "The Purloined Letter." In *The Short Fiction of Edgar Allan Poe,* eds. Stuart Levine and Susan Levine, 225–236. Indianapolis: Bobbs-Merrill, 1976.

Ray, Robert. *A Certain Tendency of the Hollywood Cinema, 1930–1980.* Princeton: Princeton Univ. Press, 1985.

CHAPTER 5

Looking Both Ways in Casablanca

Larry Vonalt

A film's visual style, its look, might seem to have little relevance to its cult status. At least, that is what we might think after reading Eco's "*Casablanca:* Cult Movies and Intertextual Collage." Though the notion of "collage" hints of a link to visual experience, Eco actually highlights not visual style but narrative situations that recall similar situations in earlier movies and, at the same time, seem to predict ones in later films. "*Casablanca* carries the sense of *déjà vu* to such a degree," Eco writes, "that the addressee is ready to see in it what happened after it as well" (6). Extending this notion of collage, Timothy Corrigan suggests that we see "cult action" as "radical bricolage, the play with and reassembly of signifiers from strikingly different cultures and contexts . . . crucifixes with motorcycles; lace over leather; Maoists in America; Woody Allen as Bogart" (92). These examples represent ways that "cult movies map a place for the viewer where she or he can act out simultaneously the vision of child and adult" (93).

Corrigan's idea that cult films contain seemingly conflicting visions—the child's and the adult's—along with Eco's that a film like *Casablanca*'s narrative situations possess the power to look both ways at once, suggests an important way the visual style of a cult film works. That style must allow the film's audience the freedom to entertain contradictions or radical views with no difficulty. It must visualize a world in which the audience can feel comfortable *with* contradiction. *Casablanca,* as a kind of archetypal cult film, well illustrates this stylistic quality. In it we find what might be described as a doubled visual style, coupled to a concern with betrayed appearances that is developed in the narrative.

Casablanca's doubled visual style results from a blending of what Richard Schickel describes as the "artfully glamorous" (35) tradition and the visual techniques of the then-evolving *film noir* form. The "artfully glamorous" has been a dominant visual guide for Hollywood moviemaking and was particularly influential in the studio era that produced *Casablanca.*

This style is designed to appeal to those whose lives might lack glamor and to those who long for the power and wealth with which such glamor is associated. The movies, as Roland Marchand points out, "usually showed life at its best. People wore the latest styles against backdrops of exquisite furnishings and the most modern home accessories. And the movie 'palaces' seemed to reveal the hunger of the audience for luxurious surroundings and the attentions of the servile class in the form of bowing ushers" (62). The "artfully glamorous" is, in fact, the visual style of the American dream. It is style as a signal of success, prestige, authority, and security—of all that we commonly desire.

The *film noir*, on the other hand, emerging during the dark days of World War II and in its disenchanted aftermath, represents the American dream's underside. Its low-key lighting, "creating areas of high contrast and rich, black shadows," J. A. Place and L. S. Peterson explain, "opposes light and dark, hiding faces . . . and by extension, motivations and true character—in shadow and darkness which carry connotations of the mysterious and the unknown" (327). This style emphasizes uncertainty, menace, paranoia, disorientation, the dark side of human existence—our dreams and desires gone wrong.

Interestingly, Rick's Cafe Americain, *Casablanca*'s primary setting, manages to express both visual styles and thus immediately keys us to look in two directions. It is a high-tone cafe, frequented not by riff-raff, but by those who can afford its pleasures. It is the favorite nightspot of those in power, like Captain Renault, the Prefect of Police. But since it operates only at night, Rick's is also susceptible to moods associated with the *film noir*. Its artificial, irregularly sourced lighting results in irregular pools of light and stark contrasts of shadow and light that typify the *noir* look. It is a place where those outside the law, such as Ugarte, illegally sell exit visas to those desperately trying to flee the Nazi menace. Though Rick himself does not sell exit visas, we gather that much illegal activity goes on there, and his cafe does have a back room for illegal gambling, which is allowed because Rick pays off Renault.

The main contributor to the film's aura of "artful glamorousness," though, is dress. That such is the case is appropriate, for, as Ann Hollander remarks in *Seeing through Clothes*, "Clothes create at least half the look of any person at any moment" (314). The look of most of the clothes in *Casablanca* might be described as classic, suggesting a world of wealth, taste, and power. In an interview thirty years after *Casablanca*'s filming, Ingrid Bergman made particular note of the contribution of her clothes in the movie: "Very often hair and hats age you tremendously and look quite ridiculous a couple of years later. But the two hats I wear [in *Casablanca*] are classical hats that you can wear today . . . [and] the clothes looked quite nice. They are really clothes you can wear today" (Anobile 7). We should note that even the less fortunate characters, such as the refugees Jan and Annina, wear well-tailored clothes. In fact, the black suit Annina wears when she asks Rick for his advice is cut much like the white suit Ilsa wears when she first enters Rick's cafe. And the men, particularly Victor Laszlo, are equally well suited, despite the heat of a North Africa setting and the chaotic times. This almost constant wearing of jackets would have suggested to many in the film's audience a world beyond their financial means, beyond their limited power.

The power expressed by these jacketed men reflects that stated by the uniforms of the military and the police. Jerzy Kosinski notes the striking effect of such uniforms in *The Painted Bird,* when he describes a boy's response to first seeing an SS officer: "The instant I saw him I could not tear my gaze from him. His entire person seemed to have something utterly superhuman about it. Against the background of bland colors he projected an unfadable blackness . . . he seemed an example of neat perfection that could not be sullied" (118–119). Strasser and Renault both have their dark and light uniforms, one apparently for day wear and one for evening, complete with gold leaf and appropriate medals that signify their status and power. Although uniforms most often designate a person's vocation, they also signal a person's special authority. Thus Major Strasser's uniforms are more elaborate in their decoration than Captain Renault's, signifying his higher power here.

We should note too that even Rick wears a uniform, after a fashion—his white tuxedo jacket with its white folded pocket handkerchief—that marks his authority over the cafe's customers. He permits or denies their cash advances, entry into the gambling room, hearing music they want played (his nod allows the band to play "La Marseillaise"), and winning at the roulette table. But unlike Strasser's and Renault's uniforms, Rick's is empty of medals and other decorations, more like a waiter's than an officer's. In effect, his jacket indicates both his power and its limitations. He can control what occurs within the cafe but remains at the mercy of Renault, who can and does close his cafe when occasion warrants a display of his power. Renault is, likewise, at Strasser's mercy. The similar dress of these three men not only maps their relative authority but also implies that they may share other qualities as well. Although most commentators on *Casablanca* have noted a likeness between Rick and Renault, we should not fail to see a similarity to Major Strasser as well—a similarity that hints of a darker side to someone like Rick. Basically, all three are players in the game of authority, waged in the glamorous arena of power. They enjoy strategy, a verbal battle of wits, the pleasure of being arbitrary in their use of power, and the amenities their positions of power give them.

The other major male figure in the film is also a player in the authority game, if less obviously so. Laszlo possesses neither the power of the state, like Strasser and Renault, nor the power of ownership, like Rick. His power comes from his commitment to a cause and from his wealth. His off-white Palm Beach suit and the way he wears it imply his wealth. In fact, almost everything about Paul Henreid's style of playing Laszlo—his impeccable but understated suits, his posture, his quiet mode of address—suggests a man of wealth who is capable, as Ilsa tells Rick, of opening up "a whole beautiful world full of knowledge and thoughts and ideals." Robert Ray has called Henreid's Laszlo the perfect embodiment of the "official hero" (98). Others might simply call him the White Knight.

Because we have long associated the color of clothes with particular moral qualities, we almost immediately link Laszlo in his white suit with the good and Strasser in his black uniform with evil. But *Casablanca* complicates such simplistic associations. Remember that both Strasser and Renault, who are most often seen in black, also appear in white or lighter-colored uniforms when they first dine at Rick's. Their actions at this time even seem to fit their clothes. They are not evil, comic-book villains. Rather, in their own way, they are attractive, sophisticated, well mannered, and capable of charm. Their ambivalence, in fact, equates with Rick's. He never appears in all white or all black. Thus, his dress suggests that he shares to some degree the qualities of both the military men and the civilian hero, Laszlo. His dress permits, perhaps even encourages, the audience to look at Rick from a double perspective, to see him, as does Eco, as a self-sacrificing hero, even as they sense in him some of the less noble character traits that would become associated with the characters of *film noir*—characters with which Bogart would later become associated.

The dress of the women follows a similar pattern, but rather than focusing on authority and noble motives, the women's dress emphasizes tensions between innocence and sexuality. That Annina and Ilsa wear similar clothes suggests, as we saw in the men, that they may share similar attitudes. An immediate difference between them shows up in their jackets' V necks. The more innocent Annina wears a white blouse under her jacket to cover the V, while Ilsa's bare skin under her jacket suggests a more worldly self. What the costumer Orry-Kelly has done in *Casablanca* with such a simple device as the V-neck dress and suit is quite revealing in disclosing certain qualities of a woman's personality along with her flesh. The teasing neckline of the V neck, which is a subtle repetition of the shape of the genital area, becomes a more or less discreet means of implying sexuality. The degree suggested depends on the depth and width of the V and on the amount of flesh exposed.

Just as this difference draws a visual parallel between Ilsa and Annina, it also visually enhances the parallel between Ilsa and Yvonne. Early in the film we see that, like Ilsa, Yvonne has a passion for Rick, one he rejects, as he will later reject Ilsa's, sending each woman off with another man. The similarity between the two women shows up especially on the day that Ilsa and Laszlo go to Renault's office and then on to Ferrari's Blue Parrot Cafe. Ilsa wears a horizontally striped blouse under a short-sleeved white dress with a V neck that plunges to her belt. That evening, when Yvonne enters Rick's cafe, she wears over a long white skirt a horizontally striped jacket that has a revealingly deep V neck. Her costume is probably the most daring in the film, but it aptly describes Yvonne's flamboyant sexual nature and is a means, she hopes, of drawing Rick's attention back to her.

Ilsa's clothes tell us that she is a woman who, like Annina, treasures "the whole beautiful world" of ideal love and, at the same time, like Yvonne, desires the sexual pleasure to be found with a man like Rick. The clothes she wears the first night she returns to Rick's and Rick's treatment of her are an early hint of Ilsa's conflicting nature. She still wears the white suit she wore earlier that evening, but now her head is covered by a long white scarf tied at her neck. Just before she appears in the darkened cafe, Rick has been getting drunk and tormenting himself with memories of his happy days in Paris with Ilsa. When she appears, backlit and framed by the doorway, she seems almost an apparition, a ghost of the angel Rick remembers and cherishes. As they talk, Rick realizes she is not the "angel" of his memory. She has not returned to him as he had believed she would, apologetic and begging for his forgiveness and love. He believes he sees through her appearance to Ilsa's real self and treats this *apparent* angel as if she were really a conniving tart.

In *Casablanca*, then, clothes help sketch an "artfully glamorous" world, a world of romance, wealth, and power beyond what most of the film's audience could ever experience. But at the same time, they also work as a kind of shorthand, enabling the audience to recognize qualities of personality these characters share. Those shared qualities, in turn, reveal a pattern of ambiguities in these people. Their clothes thus invite us to look both ways, seeing in the wearers light and dark sides, as they hint of a duplicity to all appearances here.

This duplicity of appearance is further developed by the use of a visual pattern of the sort that would become commonplace later in the 1940s with the emergence of the *film noir*. Place and Peterson suggest that "above all, it is the constant opposition of areas of light and dark that characterizes *film noir* cinematography" (330). This opposition of shadow and light speaks of a duplicity to all appearances by suggesting the hidden, the mysterious, the menace of forces inside and outside the self. Alfred Appel, Jr., asserts that shadow-striping of characters, or what he calls "the prison-bar chiaroscuro created by light projected through the slats of lattices or venetian blinds" is "the consistent signature of *noir* stylists" (223). In analyzing what he calls *Casablanca*'s metaphor of imprisonment, Sidney Rosenzweig identifies a number of such *noir* elements. Director Michael Curtiz "creates this metaphor," he says, "through his baroque imagery, crowded compositions, and chiaroscuro lighting. Throughout the film, smoke-encircled, shadow-striped figures move through pools of darkness in images similar to . . . prison scenes" (89).

Although these prison-bar shadows suggest that Casablanca is a prison from which people want to escape, they also help identify it as a kind of limbo, an in-between place of waiting, a place of uncertainty, impurity, and ambiguity. The opening newsreel-like scenes show Casablanca as a way station enroute from the Nazi menace, but it is a way station where one can easily get waylaid by uncertainties. These uncertainties are stressed in the film's first scenes: the roundup of the usual suspects and the picking of an unsuspecting tourist's pocket. Indeed, these two sequences suggest not only uncertainty but also how easily appearances can betray us.

In the roundup of suspects, a man with no identity papers is shot in the back as he flees the Vichy police. This scene's irony is intensified by his being shot in front of a huge poster of Marshall Petain, the Vichy French leader; on the poster we read Petain's boast about keeping his promises. At the end of this scene, a close-up shows the dead man's hand clutching papers that identify him only as a Free French partisan. This scene suggests that those who appear to be protecting the French are actually its betrayers, their countrymen's killers. This betrayal is underscored by the ironic image that opens the next sequence: a shot of the words "Liberté, Égalité, Fraternité" above the door of the police station, where those rounded up are taken. The inscription reminds us of the values the French police are supposed to stand for—values clearly put aside for the war's duration.

The pickpocket sequence that follows shows a small European coming to the aid of an English couple bewildered by the police's actions. While appearing helpful, warning them to be on guard because Casablanca is "full of vultures," he steals the Englishman's wallet. Besides betraying his helpful appearance, the pickpocket helps set in motion a pattern of betrayals, only belatedly discovered. The victim discovers his loss only after the event. These two early sequences also suggest the way the film moves

from the large-frame betrayals perpetrated by the Nazis and the Vichy police to the more personal, to focus, finally, on Rick's own sense of being
betrayed by appearances in Paris.

In fact, Rick's actions in Casablanca are largely based on what he sees as
that earlier betrayal of appearance. On his last day in Paris, Rick is playful
in the face of the approaching Nazis, because he believes Ilsa will be leaving with him. Even when Ilsa tells him, "Kiss me as though it were the last
time," he does not understand that it is indeed "the last" kiss. Only when
Sam arrives at the train station with a note from Ilsa, simply indicating she
will not be coming, does he begin to understand.

Unable to believe that Ilsa has been two-faced with him, Rick makes a
double of himself. In Casablanca, before Ilsa and Laszlo appear, Rick
adopts a tough mask of self-interest, one illustrated in his remark to Renault, "I stick my neck out for nobody." Yet we tend to agree with Renault's suspicion that "under the cynical shell" Rick is "at heart a sentimentalist." The clues to this sentimental self are not only those observed by
Renault, but also Rick's idiosyncrasies of not drinking with the customers
and his commanding Sam never to play "As Time Goes By." These idiosyncrasies are rituals Rick uses to keep himself aloof from this corrupt
world and to maintain the purity of his passion for Ilsa. They suggest that
Rick seems to believe, despite the evidence, that Ilsa may return to him
and love him again as she did in Paris.

When she does return and Rick joins her, Laszlo, and Renault for a
drink, the mask of toughness seems to drop away. Renault exclaims, "A
precedent is being broken." His manner seems so different that, at one
point, Renault says, "Ricky, you're becoming quite human." Although
Rick seems to be changing, the looks on his and Ilsa's faces suggest that
the change may only be superficial. Ilsa's face is, as one might expect at the
meeting again of an old acquaintance, smiling and pleasant. Rick's, however, remains somber, though he never turns his gaze from her. He realizes, like the pickpocket victim, that what he once thought he had is gone.

The scene reemphasizes the differences between Rick's and Ilsa's responses to their idyll in Paris. Ilsa truly believed, as she tells Rick later, that
she would never see him again, while Rick believed that, if he kept his love
for her pure, she might someday return and love him again. This scene also
demonstrates the irony, the looking both ways, that penetrates *Casablanca*.
Rick gets what he believes he will get by keeping his love pure: Ilsa returns
to him—but with another man on her arm. In such a situation, Rick feels
betrayed not only by Ilsa but by his belief. It seems little wonder, then, that
when he is alone with Ilsa later that evening, he should treat her so harshly.
With Ilsa's return in Laszlo's company, Rick begins to play the game of

revenge. If he cannot have Ilsa on his own terms (if he cannot get back Paris), then he will return his hurt (he will get back *at* Paris). Rick will not, of course, take overt revenge; rather, he will do it in keeping with his own ambiguous character. Only after the event, looking back, might Ilsa and Laszlo sense, as Rick did when they walked into his cafe, that what they had has been lost.

Rick's double nature now reverses; the tough, revengeful side submerges and the caring side surfaces. He will be as he believes Ilsa has been to him. He will become a pickpocket of her emotions. Interestingly, the film uses another *noir* technique to convey the two-faced natures of both Rick and Ilsa here. This technique is the mirror reflection or use of the character's shadow to suggest, as Place and Peterson put it, "an alter ego, a darker self" (335). We see this image of the double self when Rick's shadow is cast on the wall of his office as he goes to get some money and again when Ilsa's face is seen in the mirror in Rick's apartment as Carl comes to the door. These images hint of the double potential that we have already glimpsed in each of them.

Rick begins a series of betrayals with Renault, who sends Annina to Rick, expecting him to attest to Renault's honor. Although Rick does confirm Renault's word, he betrays him by letting Jan win enough money at roulette to gain his and Annina's exit visas. Rick's actions here make him seem, as the joyous response of the cafe personnel suggests, a caring hero. Yet, as his later actions testify, that appearance only goes so far. He brusquely refuses Laszlo's offer to buy the Letters of Transit and tells him to ask his wife why he won't sell. His refusal suggests that he wants to make Ilsa lie to Laszlo, as Rick has told her she would, or to make her suffer by having to tell her husband of her infidelity.

When Laszlo goes to a meeting of the underground, Ilsa takes it upon herself to get the Letters of Transit and gives Rick the chance to settle their score. Ilsa, much like Annina, is willing to offer herself for the letters, but Rick tells her he is not interested in her offer or in Laszlo's cause; his only interest is himself. His refusals keep pushing her to more drastic measures. She accuses him of being a coward, and he stares at her with a look of hurt disbelief until she apologizes. Finally, as if revealing a hidden other side of her own, she pulls a pistol, but he turns the tables on her by telling her to go ahead and put him out of his misery. This ploy shatters her resolve. He walks toward her, looking into her eyes, until she turns away and admits she still loves him as she had in Paris. Momentarily, at least, a world of glamor and ideal love seems regained.

Rick has seemingly rectified his betrayal, confirmed his belief that Ilsa would return on his terms, gotten back "Paris." Thus he embraces her and they kiss as they had kissed in the past. At this point, Curtiz inserts an intriguing gap in the scene. We see a shot of the airport searchlight glimpsed earlier in the film; then we return to the room where Rick leans casually against the wall, smoking a cigarette. How much time has elapsed and what has happened in that ellipsis are left to the imagination. (For one imaginative filling-in of this gap, see Robert Coover's "You Must Remember This" in *Playboy* of January 1985.) Ilsa continues with her story until she tells Rick, "You'll have to think for both of us, for all of us." Then, as if to affirm that "Paris" has been restored, Rick agrees to her request and tells her, "Here's looking at you," as he had done so often in Paris. Everything now seems settled. Rick and Ilsa will apparently stay together, while Laszlo will go on to continue his resistance against the Nazis.

Yet Rick's way of thinking for them all continues a familiar pattern, for it turns on the betrayal of appearance. The next morning Rick visits Renault at the police station and proposes a deal: if Laszlo is released, Rick will pretend to offer the letters to Laszlo and Ilsa, and Renault can arrest Laszlo on a substantial charge. Renault agrees and comes to Rick's that evening. When Laszlo and Ilsa arrive and a deal has seemingly been struck, Renault reveals himself and arrests Laszlo. But again Renault is betrayed, as Rick pulls a pistol on him and has him call the airport to clear the way for the Letters of Transit. Not to be outwitted in the game of betrayals, Renault instead calls Major Strasser.

At the airport, these betrayals of appearance build to a climax. The heavy fog of the airport scene establishes the appropriate *noir*-like climate, suggesting uncertainty and tension in a situation where nothing is certain—plans, motivations, resolution. It is also an appropriate backdrop for Rick's betrayals. Ilsa and the audience expect Laszlo to leave alone, and the images seem to point to such a conclusion. Rick has the orderly take Laszlo's luggage but says nothing about Ilsa's. Laszlo begins to follow the orderly but pauses, as if to ask Ilsa, "Are you coming?" When he turns back to the orderly, Ilsa, separated now from Laszlo and occupying the edge of the frame, looks expectantly toward Rick. At this point, Rick betrays all appearances, all expectations. He walks away from Ilsa and toward Renault, telling him to fill in the names of Mr. and Mrs. Victor Laszlo on the Letters of Transit. When Ilsa protests, Rick gives his explanation, while the camera tightly frames their faces, keeping them both in close-up until near the end of the sequence when Ilsa finally accepts Rick's "thinking."

We might see Rick's actions and explanations as simply a noble gesture. Rosenzweig, for example, feels Rick is acting on the knowledge he has gained from Annina's questions about "how events can force people to actions that seem to betray their feeling and belie their words" (93). Richard

Schickel interprets his actions as an "acknowledgment of the power of his best instincts, his better self, which was formed by values of the most old fashioned and, indeed, cultivated kind" (35). In effect, both critics want to see the ending in terms of a thematic that matches the film's "artfully glamorous" style, that is, as romantic almost beyond the world of everyday existence, the way we would like to be at our best.

But this film's continuing appeal derives in part from its ability to transcend the simple, to offer more than we expect—at least to offer such ideals *along with* other possibilities. Is Rick simply being noble? Given all the images of appearance betrayed and the fog-shrouded atmosphere, we might sense beneath the noble appearance a *noir* shadow, as Rick partly pays Ilsa back for having abandoned him. In this way of seeing the conclusion, he rejects her just as he believes she had rejected him. He gives her no choice, just as she had given him none in Paris. Certainly, there is a hint of cruelty in his putting her through such emotional turmoil to get her to confess her love for him and then tossing her over to Laszlo.

It is an element that also surfaces in his explanation to Laszlo. Despite Laszlo's statement that Rick need not explain anything, Rick explains, reasoning that what he says may make a difference to Laszlo later. In this speech Rick seems honestly to uncover all the secrets he and Ilsa kept from Laszlo. He tells how she came to him the night before to get the Letters of Transit, how she "did her best" to make him believe she was still in love with him, but that their love "was all over long ago," and he makes her admit to the truth of what he says. The audience wants to see this statement as a kind of beautiful lie, one that none of these characters really believes. And in a sense it is, for his love for Ilsa took on a darker coloring only when she walked into Rick's cafe with Laszlo on her arm. He tells Laszlo, "For your sake she pretended it wasn't [over], and I let her pretend." Yet in light of the various pretenses we have seen in the film, Rick's intentions here are difficult to gauge precisely. Perhaps later, Laszlo, in considering the possible interpretations of Rick's remarks, will discover that what he thought he had—Ilsa's love—is gone. For Rick's explanation, delivered for no certain reason, could well under the guise of honesty eventually undermine Ilsa's relationship with her husband.

Perhaps these possibilities suggest a Rick that most of us do not want to accept. Seen in this light, he seems too dark, too cruel—more a figure of *noir* than of the "glamorous" tradition. Yet that figure is from one perspective quite appropriate. Rick gets what he wants. By making Ilsa confess her love for him and then rejecting her, he pays her back in kind, if not in kindness. It little changes our admiration for the character. We admire his control, his skill in manipulating the situation to his advantage. He seems superior not only because of his control, but also because, like so many others in this complex and deceptive world, he knows what is happening. He is nobody's fool.

Such ambiguities and even opposite possibilities (see, for example, the lure of the camp here as well) are, of course, a large part of a cult film's special attraction. Its audience believes that only they can see certain qualities or resonances in a film, which have simply been overlooked or missed by mainstream viewers, often because those mainstream viewers look in such a conventional, *single* way. When we look at *Casablanca* doubly, though, we see a man who can get a measure of revenge and still be noble. It is the result of that wonderful magic of looking both ways, in this case, of having the glamorous and the *noir* too. This effect is achieved not simply by the film's dialogue and action, but by the doubling implicit in all the elements of its visual style. Those visual elements cue us to look two ways by pointing to the betrayal of all that seems the case in this simultaneously light and dark world.

WORKS CITED

Anobile, Richard J., ed. *Casablanca.* New York: Avon, 1974.

Apple, Alfred, Jr. *Nabokov's Dark Cinema.* New York: Oxford Univ. Press, 1974.

Corrigan, Timothy. "Film and the Culture of Cult." *Wide Angle* 8, nos. 3–4 (1986): 91–99.

Eco, Umberto. "*Casablanca:* Cult Movies and Intertextual Collage." *SubStance* 14, no. 2 (1985): 3–12.

Hollander, Anne. *Seeing through Clothes.* New York: Viking, 1978.

Kosinski, Jerzy. *The Painted Bird.* New York: Bantam, 1965, 1978.

Marchand, Roland. *Advertising the American Dream.* Berkeley: Univ. of California Press, 1985.

Place, J. A., and L. S. Peterson. "Some Visual Motifs of *Film Noir.*" In *Movies and Methods,* ed. Bill Nichols, 325–338. Berkeley: Univ. of California Press, 1976.

Ray, Robert B. *A Certain Tendency of the Hollywood Cinema, 1930–1980.* Princeton: Princeton Univ. Press, 1985.

Rosenzweig, Sidney. *Casablanca and Other Major Films of Michael Curtiz.* Ann Arbor: UMI Research Press, 1982.

Schickel, Richard. "Bogart." *Film Comment* 22, no. 3 (1986): 33–44, 46.

CHAPTER 6

Confessions of a Casablanca Cultist: An Enthusiast Meets the Myth and Its Flaws

James Card

O ver a long period of time I have come to realize that I am a *Casablanca* cultist. I had never really thought of *Casablanca* as a cult film, perhaps because I grew up with it. At age twelve I was deeply impressed by Ingrid Bergman, walking toward an airplane on a misty runway, the tears on her face just glimpsed beneath the large hat that shadowed her face. At age twenty seeing it again in a theatrical revival, I thought it was as good as I had remembered, not something I had outgrown. Later, in graduate school I saw it at the old New Yorker theater on Broadway in a showing memorable for a curious interaction of film and audience, who applauded the first appearance of each major performer, as if the film were a live stage presentation. Perhaps that response should have identified the reaction of a cult, but at the time I had never heard the term associated with film. Later, as a college professor, I have enjoyed introducing the film to students who whoop with gleeful surprise at lines like, "Major Strasser has been shot. (Pause.) Round up the usual suspects." Finally, after repeated viewings on television, I realize it is a film of which I, like so many others, never tire. A cartoon in the *New Yorker* (March 2, 1987), showing a wife discussing her stern-faced husband with a friend, has succinctly summed up my problem, "Beneath that gruff exterior, he's a sucker for reruns of *Casablanca*."

This recognition is important because cult films are defined not simply in terms of themselves but in terms of their "sucker" audiences. Danny Peary in *Cult Movies* discusses numerous cult works, *Casablanca* among them, but illustrates rather than defines the term, mostly because cult films are so hard to separate from the cul*tists*, from our experience of them. He acknowledges that they are "special films which for one reason or another have been taken to heart by segments of the movie audience, cherished, protected, and, most of all, enthusiastically championed" (xii). Assuredly, a cultist is an enthusiast, a word that more kindly describes the moviegoer attracted to repeated viewings than do other phrases often applied, such as "a sucker for reruns" or "a moron who has seen the film fifty or sixty times"; and the kind of enthusiasm that *Casablanca* arouses puts it, for Peary, in a class with such other classical narratives that have achieved this status as *All About Eve, Singin' in the Rain,* and *The Wizard of Oz*—films once "popular with the mass audience but today theatrically distributed primarily for hardcore fans" (xii). The problem is that enthusiasts or hardcore fans often do not seem able to discuss their enthusiasms objectively. Like Peary, they tend to *illustrate* their feelings by simply citing a line or recalling an image, but without shedding an understanding light on that compulsion. While recognizing the cultist traits in myself, I would like to use that very enthusiasm to reflect on *Casablanca*'s cult appeal.

As a good cultist, I must first defend *Casablanca*'s reputation. I feel more than a little indignant when a critic like Pauline Kael says "It's far from a great film" (96). How can she fail to see its special qualities? After all, it won an Academy Award and has delighted audiences for forty-nine years, constantly renewing its appeal to viewers. As a product of the Hollywood studio system, *Casablanca* does make a good case for the collaborative artistry of that system in the level of achievement attained in its directing, producing, acting, photography, editing, writing, music, and art direction. Michael Curtiz may not be recognized as a great director—for this reason Andrew Sarris calls *Casablanca* "the most decisive exception to the auteur theory" (176)—but he oversaw such memorable and diverse films as *The Adventures of Robin Hood, The Sea Hawk, Mildred Pierce,* and the underrated *The Breaking Point*—surely an honorable record. Hal Wallis, particularly in his years at Warner Brothers, was a producer of taste and distinction; in 1942 alone he produced not only *Casablanca* but also such classics as *Yankee Doodle Dandy* and *Now, Voyager.* The casting is lavish, with even the smaller roles, occupied by actors like Peter Lorre and Sydney Greenstreet, consistently memorable.[1] The cinematography is by a craftsman, Arthur Edeson, whose work is only lately being fully appreciated. The film also received an Academy Award nomination for editing; conspicuous instances of this craft in the film include the spine-tingling cut in the final scene as the airplane motor first turns, and the cut to Paul Henreid on the phrase "Aux armes, citoyens" during the playing of "La Marseillaise." Of course, the script won an Academy Award, and Max Steiner created a score that includes as a love theme his skillful variation on "As Time Goes By," while in the manner of the period, the studio sets provide a most convincing mise-en-scene. All of these elements coalesce to considerable effect, as the film industry's awards, audience dollars, and enduring appeal attest.

With a kind of self-protectiveness, though, a cultist can shrug off details in a film that confound close inspection. The British couple, for instance: what are they doing in Casablanca in December 1941? Bombs have been falling on London for two winters. How did they even get visas? If the setting were prewar or their nationality American, their presence would be more understandable, but since neither is the case, they simply are not credible among this mass of refugees. Of course, today's audience, with no immediate sense of the period, might not question the scene, because it is, after all, amusing. But then there are the swanky refugees, Ilsa Lund and Victor Laszlo. In a memo Hal Wallis questioned their manner of dress, wondering whether Ilsa "should ever appear in an evening outfit. After all, these people are trying to escape from the country. The Gestapo is after them; they are refugees. . . . It seems a little incongruous to me for her to dress up in evening clothes as though she carried a wardrobe with her" (Behlmer 212). As a matter of fact, she does carry a wardrobe with her— gowns by Orry-Kelly. But this *is* Hollywood in the 1940s and Ingrid Bergman is a star, even if on loan from David O. Selznick. She has four changes of costume, two outfits for day, each with its own hat, and two for night. One can excuse the refugees' appearance as mere Hollywood glamor, although a real *Casablanca* enthusiast might tell you that their apparent wealth is a legacy from *Everybody Comes to Rick's,* the play on which the film is based: in it Laszlo is wealthy, and the Gestapo is after him as much for the millions he has in foreign banks as for his political activity. In the film, his wealth is unaccounted for, his anti-Nazi activity stressed.

Another problematic element in the film is coincidence, but it too can be excused on the grounds that coincidence has served drama ever since *Oedipus Rex.* Moreover, one of the best defenses against an audience skeptical of coincidence is to call attention to it. To illustrate, in *All About Eve,* when Addison DeWitt tells Eve, "After tonight you belong to me," she replies, "Belong to you? That sounds medieval—something out of an old melodrama," which, of course, is precisely what the story is, melodrama of an old-fashioned kind. In the same way, Rick complains, "Of all the gin joints in all the towns in all the world, she walks into mine," baldly announcing the coincidence. A cultist accepts it with utter ease, feeling that the circuitous escape route described in the film's opening voice-over sufficiently accounts for Ilsa and Victor's arrival at Rick's Cafe Americain. Furthermore, a cultist will not feel uneasy to learn that Ilsa coincidentally received the news that her husband was alive and hiding in Paris on the very day she and Rick were to flee that city. Most certainly, a cultist can accept this and a good deal more, including the occasional blighting effect of the Production Code, seen most clearly in Rick's final shoot-out with Major Strasser, directly shaped by Breen Office interference. "Rick," notes Hal

Wallis, "was not allowed to shoot Major Strasser in cold blood, but had to be provoked" (Wallis and Higham 91). (In the script published in *Best Film Plays, 1943–1944*, Strasser has no gun, and Rick shoots him as Strasser telephones to stop the plane.) In the *Casablanca* we see, Strasser draws, but in the best Hollywood tradition Rick is faster. For a cultist like me, this moment too can pass, being seen not as something from a Western in disguise but as an instance of pleasurable recognition: of how movies, especially Hollywood movies, have their comfortable conventions, particularly when censors would not permit protagonists to take lives without being threatened or attacked first. And for most cultists, none of this really matters. Any need to excuse or justify such moments is simply ignored as a block to the pure and pleasurable enjoyment of the text.

With all cult films, one sign of a cultist is that he or she treasures the film's dialogue. No better example exists than Bette Davis's astonishment, on viewing *All About Eve* at a revival house in New York, as she observed people in the theater murmuring the dialogue. In the case of *Casablanca*, cultists not only treasure the dialogue but guard it jealously as their own special province. One example that I once treasured has now taken on larger, critical proportion; it occurs in the first scene between Louis and Rick:

> *Renault.* And what in Heaven's name brought you to Casablanca?
> *Rick.* My health. I came to Casablanca for the waters.
> *Renault.* The waters? What waters? We are in the desert.
> *Rick.* I was misinformed.

In *Talking Pictures*, Richard Corliss points out that this dialogue is Pinteresque in character (110). It is, in fact, an early example of a very modern style of speech, the put-on, exemplified especially by Lenny in Pinter's *The Homecoming*, a character who never says a straight word. In this respect, the dialogue of *Casablanca* seems ahead of its time and thus suited to an audience that finds characters of many years ago speaking their language, as it were.

Because we live in a far more ironic age, we can also see *Casablanca* with its frequently ironic dialogue as exemplifying our time's moods. Consider, for example, how Captain Renault introduces Major Strasser: "He is one of the reasons why the *Third* Reich enjoys the reputation it has today." Strasser takes this sly comment as a compliment, but Rick clearly understands its irony. For he and Renault are the film's two ironists, which is one reason why their pairing at its end seems so appropriate. Rick, we might recall, refers to the two murdered German couriers as getting a lucky break: "Yesterday they were just two German clerks. Today they're the honored dead." Renault's irony goes a step further, even becoming self-deprecating, as he notes, "I'm only a poor corrupt official," or when he learns that Rick intends to trick Laszlo and leave with Ilsa, and remarks, "You're the only one in Casablanca who has even less scruples than I." While some lines simply seem remarkably memorable understatements—"Here's looking at you, kid" is certainly the best example—others fall in the realm of calculated dramatic punctuation. For example, the climactic "Major Strasser has been shot. (Pause.) Round up the usual suspects" is simply a great *coup de theatre*.

While I admire *Casablanca*, I must confess to being an atypical cultist in some ways. For instance, I am not a Humphrey Bogart cultist, although I appreciate his Rick and would allow—scandalously to some—that there are eight or ten other performances of his worth watching. Conversely, I am a *Beat the Devil* cultist, but not because of Bogart. Essentially, I resent cultists who focus solely on Bogart's character, turning Rick into an existential hero, seeing him as a 1942 precursor of Camus' Dr. Rieux in *La Peste*, with Casablanca substituting for the Oran setting of that novel. I would save Rick from his idolaters in the same way that I would like to save Alfred Hitchcock, that master entertainer, from the critics who have tried to turn him into a metaphysician of the highest order.

I am also an atypical cultist in not accepting on blind faith, as most cult worshippers might, a number of myths surrounding the film. I use "myth" here as it is commonly defined, as a fictitious story or unscientific account, a meaning which is virtually synonymous with "legend," which is a story handed down for generations and commonly assumed to have a basis in history. Like many other cult films and more than most, *Casablanca* has generated myths or legends that are themselves partly responsible for its status. Some of the people who worked on the film have contributed such stories, and gullible cultists have accepted the colorful or improbable in the same way that Shakespeare's idolaters once embraced the notion that he never blotted a line, but wrote in bursts of pure inspiration and never revised. Many of *Casablanca*'s enduring myths are just as unlikely.

One myth, perpetuated in Paul Michael's *The Great American Movie Book* and repeated by Corliss in *Talking Pictures*, is that originally named for the leads were Ronald Reagan, Ann Sheridan, and Dennis Morgan (42). While such casting seems unlikely, an early studio press release did contain this erroneous information. But Hal Wallis notes that Jerry Wald initially suggested the material as a vehicle for either George Raft or Humphrey Bogart, and this was just five weeks after a studio worker submitted a plot synopsis of the play and before the studio even bought the property. Wald's suggestion that the piece be "tailored along the lines of *Algiers*" led eventually to the thought of Hedy Lamarr in the leading female role and thus to a change from an American girl to a European, although as studio memos show, Wallis was still imagining Bogart and Sheridan as the leads in early February 1942. For most people, the idea of Ronald Reagan as Rick is a joke (let alone the possible casting of Dennis Morgan as Laszlo) and is usually brought up to demonstrate the stupidity of Hollywood executives or to heap ridicule on Reagan by asking audiences to compare him with Bogart. But we might imagine what the film would have been like with George Raft, monotonous of face and voice, as Rick. Again, Hal Wallis states in *Starmaker* that Raft turned down the role of Rick and that Bogart was his next choice, while studio memos show that when Jack L. Warner approached Wallis about using Raft, voicing Raft's interest in the part, Wallis replied that "Bogart is ideal for it, and *it is being written for him* [italics mine], and I think we should forget Raft for this property" (Behlmer 196). The very endurance of the myth that Raft or Reagan might have been Rick, though, points to an appeal of the cult, how it represents an almost magical coalescence of elements, a nearly *accidental* creation of something wondrous.

Cultists also play this "what if" game with Ingrid Bergman, since both Hedy Lamarr and Michele Morgan were considered before she was, and, as with Bogart, the circumstances of her employment vary from source to source. In 1984, Julius Epstein, who collaborated on the script, claims that he and his brother Philip persuaded David O. Selznick to lend Bergman to Warners for the film by saying, "Oh hell, it's a lot of junk like *Algiers*" (Harmetz 1). Wallis, in contrast, recalls that he persuaded Selznick to let Bergman play Ilsa (86). Whether Wallis flew to New York to see Selznick or whether the Epsteins told the plot outline to Selznick or one of his assistants is part of the embroidery that gets stitched onto a legend. Other people mentioned for possible roles are noted in the collection of studio memos, *Inside Warner Bros.*, which reveals a major "what if" in Wallis's flirtation with changing the character of Sam into a black woman pianist and hiring Hazel Scott for the part. Fortunately, Wallis entertained the idea only briefly, but for a cultist the replacing of Dooley Wilson is almost as mind-boggling as Reagan substituting for Bogart. Again, these stories about possible casting suggest not only how important the cast is, but how crucial the sense of its *rightness*, of their almost providential coming together, is to the film's success.

Another often-repeated story that probably has some basis in fact is the anecdote about Bogart's afternoon at the studio. According to legend, Bogart went to Warner's one afternoon, did a three-second take, and returned home. All he did was nod his head. Any *Casablanca* cultist recognizes this shot as the moment when Rick allows his band to play "La Marseillaise." The story is a good one and useful for suggesting what the art of editing can accomplish in a few seconds. But as strange as studio methods of filming may seem to contemporary moviegoers, the studios were quite cost-conscious, especially with their time and stars, none more so than economy-minded Warner Brothers. It is hard to believe that Bogart would have been used in this way. However, there is a recorded instance of Bogart being brought back to the studio to film the script's final two lines. They are the final lines of the film as we hear them, but on August 7, 1942, they were only alternates. Two weeks after filming, Wallis wrote to Michael Curtiz what the final words would be, as spoken "by Bogart when we can get him."² Out of such circumstances legend is born.

That the film's final lines were written and recorded after all else was completed is certainly unusual, but they point toward the greatest myth about *Casablanca,* one that every cultist swallows whole: that the writers, players, director, and producer did not know how the film would end—that is, which man Ilsa would get on the plane with. Most reports corroborate that the scenes were filmed following the script's chronology, almost as if they were being performed in a play, so that, the script being incomplete, the players were unsure sometimes what they would be doing the next day or precisely where the narrative was leading (thus Bogart's return to do the final lines). But the idea that Ilsa would have left her husband for Rick is nonsense, because the Production Code was a major force at the time, and under no circumstances would Joseph Breen have permitted a married woman to leave her husband for another man. If Ilsa had chosen such a course, she would probably have been struck by lightning. In fact, Wallis notes that the writer he originally wanted for the script, Aeneas MacKenzie, felt that "the suggested relationship between the hero and heroine was overtly adulterous and that the Breen office, guardian of industry morals, would complain. He was right. They did" (84). MacKenzie's own memo says, "I feel the material presents very serious problems indeed . . . in my opinion the material will require drastic revision because the situation out of which the action arises (between Rick and the girl) is a highly censorable one . . . . This is a tough job for anyone it may be assigned" (Behlmer 198). Of course, a time-honored device of novelists and screenwriters existed. Killing off Victor Laszlo would have left the field clear for Rick and Ilsa and removed any doubt about the ending, but Breen would never have sanctioned any resolution but the one we have.

The myth of *Casablanca*'s ending results in part because of some self-serving mythologizing on the part of the participants and also because of the difficulty in determining who wrote what in the script. The Epsteins were hired to write the script, and they were paid the lion's share of script costs. However, early in the production they left for Washington to write government films for Frank Capra, so Wallis hired Howard Koch, who had worked for him on *The Letter,* to write an alternate screenplay. Later, the Epsteins returned to Hollywood and continued to write their version while Koch worked on his. Sometimes they worked together; as Koch notes, "My collaboration with the Epstein brothers was entertaining and, to a degree, productive" (93). Still, Wallis reports that in March of 1942 he only had sixty "satisfactory pages" of script and that on Sundays director Curtiz and the writers (presumably all three) came to his home, spread the pages out, and tried to combine them into a satisfactory draft. Koch adds that eventually the Epsteins "asked to be transferred to another assignment and the front office granted their request" (94). A Wallis memo to Jack Warner at this time states that their work "was practically all rewritten" (Behlmer 215), although in 1984 Julius Epstein recalled, "The ending of *Casablanca* was written dozens of times, none a satisfactory answer to the question of whether and how Ingrid Bergman should wind up with Paul Henreid or Humphrey Bogart. Then my brother and I were driving down Sunset Boulevard and we looked at each other and said 'Round up the usual suspects.' Somebody must have been murdered. Who was murdered? Major Strasser. Who killed him? Rick! That was the way we got our ending."[3] Yet Richard Corliss asserts that *Casablanca* "boasts some of the best dialogue to be found in an American film—which Koch wrote . . . . The script was completed at breakneck speed under appalling pressure by Koch, a junior member of the Warner's writing pool" (103). Koch himself recalls that after the Epsteins' departure, he had three weeks in which to provide the jumble of material with a narrative structure and that by the beginning date of production, he had the equivalent of the first act of a three-act play worked out with continuity for the rest. Providing the rest was "a race against time . . . . There were even several occasions when the company was on the set waiting pages to rehearse a scene" (Koch 95). Wallis adds, "Bogey complained constantly about the dialogue and the fact that new pages came in every day. The cast kept saying they had no idea what they were doing. We still had no ending. We didn't know if Rick or Victor Laszlo would get the girl and both actors were insisting they had better be the one. Ingrid kept saying plaintively, 'Does Bogey get me in the last scene or is it Paul?'" (Wallis and Higham 90). Bergman's concern is reflected in an interview with Richard J. Anobile: "I said to the writers, 'Now which of these two men do I end up with? . . . there is a little bit of difference in acting towards a man that you love and another man for whom you may just feel pity or affection.' 'Well,' they said, 'don't give too much of anything. Play it in between, just, you know, so that we can decide in the end.' Well, there was nothing for me to do but go ahead and try to play it in between" (6). Bergman further noted that there were two endings, one in which she would stay on the ground with Rick while her husband flew away and the one we know, but after the latter was shot, the actors were told there was no need to shoot the other. Finally, these differing reminiscences are confused by the knowledge that Casey Robinson, uncredited, worked on the script for two weeks; the money was paid him anonymously and listed in the budget as "script changes." Seemingly, Robinson solved the problem of Rick putting Ilsa on the plane with Victor, as his notes suggest, "a swell twist . . . he is not just solving a love triangle. He is forcing the girl to live up to the idealism of her nature, forcing her to carry on with the work that in these days is far more important than the love of two little people" (Behlmer 207). As anyone familiar with the film knows, these comments echo in the line that Rick finally uses to convince Ilsa to leave with Laszlo.

All of these stories surrounding the script are linked to two other received ideas about the film. The first is that it is based on one of the world's worst plays, as James Agee's review in *The Nation* suggested (29). Reports about the play vary: Koch says that "it died on the road before reaching Broadway" and so bears the stigma of a flop; however, a Warner's memo lists it as "unproduced" and suggests that a successful production might enhance its value as a film property. That the play may not have been produced does not discredit it, and a history of the plays produced on Broadway in this period substantiates the view that many plays much worse than *Everybody Comes to Rick's* opened and closed with rapidity, after playing for one night, a few nights, or a week or two.

Murray Bennett, the play's co-author, has made a copy available, and Warner's original story synopsis appears in *Inside Warner Bros.* What these sources indicate is that this "obvious imitation of *Grand Hotel*" and "sheer hokum melodrama of the E. Phillips Oppenheim variety," as some Warner's executives styled it, at least offered a solid structure upon which to mold the final film. Howard Koch says that at the beginning the Epsteins had "a locale, a few assorted characters and some fragments of a situation but nothing to hold them together—no story" (93), and after their departure he still had only "a miscellaneous jumble of characters, ideas for scenes and atmospheric bits." Nonetheless, the plot synopsis shows more than just ghostly demarcations for the final film. Rick, Renaldo (Renault), Sam, Ugarte, the Letters of Transit, Strasser, Laszlo, and Rick's encounter with Lois, a woman he loved in Paris who is Laszlo's companion, are all present.

Ugarte's asking Rick to hold the letters for him and his arrest and subsequent death are there, as are the girl's divided feelings: admiration for and gratitude to Laszlo, love for Rick. Jan and Annina are from Bulgaria, and, as in the film, she is a character foil to Lois. When she "confides to Rick she has agreed to yield to Renaldo (Renault) for the sake of an exit visa, Rick's cynicism is pierced; he begins to understand Lois" (Behlmer 195). Rick's line in the film, "Nobody ever loved me that much," clearly reflects this scene. Renault's closing the cafe, Rick's offer to trap Laszlo if Renault calls off the police, Rick covering Renault with a gun, and Rick's insistence that Lois/Ilsa leave with Laszlo are all there too, as is the bet between Rick and Renaldo/Renault on Laszlo's escape from Casablanca.

What we can also see is how the material needed to be reshaped by the screenwriters. Originally, Jan and Annina leave on one of the Letters of Transit, Laszlo and Lois on the other; it is a situation that resolves two plot lines simultaneously, but also dilutes the effect of the final escape from Casablanca and the Germans. The closing of the club by Renaldo is out of frustration when Rick hides Jan and Annina. Rick sacrifices himself for others at the close of the curtain and will be sent to a concentration camp. The principal changes are in the motives and personalities of characters, although some important scenes are also added or altered. Some attempt, for example, was made to "open up" what is essentially a single-setting play by adding scenes outside of Rick's cafe that enlarge the drama and flesh out the characterizations. We might think of the roundup of suspects in the opening sequence, the flashback to Paris, the visit to Ferrari's cafe, the scenes between Rick and Ilsa in the marketplace, Ilsa and Victor in the hotel room, and, later, Rick and Victor as the latter asks the former to take Ilsa away. More than simply adding "color," such scenes develop motivation and place the human actions here within a larger context. Other important changes within the two main acts of the play (that is, the two successive evenings at Rick's cafe before it is closed) are Jan winning at roulette so he can buy exit visas and Laszlo leading the club patrons in singing "La Marseillaise," which then becomes a reason for closing the club. Someone also happily moved the final scene from Rick's office to the airport.[4] What hindsight demonstrates is that all of these changes were invariably improvements over the play. Perhaps it is another case of a principle often demonstrated: just as second-rate novels often make first-rate films, whereas great novels translate to the screen with difficulty, so second-rate plays translate well to film, while those finely crafted for the stage resist that adaptation.

The myth of *Everybody Comes to Rick's* as a dreadful play leads to a second received idea—that *everything* surrounding *Casablanca*'s creation was a matter of happy circumstance. Hal Wallis's account of the film's production history furthers this belief by leaving us marveling that the film was made at all, while Howard Koch has remarked, "I still wonder how the film emerged from the chaos of its birth" (Koch 95). Yet clearly decisions were made by people like Wallis and Curtiz that were hardly accidental. In effect, two seasoned professionals who had already produced a number of distinguished films were in charge of the filming and made the final decisions. There were, as we have seen, four writers who contributed in some way to the script, but one need only compare the more convoluted history of the *Gone with the Wind* script to see what collaboration, often with writers uncredited, could accomplish. The stable, continuing, professional elements of the photography, music, and set decoration did not, unlike the script, require reworking or rethinking. As indicated earlier, the vital concerns of cultists tend to be with dialogue, casting, and production changes, particularly in the script. On all of these counts, someone made a decision, and for enthusiasts like me, those sometimes faceless Hollywood collaborators made the right decisions: they cast Bogart, Bergman, and Dooley Wilson; Lois was changed to Ilsa; Rick puts Ilsa on the plane with Laszlo, as in the play, but for very different reasons; he says, "Here's looking at you, kid" and other long-resonating lines. None of this can be accounted for solely by accident or luck. Skill had to do with it, mostly. The talents involved can say to detractors, as Liza does to Freddy in *Pygmalion*, "Here you, what are you sniggering at? I bet I got it right."

In the end, of course, it may be that for the cultist the heart and not the head, the feelings not the intellect prevail. Indeed, that may be sufficient. I cannot fully explain why *Casablanca* remains one of my favorite films. Certainly Peary's simplistic explanation of "pictures for which we have nostalgic feelings because they had great impact on us when we were kids" (xiii) does not hold, because viewing many of those films today is disillusioning, while seeing *Casablanca* is not. Still, I know that it lacks the visual brilliance and narrative style of *Citizen Kane*—as do most films. In reaching for some objectivity, I think that the triumph of feeling over intellect is, after all, a good bit of what this film is about. Hal Wallis early on thought that Jerry Wald's assessment of the story "had gotten to the heart of the matter . . . a romantic story in an exotic setting" (Wallis and Higham 84), and the film is certainly most romantic when its love triangle reaches an emotional impasse that is not resolved by the killing off of one of the three, as was often the case in classical Hollywood narratives.

For the audience, there are certainly divided feelings between those old terms "love" and "duty." The screenwriters may have made their most effective addition to the play in a scene that foregrounds this conflict—

when Ilsa comes to Rick to demand the Letters of Transit in the name of their "cause," threatens him with a gun, and then dissolves into tears. She asks him to do the thinking for both of them, and he remarks that "This is still a story without an ending." There follows the scene in which Laszlo asks Rick to use the letters to take Ilsa away, replying when Rick asks, "Do you love her that much?" "Yes, I love her that much." At this point, however much we might want Rick and Ilsa reunited, we realize that such a reunion could only be at the expense of Laszlo and the ideals he represents. Pulled in these different directions, *Casablanca* finally leaves the claims of its lovers unresolved, substituting for them a memory ("We'll always have Paris . . . we lost it . . . We got it back last night") and a larger commitment that effectively ennobles that irresolution. In the end, Rick puts their love in a global perspective ("It doesn't take much to see that the problems of three little people don't amount to a hill o' beans in this crazy world"); but it seems the *right* perspective, since it is, after all, the one the film began with—its first image the turning globe. In this larger context, with the stronger than personal claims made on the characters, Ilsa and Rick can part, going off to make their respective contributions to the war effort, while satisfying the Breen Office in the bargain.

It is a thoroughly romantic ending, one that serves the heart if not the head. The head, nonetheless, holds its reservations, asking the nagging question that Lucy once posed in a *Peanuts* cartoon as she watched Snoopy ecstatically dance and play the violin at the same time: "Yes, but is it art?" In 1984, lauding his script for *Reuben, Reuben*, which he also produced, Julius Epstein compared the old Hollywood with the new, declaring, "There wasn't one moment of reality in *Casablanca*. We weren't making art. We were making a living. Movies in those days were prevented from reality" (Harmetz 1). For Epstein, obviously, *Reuben, Reuben* is art, but this cultist, like many others, needs and is thankful for the gift of unreality; he will take *Casablanca*.

NOTES

1. A listing of the "contract talent" by studio budget compilers cites only Humphrey Bogart, Sydney Greenstreet, Paul Henreid (who was a Warner's newcomer), and Madeleine LeBeau as regular contract employees. Still, Claude Rains, S. Z. Sakall, Peter Lorre, Helmut Dantine, Dan Seymour, Ludwig Stossel, and Ilka Gruning are often associated with roles they played in the studio's pictures (see Behlmer 209–211).

2. Behlmer 216. In one treatment cited by the *Casablanca* memos included in this volume, the film's final line was to read, "Ricky, I was right. You *are* a sentimentalist."

3. Harmetz 15. Koch insists, to the contrary, that he did not know where the story was going. We might question, therefore, the Epsteins' assertion that they wrote the ending. They had left the project by this time, and Koch holds that no ending yet existed.

4. Gassner and Nichols 691–694. The published script seems to be a working version, since many scenes differ in detail from the film. In the script, for example, Rick runs the roulette wheel when Jan wins. Sam, Carl, Sascha, and Abdul pound at the door of Rick's office as he struggles with Strasser, and the final scene, as in the play, takes place in Rick's office, with a beacon light and a plane's roar—as in the original play—the only signs that Laszlo and Ilsa have flown away.

WORKS CITED

Agee, James. *Agee on Film.* vol. 1. New York: Grosset, 1967.

Anobile, Richard J., ed. *Casablanca.* New York: Darien House, 1974.

Behlmer, Rudy. *Inside Warner Bros.: 1935–1951.* New York: Viking, 1985.

Corliss, Richard. *Talking Pictures.* New York: Penguin, 1975.

Gassner, John, and Dudley Nichols, eds. *Best Film Plays of 1943–1944.* New York: Crown, 1945.

Harmetz, Aljean. "Hollywood Survival: Fifty Years of Success and Oblivion." *New York Times,* Feb. 5, 1984.

Kael, Pauline. *5001 Nights at the Movies.* New York: Holt, Rinehart, 1982.

Koch, Howard. "Notes on the Production of *Casablanca.*" In *Persistence of Vision,* ed. Joseph McBride, 93–95. Madison: Wisconsin Film Society, 1968.

Michael, Paul, ed. *The Great American Movie Book.* Englewood Cliffs: Prentice-Hall, 1980.

Peary, Danny. *Cult Movies.* New York: Delta, 1981.

Sarris, Andrew. *The American Cinema.* New York: Dutton, 1968.

Wallis, Hal, and Charles Higham. *Starmaker: The Autobiography of Hal Wallis.* New York: Macmillan, 1980.

CHAPTER 7

The Cult Send-Up:
Beat the Devil *or Goodbye,* Casablanca

T. J. Ross

When released in 1954, *Beat the Devil* was publicized as "another *Casablanca.*" If this was to suggest a further spin on the romantic themes and mood of the earlier film, no claim could have been more misleading. Certainly, the publicists were not looking ahead to the day when both films might be paired through their mutual cult attraction. And just as certainly, they were not concerned with playing up a *technical* correspondence: both films' sketchy plot lines and bumptiously arbitrary plot devices. In fact, each film violates both narrative norms and viewer expectations; yet each does so in a way that incorporates, while giving a fresh twist to, the myths of its own time and the moods engendered by those myths. For similar reasons, then, both films have found a celebrated place in the canon of cult cinema. However, *Beat the Devil,* because of the way it evokes the very tradition in which it works, offers a keen insight into the cult film phenomenon, particularly as it points toward the emergence of a cult narrative that seems almost self-conscious, as if reveling in its own difference from mainstream Hollywood films.

Even today, a film like *Beat the Devil* may baffle those in the audience unprepared for its departures from traditional plotting and tone—from the linearity, cause-effect logic, verisimilitude, psychologically defined and goal-oriented characters, and closure typical of classical film narrative.[1] Yet as was the case in 1954, some will be drawn to further viewings, lured by the film's buoyant if elusive tone and its compelling "human interest," despite its apparent heedlessness of plot grids usually employed for exploring human character. Such repeated viewings involve more than a ritual behavior—and more too than reinterpretation, seeking to add to the freight of a work's possible meanings. What one chiefly gains in returning to this film, as a kind of cult devotee, is a feeling of being more closely in tune—to the point of complicity—with a kind of borderline sensibility, one that skirts the standard domain of popular culture.

As director John Huston himself saw, his film has asserted a life of its own in defiance of initially glum reviews and sluggish viewer response. That life springs from its ability to attract splinter groups which, in their sense of complicity with the film's slant, developed the dedication of a cult. As Huston explains,

Bogey sent me a copy of an advertisement an exhibitor had taken out in a newspaper saying that this was the worst picture he had ever had in his theater. It was generally conceded to be a minor disaster, frivolous, self-indulgent and all the rest of it, at a time when such qualities were not accepted. Then presently people began to talk about it and say, "You know I liked it. I don't care what people say, I think it's good." More and more of these voices were raised, and then I discovered it had a following . . . particularly in university towns. It was one of the first "underground" films in the sense of appreciation rather than production. Then people would come up to me and say, "I've seen *Beat the Devil* eleven times." One said he had seen it a grand total of thirty-eight times, or something like that! There were those who actually went after a record for how often they'd seen it. It has its cult following and the audience actually knew the dialogue and would say the lines along with the actors. So it just grew and grew until it has its present status. (Prately 101)

To get our bearings on *Beat the Devil* as a prototypical cult film, we should first compare it with the sort often designated as "camp." An immediate distinction shows up in plot structure. The plots of camp films tend to be all of a piece; they rarely present "difficulties" in content or style. What holds for plot also holds for characterization. The characters played by, say, a Maria Montez or, more recently, Arnold Schwarzenegger prove as integrated and as "easy to follow" in their psychological, moral, and emotional makeup as the plots that provide such characters a perfect fit. It is the same characters who, to be sure, appear most "to have their act together," who most quickly fall victim to the passage of time and changing fashions. Changing theories of character are bound to affect our perceptions of fashion and manners; thus Robert Jay Lifton has detailed the "protean" nature of contemporary character and the uncertain, if even locatable, nature of the self. In light of such views, the screen image of a Maria Montez comes across as dated to a degree that seems innocent—and thus curiously appealing. Montez indeed exemplifies the sort of retrograde "innocence" that Susan Sontag, in her classic essay on the subject, identified as a hallmark of camp, that which it both "rests on" and "discloses" (284).

For a film like *Beat the Devil,* no word seems less applicable. Not "inno-cence" but rather the sort of "difficulty" in style and characterization asso-ciated with modernist texts typifies it, although *Beat the Devil* too might be said to both "rest on" and "disclose" certain characteristics of its narrative form. Of the pair who collaborated on the film, Huston and Truman Ca-pote, neither is known for dealing much with characters who are models of autonomy and integration. Like Capote in his fiction, Huston has often focused on characters who seem hazily adrift, their deportment and man-ners so difficult to get a grip on as to seem indeed "protean." Sam Spade of *The Maltese Falcon* (1941), for example, proves far more slippery and unpre-dictable in manner than Dashiell Hammett's original. Nor could the protag-onists of *The Asphalt Jungle* (1950), *The Red Badge of Courage* (1951), *The Mis-fits* (1961), or *Fat City* (1972) be described as classically rounded characters.

Although the Huston hero may be obsessed, the self-consuming drive of his obsession precludes the capacity of the autonomous character for either transcendence or self-sacrifice. In Casablanca (1942), Bogart and Ingrid Bergman exemplified a romantic ideal of the forties, and indeed of classical film narrative in general, in their capacity for self-sacrifice. Their emotional bond as lovers sustains and complements their loyalty to the greater public good. Where Bogart's motive as Sam Spade in *The Maltese Falcon* in "sending over" the femme fatale whom he loves is, as he explains, strictly personal, Bogart's Rick in *Casablanca* acts nobly and impersonally, for the greater good, as well as out of some respect for the "other man." Given its object, Spade's attachment to Brigid inevitably seems an arid pas-sion, while Rick's love for Ilsa, even if illicit, seems both understandable and human. It is the healthy passion of an integrated man who, for all his cynical surface, will always do the "right thing," which is to say, that which both reflects and reinforces civic virtue. Thus the hero is very much part of a busy social world; for all his aloof poise he is a social being whose success as a cafe owner depends on his social skills. Spade, on the other hand, slith-ers from one milieu to another, each no more social than a boxing ring. The "neutrality" of *Casablanca's* hero is clearly a painfully worn mask; in fact, his commitment to the Allied cause determines much of the film's mood and dramatic action. But in Spade we find true alienation, which marks the lack of the sort of integration in character and outlook that typi-fies the hero—and lover—of most classical narrative. Not that the roman-tic passions of the alienated hero were denied in the forties; they would be played out in every *film noir,* where matters of civic virtue, when they were introduced at all, were severely tested by the lure of passion.

Still, *Casablanca* remains the film that first comes to mind as the key romantic work of its decade and as a kind of model for the character and action of classical film narrative. One reason may be that its characters reach us through complexities in their depiction that add both depth and toughness to the film's overall tone. In the natures of the lead couple there are evident problematic edges. If not as much as in a film like Hitchcock's *Notorious* (1946), Ingrid Bergman's continuously quivering stance borders on the masochistic. As to Bogart, his stoic hardihood comes across as a touch jaded, well matching the world weariness of his buddy Louis (Claude Rains), with whom he walks off into a fogbound future at film's end. Neither Bogart nor Bergman shows the unselfconscious assurance and assertiveness of the camp character. Their approach to one another is marked rather by a tentativeness reflected in the defensively clipped speech of the hero and by his self-conscious hipness—just the sorts of things Woody Allen picked up on in his celebration of *Casablanca*'s mood and style in his cult-inspired *Play It Again, Sam*.

Despite these differences, a kinship clearly exists between Bogart's Rick and his Sam Spade, and it is one that points toward his later, clearly far more baffled character, Billy Dannreuther, in *Beat the Devil*. In no film in which he starred does Bogart seem less in control, either of the action or of the other characters, especially the women. In no film does he seem so tentative and so uncertainly aloof from the action. Nor is he set off from the others in his orbit by a moral probity that shines like a beacon on mean streets. Through long experience with the figures of classical narrative, even with its more alienated protagonists, we expect a popular hero—and especially Bogart—to live by a strict personal code, the violation of which stirs him to action. But in *Beat the Devil* that code is simply absent. In fact, the other characters take turns in urging him, much as the audience itself might, to show "where he's at"; repeatedly, they hector him on the need for a clear stance, a solid attitude. When Jennifer Jones as Gwendolen Chelm remarks of her husband, "Harry has a sense of dignity," Bogart's response is, "I have a sense of survival," which he later reinforces with a remark that suggests how much our own sense of his usual character is being invoked here, "It's my expectations that hold me together." Unlike strict codes that can close one off to possibility, that can serve as blinders to one's perceptions, "expectations" keep one open to experience, alert to possibility. At the same time, calling our attention to how much the Bogart character is fundamentally "constructed" from our own "expectations" also helps keep *us* on our toes, alert to the new narrative possibilities this character might hold out.

In contrast, each of the other characters here seems almost conventionally—if too one-dimensionally so—defined and driven: by a quest for the perfect scam, the perfect love, the perfect social scene. Yet for their quests to have a chance at success, these characters would need to be in a different, more conventionally plotted movie than *Beat the Devil* proves to be. For it is so loosely mapped that strict codes and patterns of behavior seem only odd, out of place, unavailing.

Consider so iconic a villain as Peter Lorre, who mutters "My feet are on the ground—both of them," as he urges Bogart/Dannreuther to plant his feet likewise and so adopt a stance that would allow him to play a conventional role, "to act honest." But as with most of the characters here, Lorre's "honest act"—his performance in the film—comes across from the start as somewhat askew. Thus his name, O'Hara, hardly squares with his Teutonic accent. He seems to illustrate Stendhal's view that one may as readily change one's name as one's clothes.

But Lorre is just one of many such figures here, part of a quartet of racketeers who refer to themselves as a "committee," at work on a deal involving a uranium field in British East Africa, with Bogart serving as their point man. Robert Morley as Petersen, their chairman, is among the most obsessed of the characters, suspicious of everyone in sight and always misreading everyone's motives. As Petersen, Morley does an exaggerated turn on another established character type, the stage Englishman. His continuous fuming in mixed clichés and general bombast are among the various kinds of put-on the film revels in and its audience especially responds to—a large aspect of the film's cult appeal. While Petersen and the other characters prove to be by turns edgy, morose, prissy, hysterical, and fanatic, these traits are all pushed beyond the bounds we normally associate with such types; but such was Huston's idea, for as he notes, there was supposed to be something "slightly absurd" about each of them. If *Beat the Devil* is a work of consistently high spirits, it is largely due to this absurd element it injects into the ideals we expect to see revealed in these characters—ideals here juxtaposed with their opposites and rendered contradictory: teamwork, individualism, commitment, entrepreneurship.

Yet what contributes even more to the film's cult appeal is the sustained fun it has with the quests of its leading female characters: one for gracious living and the other for romantic love. These quests engage our interest more than the uranium field plot does; the latter serves mainly as an arbitrary reference point, like a Hitchcockian MacGuffin.[2] The film's chief plot interest is rather its perspective on human relations (especially romantic relations) in a time grown less secure about clear-cut codes of value and action, and so all the more improvisatory and tentative in its behavior and "moves." To define the women here in their temperaments and quests, a more improvisatory, freewheeling narrative was required than the linear, progressive logic that carries the classical film's action. As David Bordwell explains, "In the classical cinema, narrative form motivates cinematic representation. Specifically, cause-effect logic and narrative parallelism generate a narrative which projects its action through psychologically-defined, goal-oriented characters" (57). Yet in *Beat the Devil* we find the characters who come across as the most compellingly attractive are also those most resistant to a conventional psychological explanation or presentation. Nor do their wild quests and dreams finally betray any sort of sensible goal.

We first see Bogart and Gina Lollobrigida in a quite traditional role, that of the old married couple, the Dannreuthers. From the start, we see him as habituated to his domestic role—a role far removed from his Rick and Sam Spade. And she, meanwhile, hardly conforms to the cool woman-of-the-world sort we expect opposite Bogart. In contrast to, say, the smooth gait and presence of a Lauren Bacall, Lollobrigida's overheated manner, blunt walk, and high-pitched voice combine to reflect a certain suburban provincialism, a mental set cast in the images of *Better Homes and Gardens*. Lollobrigida enacts this role with a zest and aptness that may mark her pleasure in a role requiring something more than the mere languor of a sex kitten. Certainly the Dannreuthers appear in no exotic or glamorous light. Both are shown strictly according to what seems to be the scenarist's idea of a standard domestic relation: they appear to be living in a state of mutual, if impatient, toleration. Thus, even when they argue, the temperature between them remains lukewarm, as if these characters had only partially assumed their roles.

This characteristic also holds for the complementary couple, the Chelms, played by Jennifer Jones and Edward Underdown. No Gregory Peck storming across the prairie after Jennifer Jones in *Duel in the Sun* (1946), Underdown continually mopes over his misplaced hot water bottle, while Jones, the "dark and sultry" woman of the western, here appears as a mature blond, militantly assured in manner. Like roly-poly Morley, the tall, gaunt Underdown plays another exaggerated version of the stage Englishman. He is keenly survival conscious and lectures his wife on the need to adapt to new conditions, even if it means catering to Americans like Dannreuther: "One can't afford to dismiss people only because they're not one's sort. After all, it is a new world we've gone into . . . . Try to bridge the gulf, face it, use it, master it." But while the American is not the Englishman's "sort," he proves decidedly the wife's type. If Gwendolen's husband is, as she puts it, "the best of his type," she longs for a quite different type, as she suggestively tells Bogart, "Someday I shall meet my type."

Most of her dialogue, however, is hardly so straightforward; rather, she is given to inspired lies. Her favorite introductory phrase, "in point of fact," for example, invariably precedes some elaborate fabrication, designed to help her achieve her desire of the moment. To the man she sees as her long-sought "type," she prophesies: "You're going to found a new empire and I'll be your empress." And while she can go on about her husband's aristocratic background, we are not surprised to learn that he is actually "a ruddy refugee from Earl's Court," or rather, "the son of a boarding house keeper from Earl's Court." The slippery identities and confused longings of such characters, though, are simply reflections of the plot's own hazy structure. In fact, we might read Gwendolen's improvisations as mirroring the scriptwriters' desperate sense of how they were working. Her tall stories reflexively comment upon the film's own tall and seemingly wildly improvisatory script.

That the characters here prove easy prey to such false reports and rumors also points up a general unreliability of point of view that distinguishes this film from most classical narratives. That traditional form depends on a single and reliable viewpoint, normally that of a trustworthy protagonist whose actions unfold in a linear—and logical—fashion. By dispensing with a fixed narrative pattern and rendering practically every character a *poseur* of sorts, then, *Beat the Devil* undermines the sense of objectivity and observed truth, the level of verisimilitude we expect in the classical narrative. For here there simply is no central—or dependable— point of view; and each character, in his or her whimsy, is liable to direct us along some false narrative trail.

Beat the Devil thus offers an ensemble of characters, each given pretty much equal weight, and no protagonist with whom we are invited to identify or even sympathize—and certainly no one whose point of view or logic governs how we perceive the action. If the plot is hesitant and jerky in its movement, so are the characters in their moves—almost as if they were its products rather than, as in classical cinema, its causal agents. But at the same time, to describe *Beat the Devil* as a film in quest of a plot is to note what often appears to be the case in cult films. A similar meandering development, a zigzagging in both plot line and tone, typifies such other cult works as *Casablanca, Easy Rider* (1969), *The Wild One* (1954), *Johnny Guitar* (1954), and *2001: A Space Odyssey* (1968). And this trait may well explain why fans of cult films rarely spend time recounting the plots—or find such an activity almost frustrating. Since cult films provide a treasure house of what François Truffaut called the "privileged moment"—the image or scene that redeems an otherwise routine film or enhances a good one—cult fans prefer to single out particular scenes or snatches of dialogue. Jack Nicholson's telling off of the waitress in the diner scene of *Five Easy Pieces* (1970) is an obvious example. So too is the scene of the lovers' airport parting in *Casablanca*.

Certainly we can find semblances of such moments in *Beat the Devil,* such as when the camera briefly holds Lollobrigida and Jones in medium shot as they disport in the sun, Jones stretched sideways, doing arm and body bends, while her companion faces the camera, impatiently pouting. The image contrasts the dark and blond beauties, and at the same time sums up Jones in her heedless flair and Lollobrigida in her sullen restiveness. But what clearly distinguishes it from scenes like that which concludes *Casablanca* is that it reflexively comments on the classical image of the "love goddess," and thus on the general function of the sort of characters typically played by Lollobrigida and Jones. In particular, the two-shot recalls the celebrated shot of Rita Hayworth on a ledge overlooking the beach at Acapulco in Orson Welles's *The Lady from Shanghai* (1947)—itself in part a send-up of that staple image of Hollywood. However, where the focus on Hayworth also brought out her dangerous character (the complete fatal woman), the image of the Lollobrigida-Jones duo mainly abstracts their exaggerated characteristics, their jadedness and impetuosity, in keeping with the film's comic and reflexive character.

In contrast to this scene is the one in which Bogart and Morley are bounced up and down in the back seat of a jalopy as it hits one pothole after another on a road winding precariously over the sea below. Hardly a glamorous situation, the car stalls on the crest of a turn, and when they get out to push, they only manage to set it rolling over the edge. But this scene foreshadows a series of similar failures that also takes on a reflexive weight, commenting not only on the abilities—and our expectations—of the film's leading men, but also on the very plot of the film. For just as the car fails to reach town, the ship on which the group later embarks fails to reach its intended port, as it founders and threatens to sink. Both the bouncing car and the stalled ship, neither of which directly reaches its goal, are analogous to the narrative's own movement by fits and starts, as it too seems at times to founder or to "bounce" characters out with its meandering movement. An underscoring of this reflexive impulse occurs when the ship finally arrives at a port and the customs official turns out to be a worshipper of Rita Hayworth, in a scene that follows through on the earlier evocation of her image in the above-cited "love goddess" scene.

Just as the characterizations of the principal male and female figures mark the sort of "deviation from the classical canon" that Bordwell posits as one of the features of an "art-cinema" (59), a further—and clearly calculated—"deviation" shows up in the resolution of *Beat the Devil*'s plot, particularly in its resistance to the standard turgid parting scene of romantic melodrama. We might note that in 1952 both Capote and Jennifer Jones had been involved in the Vittorio de Sica film, *Indiscretion of an American*

Wife. That film is something of a tour de force in the melodramatic, as its action consists entirely of a parting-forever at a railroad station between an adulterous wife (Jones) and her anguished lover (Montgomery Clift). In *Beat the Devil*, though, the writer and actress conspire with Huston to deflate this sort of dramatic routine—and sure-fire commercial fare—in effect, to give an "art" twist to a classical narrative line.

We may note a further ironic play on narrative expectations in the fate of Chelm. While Dannreuther is presumed lost in a car accident, Chelm is thought lost at sea when the ship headed for East Africa has to be abandoned. But rather than miraculously showing up for a happy reunion, Chelm remains offscreen, popping up only at the film's conclusion in a telegram that announces not only his survival but also his taking over of a real uranium field. It is a rather obvious contrivance, clearly a flaunting of narrative probability, as someone who had been described by his wife as a "wonderful loser" is allowed a lucky finish. Not so the other crooks, who are apprehended by a Scotland Yard man named Jack Clayton. Jack Clayton, we might note, was the film's producer—soon to be a successful director with films like *Room at the Top* (1959)—and, as keeper of the budget, the person ultimately responsible for the "finish" of the film.

Beat the Devil thus gains in interest and weight not so much for what it looks back to, but for what it points toward. Its disenchanted yet not unsympathetic perspective on romantic love, combined with its persistent reflexive turns, certainly anticipates the more somber and definitive treatment of this theme in an equally self-conscious work that many see as the culminating masterpiece of the fifties, Antonioni's *L'Avventura*—a film that, by turns, also reveals a classical and an art aspect. In the lassitude of its couples, the desperate maneuvers and hopes of the women, the hapless fumblings of the men, the seaport settings, the quests over a beautiful yet arid landscape that proves oppressive rather than inspiring, a hothouse atmosphere languorous to the point of decadence, characters of vague definition and dimension, and a plot that ultimately leads nowhere, *L'Avventura* marks a further exploration, although in a different register, of terrain more roughly mapped out by Huston's film. For Antonioni, the adventure of our time is that of the couple in an age no longer certain of the guidelines in their relation, and it is matched by that of the filmmaker, whose conventional guidelines also seem to have vanished or been proved incommensurate for depicting the contemporary experience.

Beat the Devil, of course, is a film that is far more surface, not yielding much to the sort of psychological and sociological speculation that a film like *L'Avventura* invites. Yet it shares affinities with works as distinctive as Antonioni's, particularly as it seems to search for forms of resistance to the brute certainties and nihilism of our own "iron time." "It's solutions that kill us," says a scholar in a detective novel by Reginald Hill (35), and that remark could well be spoken by many of the characters in Huston's film, which seems resolutely set against the pat solution: the certainties of political fanatics, the nihilism of the con men, the narrow fantasies of sexual or social romance our films commonly provide, and even the very patterns by which we conventionally depict our world.

Beat the Devil establishes from the start a different, even flip tone, one perhaps best demonstrated by the film's most often quoted line, Jones's quip about the committeemen, "I knew they must be desperate characters—not one of them looked at my legs." It is a remark at once both engaging and self-conscious, inviting interest in her character but also pointing up her place in a pattern of filmic conventions. Yet the film's reflexive notations never quite block its emotional currents, just as its deliciously absurd characters and plot never manage to dispel our larger sense of what Bordwell terms a "perceptual play," characteristic of modernist cinema (61). Indeed, much of the film's cult appeal, I would suggest, derives from its ability to walk a line between these different pulls—and at various points to draw them together. It is, finally, an open film—open to various vantages, open to both a classical and a modernist perspective, open as well to a continuation of its events beyond the film's running time—and in that respect very much like the other cult films we have noted. However, that characteristic allows those of us who make up the cult audience to return more easily for another helping, to view repeatedly films that seem indefinitely open—and perhaps timeless in their appeal.

NOTES

1. For the most detailed examination of the various patterns and conventions of classical film narrative, and particularly its reliance on a stable and unquestioned point of view, see Bordwell, Staiger, and Thompson's *The Classical Hollywood Cinema* (24–41).

2. We might make special note of Hitchcock's *Notorious*, which employs its champagne bottles filled with uranium dust in much the same way that Huston, perhaps with a nod toward the earlier film, would use his uranium field.

WORKS CITED

Bordwell, David. "The Art Cinema as a Mode of Film Practice." *Film Criticism* 4, no. 1 (1979): 56–64.

———, Janet Staiger, and Kristin Thompson. *The Classical Hollywood Cinema: Film Style and Mode of Production to 1960*. New York: Columbia Univ. Press, 1985.

Franchi, R. M, and Marshall Lewis. "Conversations with François Truffaut." *New York Film Bulletin* 3, no. 3 (1963): n.p.

Hill, Reginald. *Another Death in Venice*. New York: Signet, 1987.

Lifton, Robert Jay. "Protean Man." In *History and Human Survival*, 311–332. New York: Random House, 1971.

Pratley, Gerald. *Huston*. New York: Barnes, 1977.

Sontag, Susan. "Notes on 'Camp.'" In *Against Interpretation*, 277–293. New York: Dell, 1969.

CHAPTER 8

The Star as Cult Icon: Judy Garland

Wade Jennings

The audience on its feet, some laughing, some crying, all caught up in a frenzy of emotion and instinctively pushing toward a stage where a tiny woman stood blowing kisses, bowing awkwardly, ready to touch and be touched by the adoring monster she had created—Judy Garland lived at the center of such storms of public love and hysteria through the last eighteen years of her life. On the nights she sang well, the audience loved her because she was one of the great performers of her time. On the nights she sang badly, they loved her because she was Judy. In either case, she was theirs and they were hers. Garland and her audience shared an intimacy that was unparalleled, mysterious, and in many ways neurotic. While some simply admired her talent, many in her audience were Garland fanatics, initiates in one of the largest and most lasting cults in show business history, part of what might be seen as a paradigm of the cult star experience.

Cult stardom is a relatively recent phenomenon, mainly surfacing in the fifties, and today we are still trying to discover its meaning for our culture. Though such stardom begins like more traditional film stardom, over time it can emerge as a quite different phenomenon. Traditional film stars may generate intense adulation for a cultural moment (Frank Sinatra, Tony Curtis), may produce a body of work that continues to intrigue subsequent generations (Greta Garbo, Lilian Gish), and may remain a pleasing and permanent part of popular culture (Clark Gable, Bette Davis). But after the occasional explosion of hysteria that they may initially generate, these stars become relatively unimportant parts of the day-to-day lives of those who admire them and their work.

Camp stardom is mainly a variation on this process, a recognition by part of the audience of the inherent absurdity of certain star masks and the values that they project. Camp stars may be in on the joke, as with Mae West, or an unwitting source of humor, as with Joan Crawford, but their significance is relatively minor to those who find them amusing. The only real similarity between a camp star and a cult star is that both belong to relatively small initiated audiences that share attitudes and values in some ways associated with the stars.

The cult star, however, becomes a central and engrossing part of the lives of the initiated. The merest scrap of memorabilia becomes precious; anecdotes are preserved and retold, becoming part of the developing "legend," a body of information and interpretation that becomes the credo of those in the group. Instead of being a minor and segregated part of cult members' lives, the relationship to the star performer permeates those lives, helping to shape them in surprising numbers of ways. Woody Allen's *Play It Again, Sam* treats this sort of situation comically, with its Bogart-haunted and advised protagonist, but that play and film nonetheless suggest the powerful emotional needs that bind those in the cult to the star through whom they live vicariously.

James Dean, Marilyn Monroe, Humphrey Bogart, Judy Garland—what qualities of talent, personality, and physical appeal make them so fascinating to so many, even decades after their deaths? Why have they, unlike most other film stars, outlasted the particular moment in culture that in some ways they typified? In Garland's case, the scores of books, essays, reviews, and anecdotes continue to add depth to the legend. We know more and more about what she said, what she did, where she went, how she performed, but the information only deepens the intrinsic mystery of the star's fascination. Examining the Garland "mystery," though, reveals several basic principles that characterize most cult cases, and thus provides a start for understanding the whole cult phenomenon.

Cult stardom seems so intensely human in its origins and meanings that we may be surprised to recognize how much it is in fact a product of technology, our ability to record and thus preserve performances. Although stage performers may in their own generations elicit adulation and emulation, their power to enthrall usually dies with their careers. They may be remembered, but even the greatest quickly become paragraphs in show business history. Cult stardom, by contrast, grows and even intensifies after a performer's death, largely because the performer's work lasts. As technology has improved, particularly after World War II, the possibility of cult stardom has thus also expanded.

Although Garland was an electrifying stage performer, the Garland cult, like those of all major cult stars, is firmly rooted in a body of indelible, unchanging performances recorded on film, tape, and records. But the performances are more than historical records; they remain in compelling ways alive. If they did not, cult stardom would be impossible. These performances belong as much to children seeing *The Wizard of Oz* for the first time today as they did to the 1939 audience. The recording of her Carnegie Hall concert is as vital and fresh today as when it was first performed. We have discovered an even more intriguing truth in the past few decades: recorded performances not only continue to live, but in some cases become more interesting with time.

Cult stardom depends, in fact, on the accident of the particular star qualities in the performer being the ones that the recording medium captures and enhances. If the camera and microphone are "sympathetic," then the living work lasts. In Garland's case, some of the acting in the early films now seems dated, but the musical performances are for the most part whole and vital. When she sings, she is never less than a compelling figure in film, in television, on record.

Another fact of recorded performance, visual and aural, also contributes to cult formations. In Garland's case, virtually the whole career is preserved as a whole, an established canon of images and sounds that can be known and shared. One has available simultaneously the entire Garland career and all the masks and voices of the performer: the wide-eyed girl of the early MGM musicals, the strained but gallant Garland of the television years, the powerful and confident Garland at the time of the Carnegie Hall performance, the tiny wraith of the last pitiful years.

The profound irony created by such easy juxtapositions is not lost on the cult audience, who do not hear vibrant young Garland playing the Palace in 1951 without inevitably calling to mind the ruin of Garland playing that same theater in 1968, who inevitably see Dorothy's eyes in the pudgy face of the frightened German housewife at Nuremberg. Charles Affron offers an image that encompasses this peculiar feature of recorded performance: "Garland walks down the yellow brick road, and then back down it year after year, in St. Louis, in the Easter Parade, and most unnervingly in the Nuremberg Courtroom" (7). Even when the career of a performer stretches over such a long period and encompasses as many changes as Garland's, all the individual recorded performances interconnect and comment upon one another. The accumulated performances thus take on a deeper resonance than they could have otherwise and produce more complex emotions in the initiated audience than could have been imagined when they were recorded.

Yet another important effect of recorded performance is intimacy. We can study the magnified face of the performer closely, over and over if we like, until we know it better than the faces of the most familiar people in our lives. Moreover, we can hear in modern recordings every nuance of the voice as it speaks or sings, again as often as we like and as loud or soft as we like. Equally important is the psychological effect that technology produces—of owning the record or tape, having that star in one's own living space instead of sharing him or her with a mass audience, recreating the relationship with the performer at any time. Although cult stardom is most manifest when those in the group react as one to the star's public performance, it is most often born in private moments in private places. Each person finds his or her own singular meaning in the star and the recorded performance.

Although it may not please us to admit so undramatic a truth, then, the development of a cult stardom also depends heavily on the quality of that technology, on how well the performances were recorded in the first place. Fuzzy, scratchy, incomplete records do not invite intimacy or repetition. Throughout her career, Garland had the best production teams of her time record her performances, so current audiences do not have to imagine what it might have been like to see or hear her—they know in complete detail. The films from MGM and Warner Brothers, the records from Capitol, and the CBS television shows were all done with care and with respect for her particular talents. The television shows from the early sixties are an especially important record of the concert years, the period when her cult reached its most emphatic development. In some of these performances, Garland is at the peak of her performing powers, delivering knockout one-woman shows that drive the studio audiences into a frenzy. In other shows, she is an obviously frail, uncertain performer, trying too hard to charm her audience, upstaging some guests, and clinging to others for support. By capturing both the star's best work and the underlying human weakness, these video recordings provide an illuminating insight into the paradoxical nature of the Garland cult. As memories of live Garland performances have faded over the past two decades, the cult continues to find adherents in another generation—which most convincingly demonstrates the power and importance of a recorded legacy to the cult.

A second element necessary to cult stardom is also ancillary to the star herself; it is the audience's knowledge of powerful contradictions in the star's life and work. Even the general, uninitiated audience knows something of the ambiguities and ironies inherent in such cases, but those in the cult find part of their identity in their detailed and considered knowledge of the contradictions, the differences between the publicized career and the reality, between the human being and the performer, between the public performance and the private agony. In the case of every star who becomes a cult figure, there is some variation of the notion of "the suffering artist," a belief that the achievement of the performer has grown out of his or her confrontation with personal defeat and despair that the moment of performance somehow transcends. No star more completely embodied the "suffering artist" than Garland.

Garland's relationship with her audience falls into two clearly contrasting parts, divided by her first publicly acknowledged suicide attempt in 1950. In the years at Metro-Goldwyn-Mayer from 1936 to 1950, Judy was the eternal adolescent, the girl-woman who was youth, energy, sweetness, and pluck incarnate. Although her early pictures acknowledged that she was no glamor girl like Lana Turner or Hedy Lamarr, she was obviously something better—the girl next door, loyal, patient, loving, achingly innocent, and wholesome. After the success of *The Wizard of Oz,* a persona was established on record. Dorothy's wistfulness and childlike candor became permanently tied to the Garland screen persona. As Aljean Harmetz observes, "Once an actor was a star, the clay was considered permanently fired" (103). One by-product of this system was that stardom usually had a limited duration; most careers lasted no more than about fifteen years, unless audiences began to find surprising and unexpected new qualities in the star, even qualities that contradicted those in the previous image.

Although the parts Garland played at MGM were repetitious, thin, even trivial, they appealed to the paying audience, and the studio was not interested in taking any chances with a sure-fire money-maker. For this reason, even after she had been married and divorced, Garland was still cast as adolescents or Cinderella-like innocents in such major hits as *Meet Me in St. Louis* and *The Harvey Girls.* The MGM publicity department, one of the industry's best, carefully nurtured the wholesome image, creating its own record of stories about Judy's normal adolescence, her happy marriages, her motherhood.

Even after the Hollywood insiders knew about Garland's increasing difficulties—chronic lateness, missed shooting days, tantrums on the set, various addictions—MGM continued to cover up the facts as much as possible. When projects announced for her went instead to other stars, the news stories and fan reports spoke only of fatigue and overwork. Not until she was pulled from the starring role in the much ballyhooed *Annie Get Your Gun* did the public learn that Garland was seriously ill and would have to be hospitalized indefinitely. At this time, veiled hints of emotional difficulties and perhaps even a drinking problem surfaced, but these were subordinated to the official record, which described her as "poor Judy," the victim of a demanding career.

When Garland returned to the studio to do *Summer Stock,* the public was led to believe that her physical problems had been resolved and that

she was the old Judy again. After she began her next film, shocking headlines suddenly announced first that Judy had been fired by MGM and then
that she had attempted suicide. As Vincente Minnelli, her former husband
and director, later pointed out, these events "forever destroyed Judy's
wholesome image" (223). The image so carefully nurtured during her studio years did not merely disappear, however. It became part of a new public perception of the star. Ironically, the studio became the victim of its
own success in fashioning and recording an image. If the innocent, talented girl-woman was in such desperate straits, who was to blame? Who
was the wicked witch in this episode? The answer was obviously the studio
that had worked her to exhaustion and then callously cast her aside. This
view became a major ingredient of the new Garland legend, which Garland herself embellished almost to the point of absurdity.

Had Garland's career ended in 1950 as many predicted, she would still
have a place in film history because of her accomplishments—surely the
best body of work by a female musical performer in film history to that
time—and because of the symbolic meaning she had acquired as a glaring
instance of the suffering artist. She would not, however, have been a likely
figure around which a cult might form. For in spite of the rich pathos it
evoked, the new Garland persona still lacked depth and real contradiction.
Judy as victim was an intriguing addition to the earlier girl-woman persona but did not really challenge it.

The *cult* stardom clearly had its major boost in the events of the next
year. Unable to work in Hollywood, Garland and her advisors decided
that she would return to the stage; moreover, she would do it in a revival
of vaudeville, a medium long thought dead in America. It was a serious
gamble: few film stars had successfully returned to the stage, and no one
was certain that Garland had the stamina or even the abilities that stage
performances demand. After the initial novelty, would the audience be interested in a washed-up movie star?

The show that Garland presented, first at the London Palladium and
then at the restored Palace Theater in New York, was one of the great personal triumphs in show business history. Garland discovered that she had
the rare ability to draw an audience to her, to make it listen to the lyrics of
a song and feel them, to build with her to a carefully calculated climax that
blended present and past, pathos and hope, pain and triumph. Sitting on
the edge of the stage in the tramp costume she had worn to romp through
"A Couple of Swells," Judy would begin to sing in her light, unforced
Dorothy voice the familiar opening to "Over the Rainbow." The only light
in the darkened theater was a pin spot on the smudged face, dominated by
the large and glistening eyes. As the performance developed, the voice be-

came larger and more urgent, intensely dramatic instead of childishly wistful. Garland invited those in her audience to summon all that they knew of her—her career, her failures, her uncertain future—and to make that part of understanding the song she sang. In the last few bars, tears would finally spill from her eyes, as she asked why she could not complete the journey from reality to a place of dreams. As she took breath for the last phrases, a slight catch suggested that perhaps she could not complete the song, but in the final moment the voice came back true and soaring to ask "Why, oh why can't I?" and then the spotlight went off while the last note echoed, leaving the house in darkness.

In the hands of a less convincing performer, someone less skilled at shaping her own image, the blatant theatricality would be cloying and absurd. But Garland's audiences identified with and believed in her, leaving no space for detached judgment. Although the term *comeback* was frequently used to describe the triumph, it was misleading: Garland did not return to her previous relationship with her audience but transcended it, incorporating only a small part of that previous identity in the new persona that exploded into being on the stage. In fact, the transformed Garland had a quality that the screen Judy never had: the power to take thousands of individuals and, through sheer force of personality and talent, fuse them into one, focused solely on the emotions she created.

The triumph of the stage appearances added the necessary contradiction. Judy was both victor and victim, survivor and crushed innocent. The audience could pity her, share her well-publicized pain, feel grateful to her for giving so much of herself, while at the same time being stunned by her performance, the emotional and physical resilience, tbe overwhelming personality in the small body. One could pity her and be awe-struck at the same time. The strongest evidence was the audience reaction after her performances: after the ovations and the curtain speeches, they would approach the star who had moved them to extremes of emotion, needing to touch her, needing to be acknowledged individually, and—most important of all—needing to reassure her of their love and loyalty. If they needed her, they were equally sure that she needed them, both en masse and individually. Over the years, this part of the performance became as important as the singing, a fact Garland accepted and often seemed to welcome.

The only major film role that Garland was to play after 1950 capitalized on this new perception of her as both victim and survivor. In *A Star Is Born* (1954), she plays a familiar character, a plucky, pleasantly talented girl not unlike the one Garland had played in *Summer Stock* four years earlier. But the film quickly shows us the new Garland as well, the one who stuns with the range and power of her talent. The character played by James Mason recognizes, as does the audience, that this girl's talent sets her apart from the rest of us, makes her a star whether she wishes it or not. But in a curious reversal, the Garland character in the film witnesses the self-destruction of the man she loves, an actor who suffers much the same fate in the film as she had in real life.

When the Garland character identifies herself at the end as "Mrs. Norman Maine," the moment has emotional power because the audience understands how many contradictions that identification implies—loss and triumph, pain and renewed commitment, a fusion of the star's private and public realities. Garland in the film had fused her old screen persona with the larger and more compelling star who had been discovered on stage. Equally important, the obvious parallels between events in the film and events in Garland's well-publicized life invited the audience to bring its knowledge of Garland the human being to its understanding of the character she played in the film and to its sense of the new star she had become.

One sequence in the newly restored version of this film illustrates this process well: Vicky Lester, Garland's character, films a musical number, "Lose That Long Face," playing the familiar gamin with a touch of the tramp, selling the virtues of optimism and hope. As the number ends, Vicky rushes to her dressing room where she dissolves in a devastating moment of anger, terror, confusion, and love, telling the studio head of her hopelessly tangled emotions concerning her self-destructive husband. When called back to the sound stage, she reapplies her freckles and once more prepares to entertain with apparent joyful abandon. The scene memorably illustrates what the audience would come to accept as the truth of Garland's life with all of its startling contradictions. Even this film's aftermath added another layer of irony to the Garland legend, when she lost what seemed an almost certain Oscar, to again become in the eyes of many the victim of a ruthless system that misunderstood and undervalued her talent.

In the years that followed, Garland faced crisis after crisis, all thoroughly documented in the public press: a near fatal bout with liver disease, another broken marriage, child-custody suits, film deals that never materialized, missed performances, speculation about alcohol and drug addiction. During those same years, she recorded successful albums and gave sell-out nightclub and vaudeville performances, winning audiences even when she was desperately ill and bloated almost beyond recognition. By the late fifties, however, it seemed that the Garland phenomenon was near an end. Told by doctors that she could never sing again, she retreated to London, always a haven for her, and prepared to live quietly, or so the legend goes.

Had Garland's career ended at this point, as many thought it must, the cult would have certainly been firmly enough established that it would have continued. But the Garland career drama had a final act, the most astounding of them all and the one that would provide the final impetus in forming a major cult.

According to Garland's account (and she eventually became the most important single source for her own developing legend), she discovered one day in the shower that her voice was back, as full and rich as ever. On the spot, she sang song after song, creating in her mind the concert act she would later perform all over the world. This time there would be no comedians or dancers, no warm-up acts—just Garland without props, tramp makeup, pin spots, or other gimmicks, a singer and an orchestra in a program that would last nearly three hours. No popular singer had ever attempted such a sustained independent performance before. It would require phenomenal endurance and a sense of dramatic development and pace if it were to work. More than anything she had ever done, this was to be Garland's own creation; she worked on arrangements, costumes, lighting, drawing on a lifetime of experience in the business.

The opening night at the Palladium was a total triumph, as Dan Slater reported in *The Daily Herald:* "They stood in the aisles. They stood at the back. They stood anywhere last night to hear Judy Garland. Garland the Great. Her reception at the London Palladium shook stagehands hardened by years of hysterial audience reaction . . . and Judy, the girl who found happiness through tears as audiences all over the world wept and laughed with her, gave them all she had" (quoted in DiOrio 134).

Although other reviews also referred to Garland's previous image, the reaction to her concert tour was far less a reaction to the previously established reputation than an almost surprised response to the brilliant achievement of the concert itself. In city after city, the critics used superlatives to characterize the performance and the overwhelming audience response to it. By the time of her scheduled Carnegie Hall appearance, anticipation was intense—anticipation mixed with apprehension that illness or emotional collapse would rob star and audience of what seemed a natural climax to the comeback tour, perhaps to her entire career.

After the usual delay and overture of familiar songs, Garland appeared, greeted by the now mandatory ovation. The opening bars of her first song settled the preliminary apprehensions. The voice was rich and true, the mood confident and infectious as she sang a familiar arrangment of "When

You're Smiling." The songs that followed were equally good, sometimes brilliantly sung. For example, she hit the final high note in "Alone Together" with an amazing power and resonance, a fitting climax to any performance, but Garland had only begun. Through a long and complex program, she was in control, forgetting lyrics at one point but turning it into part of the act, sailing through standards, creating a hushed intimacy while singing ballads with only piano accompaniment, doing a persuasively dramatic version of "Stormy Weather" and a hilarious parody to introduce "San Francisco," never repeating an effect, never wavering in focus, driving toward a cathartic conclusion.

The recording of the performance captures much of the sense of almost frenzied reaction to the last few numbers. When Garland comes out after several encores and asks, "Do you really want more? Aren't you tired?" the audience roars, demanding as much as she can give.

Although Garland went on to several further screen performances, a television series, and numerous concerts in her final seven years, the Carnegie Hall performance and its recording established the final part of the legend around which the cult would grow. Garland was more than a lovingly recalled musical-film star, more than a memorable vaudeville performer, more than a fine dramatic actress. She was—beyond praise or criticism—a great performer. She had earned respect as well as adulation. Judy was now also Garland.

In the final years, her voice would come and go, sometimes almost as good as ever, other times little more than a croak. Although audiences might occasionally turn hostile if she appeared very late or seemingly drunk or dazed, for the most part it was enough that she appeared at all to allow them to love her and share that emotion with her. As William Goldman wrote of her final appearance at the Palace in 1968, "Judy floats" (78). Other critics disdainfully noted the almost maniacal response of her cult members who came to worship, not to hear a singer.

Although people of all ages and types became members of the cult, male homosexuals were perhaps the largest single identifiable group. Estimates are that up to twenty-five percent of the audiences at the concerts were gay men, and Garland photographs and recordings became features of some gay bars and specialty shops. There have been a number of explanations of Garland's particular appeal to this group, the most common of which argues that gay life is so inevitably fraught with pain that those in it naturally identify with her intense personal suffering.

However, the suffering Garland belonged to the entire public, not just to the cult or a gay component of that group. Garland's appeal to the supposed gay sensibility also rested on her particular brand of humor, her sly, ironic, campy, sometimes lacerating, often self-deprecating wit that the gay members of the cult knew and valued more than did others. Of all the cult stars, Garland was the only one who lived long enough to see the full formation of her cult and even to help shape it. By all accounts an intelligent and witty woman, Garland in private often enjoyed the cult absurdity, making a mockery of it and herself part of her private and very amusing performance for the initiated.

Later, others in the cult, especially its gay members, circulated stories that Judy herself first told, stories that weren't printed until years after her death. In all of them, Judy has the punch line, of course. Rushing to a court date, she had thrown on a colorful but mis-matched outfit. Asked by a sneering reporter who her designer was, Garland crisply replied, "Walt Disney." Told by a drunken fan in a ladies' room that she must never, never forget the rainbow, Judy assured her, "Lady, I'm up to my ass in rainbows." Even the legendary suffering came in for its share of Garland put-downs. When Liza Minnelli asked her mother after one particularly tearful evening why she led others to believe that she was so unhappy when in fact she enjoyed life so much, Judy drew herself up to her full five feet and replied, "Suffering is my business." She also gently ribbed her gay followers, noting: "When I die, every flag on Fire Island will fly at half mast." Garland was especially likely to share the insider jokes with those in the cult who followed her from city to city, often breaking them up during the performances with special looks or gestures meant just for them. The one thing Garland never kidded, however, was "Over the Rainbow." She knew the complex and highly personal associations the song had for many in her audience, and she never distanced herself from those emotions.

But neither suffering nor humor are finally as central to the Garland myth as is her quality of transcendence. Writing of her MGM films, Leo Braudy observes, "With Judy Garland we feel that the song and dance allow her to transcend her personal problems in a real liberation" (161). In her later performances, it is not just personal suffering that is transcended, but the ironies of time and age, the cycle of triumph and defeat. Even the performance's absurdity—thousands of people deeply moved through a series of conflicting emotions by a frail little woman singing old songs—is transcended over and over again in the concerts and the records of those concerts. Christopher Finch convincingly summarizes the symbolic significance of the Garland legend, especially for those in the cult:

It's been suggested that Judy's audiences were sick—that they came in the hope of seeing her disintegrate before their eyes. Some people have argued that even the adulation displayed toward her was unhealthy. Undoubtedly there is some truth to this, but ultimately it is too simplistic and cynical to provide a satisfactory explanation of the whole phenomenon. Certainly many people in the audience identified with Judy because of her problems—as I have said, it was precisely her much publicized vulnerability that made her so accessible to her public. It is nonetheless true that they returned faithfully because of her ability to rise from the ashes again and again . . . Judy had become, it seemed, for her admirers, a unique natural phenomenon, following a cyclic pattern that was as established as the phases of the moon. She had become a symbol of regeneration. (234)

The release of the newly restored version of *A Star Is Born* and of some of her recordings in the CD format have recently led to glowing critical reassessments of Garland's work. Her reputation as an actress and singer has never been higher. However, as this essay has suggested, a cult star does not really depend on such periodic rediscoveries. A cult star—and Garland is paradigmatic of the type—quite genuinely lives in the minds and hearts of those to whom she is more than personality, more than great performer, more than star, more than symbol. She is theirs. In this case, she is Judy.

WORKS CITED

Affron, Charles. *Star Acting: Gish, Garbo, and Davis*. New York: Dutton, 1977.
Braudy, Leo. *The World in a Frame*. Garden City: Doubleday, 1976.
DiOrio, Al, Jr. *Little Girl Lost*. New Rochelle: Arlington House, 1973.
Finch, Christopher. *Rainbow: The Stormy Life of Judy Garland*. New York: Grosset and Dunlap, 1975.
Goldman, William. "Judy Floats." *Esquire*, Jan. 1969, 78–80.
Harmetz, Aljean. *The Making of* The Wizard of Oz. New York: Knopf, 1977.
Minnelli, Vincente. *I Remember It Well*. Garden City: Doubleday, 1974.

PART III

The Midnight Movie

With the term "midnight movie," I already suggest what is probably the most important consideration for the last group of cult films to be considered here. They are works identified primarily in terms of their rather special viewing conditions. We go to see these films not just after dark but at a kind of magical time: the "witching hour," the point when one day becomes another. And while we often view them at conventional theaters, even at the ubiquitous suburban shoebox multiplexes, they also mark a point of magical change or transformation for their venues. For when this sort of cult film plays—whether *The Rocky Horror Picture Show*, *Eraserhead*, or *Liquid Sky*—the theater itself quickly shifts in character, from a model of industrialized and efficient exhibition practices to a kind of "underground" cinema, an urban (or suburban) site of ritualistic activity, wherein the celebrants are less likely to consume the refreshments sold in the theater than to employ them as props in their cultic practices.

Of course, the films also represent a level of difference, since they tend to challenge not only our conventional viewing practices but many norms of cinematic subject and style. Consequently, they at times suggest another sort of transformation—one in traditional film narrative. Normally taboo subjects—transvestism, homosexuality, the drug culture, etc.—freely surface in this "other" context, affording viewers a voyeur's brief pleasure, as well as a kind of symbolic association with divergent elements of modern culture. At the same time, the narratives themselves often work in strange ways, as seen in *Rocky Horror*'s curious pastiche of science fiction, horror, and musical genres; *Pink Floyd: The Wall*'s interweaving of animation, fantasy sequences, and rock performances; or *Koyaanisqatsi*'s nonnarrative exploration of America's natural and man-made vistas.

To describe and evaluate such a different film experience, this section groups essays that focus on a wide array of midnight movies and that represent the variety of vantages critics and reviewers have successfully used on these films. While many of these pieces treat what is clearly the proto-type midnight movie, *The Rocky Horror Picture Show,* they also range over the camp productions of John Waters, "new wave" genre films, imports such as *La Cage Aux Folles,* and mainstream films like *The Man Who Fell to Earth* that have belatedly found a following in the midnight audience. Be-cause they deal with such a range of films, the essays in this section may well be the liveliest and most diverse of the volume. In addition to more traditional auteurist and thematic explorations, we here find ideological, feminist, and even statistical studies of the cult film—all of them trying to sort out the appeal and significance of this alternate cinematic practice.

The first two essays in this section attempt to define, from quite differ-ent vantages, the broad cultural function served by the midnight movie narrative. Allison Graham focuses on the nostalgic, alien, and generally un-usual images on which the cult film so often capitalizes. In isolating a 1950s nostalgia that surfaces repeatedly in our cult films—and most notably in the work of John Waters—she finds in these works a peculiar awareness of cultural values. Particularly, she suggests that our midnight movies speak directly about our culture's embrace of a kind of pseudoculture, a false real-ity complete with false values. By deploying an ideological methodology, Barry Grant reveals a more specific pattern that underlies this embrace. Ranging over a variety of the most popular midnight movies, he describes the consistent play of imaginary relationships within these narratives, and in the process lays out the far from radical agenda that actually propels many cult works.

The essays by Gaylyn Studlar and Robert Wood examine various ways in which the midnight movie effectively *constructs* its audience. Represen-tative of current trends in feminist analysis, Studlar's piece looks at how films like *Rocky Horror, Pink Flamingos,* and *Liquid Sky* craft what might seem like a progressive, even liberating sense of gender. In each case, though, she reveals a series of contradictions underlying their depiction of sex roles and undermining what are often taken to be radical gender im-ages. In the essay that follows, Wood explores one of the most distinctive characteristics of the *Rocky Horror* phenomenon, the way in which it has inspired emulation, through its audience's ritualistic "performance" of the film. Drawing on contemporary developments in dramatic theory, he de-scribes the film as a kind of hybrid of cinema and theater, and argues that the film's extension of performance beyond the screen to the audience itself was less a happy accident than the product of a dramatic experience that, in our time, has undergone radical redefinition and redesigning.

Gregory Waller and David Lavery take very different approaches to ana-lyzing the nature of the cult film audience. Waller uses market research to shed light on the cult film's ever-shifting patterns of distribution and exhibition—patterns rendered even more inconstant today by the widespread penetration of the video rental business. By focusing on several small markets, he is able to chart the marketing strategies and changing popularities of the "midnight movie" during the period 1980–1985, arguably its most popular era. What those strategies in particular reveal is a portrait of the midnight movie audience as the film industry has come to see it. As a fitting conclusion to this discussion of the cult context, Waller ends with a filmography of the most popular midnight movies, drawn quite practically from the playlists of theaters in his research markets. In a rather more fanciful yet equally telling vein, David Lavery also explores this "image" of the cult audience. He does so by approaching the cult phenomenon from the vantage of a future cultural historian who wants to make sense out of certain film types that seem to belong to no familiar or traditional generic pattern. Having uncovered a group of films labeled "cult" works, his hypothetical explorer discerns the traces of a long-lost religion, quite literally a *cult* centered around the midnight movie and one whose characteristics suggest much about the cult film devotees of our own time.

The banal vision of order in *Plan 9 from Outer Space:* the police, the military, and the average couple. (DCA Films)

Divine plots her excesses in *Pink Flamingos.* (New Line/Museum of Modern Art)

The Rocky Horror Picture Show as horror film—Brad and Janet hesitantly enter the "old dark house." (Twentieth Century–Fox)

The Rocky Horror Picture Show as science fiction film—Riff Raff and Magenta reveal their alien origins. (Twentieth Century–Fox)

A model for its own cult activity: the cast dances "The Time Warp" in *The Rocky Horror Picture Show.* (Twentieth Century–Fox)

Liquid Sky's charade of androgeny: Anne Carlisle, as Margaret, confronts her own image, as Jimmy. (Z-Films/Museum of Modern Art)

Gay masquerade: Renato and Albin of the *La Cage aux Folles* series. (MGM)

CHAPTER 9

Journey to the Center of the Fifties: The Cult of Banality

Allison Graham

I think that Warhol's films are historical documents. One hundred years from now they will look at *Kitchen* and see that incredibly cramped little set, which was indeed a kitchen. . . . You can see nothing but the kitchen table, the refrigerator, the stove, and the actors. The refrigerator hummed and droned on the sound track. . . . The dialogue was dull and bounced off the enamel and plastic surfaces. It was a horror to watch. It captured the essence of every boring, dead day one's ever had in a city. . . . I suspect that a hundred years from now people will look at *Kitchen* and say, "Yes, that is the way it was in the late Fifties and early Sixties in America. That's why they had the war in Vietnam. That's why the rivers were getting polluted. That's why there was typological glut. That's why the horror came down. That's why the plague was on its way.

    —Norman Mailer, *Edie: An American Biography*

I was in no mood to argue. All I wanted to do was watch *Twilight Zone*.

    —Jerry Lee Lewis, concerning his fifth wife's death

Toward the end of his career, Edward D. Wood, Jr., who has been proclaimed both "the worst director of all time" and "the ultimate cult director" (Medved and Medved 180; Hoberman and Rosenbaum 265), produced a rare exercise in reflexivity. His 1960 antipornography film, *The Sinister Urge*, which focused on the tragic final weeks of Johnny Ryde, a talented director reduced to grinding out smut for the "dirty picture racket," offered not only a passionate attack on exploitation films but an apologia for a lifetime of cinematic mediocrity. "You know," a cop muses as Ryde's bullet-riddled body is carted off at film's end, "if Johnny'd stayed honest, he might have been a big man in the motion picture business." That Ryde is Wood's alter-ego (his Mr. Hyde) is obvious; his office is plastered with posters from Wood's films of the 1950s. Halfway through the film, as he screens his latest feature for the queen of the porn racket, Ryde poignantly assesses his own work: "I look at this slush," he says, "and I try to remember. At one time I made *good* movies." But the porn queen, Wood's apparent stand-in for Hollywood's commercial philistines, replies, "You're making more money now than you ever made in your life. Who needs good films in this business anyway?" The one problem here, of course, is that Wood never really made any "good movies"; "slush" was his forte.

The porn queen's one suggestion for Ryde, "Get some new girls, get some new angles, but the amount spent for each reel stays the same," might easily be the mass production credo of the low-budget thriller/tingler/potboiler of the fifties, a form mastered by Wood and enshrined by two generations of cult fans. Wood's reflexive protestations notwithstanding, it is his very lack of talent that ensures his place in the cult pantheon. For unlike creative heroes of the romantic tradition (whose genius is seen as at odds with contemporary values and aesthetic norms), directors like Wood finally show little resistance to either their recalcitrant medium or the historical moment. In fact, the cult activity surrounding them seems to stand auteurism on its head: instead of celebrating individuality's triumph over genre, the cultist celebrates genre's triumph over individuality, as originality is assaulted and defeated by forces of culture, convention, and, ultimately, cliché.

Wood is just the clearest case in point. The moment one of his films begins, even an inexperienced filmgoer knows something is amiss. Subtlety, ambiguity, and wit play no part in these "narratives," all of which (but especially the Bela Lugosi vehicles *Bride of the Monster*, *Plan 9 from Outer Space*, and *Glen or Glenda?* seem incredibly inept. It is hard to imagine more sloppily constructed and conceived films: plots seldom make sense, bits of footage recur repeatedly, actors forget or stumble on lines that are trite to begin with (or, in the case of the terminally addicted Lugosi, lines are misread to render pathetically personal Freudian slips), blocking of actors is nonexistent, editing produces grotesquely mismatched shots, film stock is incorrectly exposed, continuity is botched, and sets are hastily arranged, minimal collections of objects. But like fifties sitcoms, his work carries on somehow despite the technical lapses and thematic simple-mindedness.

Wood's films, like those of Roger Corman and Andy Warhol ten years later, were ground out as fast as he could make them (although his output was relatively small, since he understandably had a difficult time rounding up investors). He worked in Hollywood's Poverty Row, an older area of low-budget houses, at a studio called Sunset Stages, where, as a Lugosi biographer notes, "It wasn't unusual for a director to have to shoot around the noisy rush-hour traffic on Sunset Boulevard . . . the walls were paper-thin, and burlap bags strung across the rafters doubled as the roof" (Cremer 223). But while a kind of poverty-induced realism and carefree cinematic rule-breaking resulted, the end product differed greatly from the work of an honored B-film director like Edgar G. Ulmer, whose understanding of the mechanics of filmmaking and of popular American genres let him play productively with the bare bones of a story or structure. Wood, it seems, is worshipped by cult audiences precisely for his failings, and especially for displaying his own and his materials' limitations so very clearly.

This mystique of failure, as we might term it, has proved a remarkable lure for cult fans and has found its apotheosis in the work of self-styled "sleaze-master" John Waters, whose *Pink Flamingos* (1973) is often considered the quintessential cult film. But Waters has given his obsession with 1950s "trash culture"—with the world of Wood and his ilk—a great deal of thought. In fact, he has concluded that "bad" art is valuable precisely for the transparency of its intentions, for the nakedness of its desires: "bad taste is what entertainment is all about," he theorizes, "but one must remember that there is such a thing as good bad taste and bad bad taste. . . . To understand bad taste one must have very good taste" (*Shock Value* 2). In other words, one must be thoroughly conversant with the forms of cultural concealment in order to "see" their true motivations. What one "sees," of course, is the opposite of every cliché, the reverse of every expectation—neither of which is any more "true" than the cliché itself; as Waters says, "Good is bad; ugly is beautiful" (MacDonald 56). Yet Waters has fared far better with critics than Wood. The cliché-reversals in his "celluloid atrocities," as he calls them, have been termed everything from "Buñuelesque" to "proto-punk." "His plots," one critic writes, "which seem like genetic malformations of traditional Hollywood plots, involve attacks on conventions and also on the traditional audience relationship to film" (MacDonald 53).

The reason for this difference, of course, is that, in contrast to Wood, Waters' "badness" seems intentional. However, the difference is not just in technical or stylistic competence. As I have suggested, it is the *appearance* of Wood's intentions that so engages cult audiences—the perceived distance (foregrounded in *The Sinister Urge*) between his desire to create compelling narratives and his inability to do so. In that embarrassingly wide gap between intention and act, every spectator sees the painted cardboard monster that fails to horrify, the strings and plastic of the dinner-plate UFO that fails to amaze, the misapplied makeup and faded allure of a blonde "bombshell" who fails to arouse. And it is in this perceived gap that cultism reveals its peculiarly postmodern aesthetic. For while the hip know-ingness of the cult audience, reveling in its suspension of belief, may ap-pear ironic and seem to stand outside the "naive" spectacle of postwar popular culture, it is deeply rooted in the very culture it mocks. Like Wood himself, our modern cult sensibility is an inevitable product of that banal culture.

The cult fascination with 1950s "bad art" seems largely to stem from the commonplace assumption that the era was repressive. Certainly, since the 1970s the decade has been depicted almost as if it were a patient in the first stages of a twenty-year psychosis. What else, the conventional wisdom of popular culture now asks, were Cold War fears, segregation, sexual pu-ritanism, and suburban conformity if not manifestations of paranoia, pro-jection, and repression just waiting to be diagnosed and "cured" in the Age of Aquarius? For, to be sure, while the sixties drug culture seemed obsessed with mysticism, its primary project was the irreverent *demystifica-tion* of American culture. The trip inward was inherently a journey toward latent "truths" that seemed to lie far beneath the surface of consensus real-ity, and although this search for a superior inner reality was hardly a novel phenomenon in world history, in the context of American culture it as-sumed immediate political dimensions: what was "hidden" was a sense of life and self directly at odds with postwar morality. The belief that, as "inner space" guru John Lilly says, "all and everything that one can imag-ine exists [when] one is tuned into the cosmos with all of its infinite varia-tions" (51) could not be further from the materialist creed of the fifties "or-ganization man." The most concrete "facts" became merely transparent masks of hypocrisy, impotence, and cruelty; all that was solid dissolved in outrageous irony: in one popular poster LBJ became a Hell's Angel, while in another Nixon's face sat atop a nude woman's body; the Yippies dumped money onto the floor of the Stock Exchange, nominated a pig for presi-dent, and, in the most inventive mockery of Establishment substantiality, tried to levitate the Pentagon. The revered symbols of fifties morality, bat-tered by such persistent mockery, easily dissolved into comic stereotypes—and cult icons.

Our rage to "re-vision" the era, as well as our cult embrace of it, ulti-mately springs from a kind of tragic irony. The perceived distance between a so-called fifties "innocence" and a contemporary cynicism is almost al-ways interpreted psychoanalytically as the distance between latency and maturity. This is understandable to some degree, since most of the "Ameri-kitsch" directors—cult auteurs like Waters, Paul Bartel, David Lynch—grew up in the forties and fifties, and believe, like Lynch, that "because I was little then, it's an innocent time for me" (Edelstein 20). Director Susan Seidelman, for instance, claims that she wanted her *Making Mr. Right* (1987) to have "a *Jetsons* look," because "it was this impression I had about what the future was going to be like from watching these shows . . . back then we thought robots would be our friends." Her movie, about a woman who falls in love with an android, "was meant to be somewhat dark," since today "we're much more cynical" (Edelstein 18), which is another way of saying that such stylish eighties images are supposed to be knowing and ironic. But when the repressed double of childhood turns out, under adult analysis, to be exactly what it seemed all along—a cartoon clone—the only true irony in the situation is that the future *has* turned out to be like the past, and that one's supposedly surprising inner life, like a chain of Holiday Inns, contains no surprise at all. Recreating the style of repression implies some understanding of the dynamics of repression (i.e., something "hidden" is covered up or denied). Yet if what was repressed to begin with was an inability to fantasize or believe in any other way of life, if the imagination, in other words, was already colonized by consumer culture, then our fashionable fifties simulacra, today's cult successes, can easily become—if unwittingly—open confessions of failure.

If the cult sensibility of the 1970s and 1980s, epitomized by films like George Romero's *Living Dead* series, Waters' *Pink Flamingos,* and Lynch's *Blue Velvet,* has brought this kind of psychological colonization to the surface, it has not done so solely from a desire to be cynically "hip." Such films seem weirdly autobiographical, revealing an intimacy with the arcane nuances of postwar rites of passage that could only come from experience. The relationship between cult filmmakers and American mass culture is indeed familial, for both "came of age" together. (As Waters says of the televised dance show in *Hairspray* [1988], "You learned to be a teenager from watching the show" [*Crackpot* 89].)

This intimate connection was, in fact, foreshadowed in the 1956 *Journey to the Center of the Earth,* a work whose vision is strangely close to that of contemporary cult films. Unlike most science fiction films of the fifties, this work, which describes an expedition to the earth's core, found absolutely nothing alien or repressed at the "center" of life. Plenty of prehistoric monsters seem to roam the periphery of the center—enough to suggest that whatever lurks at the epicenter must be a psychic leviathan. But at the very center of planet Earth, the anticipated site of original trauma, there is only a roiling whirlpool which, when approached by the intrepid explorers, catapults them right back into the trees of their hometown. The unconscious is hardly a region here; it is merely a *force* that propels one outward. What is inside is simply the energy to externalize, with inner life just a self-reflexive joke. Like the roundabout adventure in this oddly pre-scient film, the cinematic plunges of later cult directors into a "taboo" underworld, seeking new images and secrets, have discovered only souvenirs from the overworld. As Waters puts it most succinctly, "I stopped taking drugs when I realized that pot smelled bad and LSD trips were becoming like TV reruns. I had had enough inner journeys" (*Shock Value* 94).

Waters' association of psychic depths with television is not as flip as it seems, for television more than any other medium embodies the cult vision's one-dimensionality. "Like the blob," as J. Hoberman observes, television "oozes out in all directions"; it is "an eternal now in which history is the history of style" (8). In a medium that obliterates distinctions between news and advertising, fiction and nonfiction (the "docudrama"), film and video (the "telefilm"), and in which all events aspire to self-promotion, neither tragedy nor irony seems possible, for neither exists without critical or psychological distance. This sort of obliteration of distinction is the case for Waters, too, who roams the movie theaters, television channels, radio stations, and newspapers of his past for inspiration. Unlike British punk fashions of the seventies, which, in Dick Hebdige's words, "gestured towards a 'nowhere'" (120), the American cult vision, growing at the same time but informed instead by "communication" and media addiction, seems to gesture everywhere. The former asserts the complexity of culture and focuses on deep structures—of class and psyche—if only to find an abyss; the latter sees culture at a glance, as a network of television dials, movie projectors, and magazine racks. There are no depths in the outlaw aesthetics, for the procrustean bed of mass media effortlessly compresses cultural contours into a truly "median" vision; everyone and everything become middle class. However, a flattened, self-referential world is inherently immediate and ahistorical. Thus when Lynch says that his *Blue Velvet* "was like the '50s meeting the '80s" (Edelstein 20), he might as easily be describing almost any cult film of the past fifteen years. This confusion of decades inevitably results from several generations' experience of thirty or forty years of personal and public history as a "media blur."

Probably no cult director is more aware of our general residency in these prime-time precincts than John Waters. "As soon as I entered high school," he claims, "I decided I was a beatnik . . . in homage to my favorite beatnik TV character, Maynard G. Krebs, on *The Dobie Gillis Show*" (*Shock Value* 36). And Waters' films are filled with references to series like *Leave It to Beaver* and *Father Knows Best*. But it is not simply an affectation of "kitsch consciousness" that generates a cult fascination with the fifties and its television artifacts. A quick trip through the "nostalgia" cable channels reveals a menacing sense of frustration that Waters has accurately gauged undermining the oppressively cheerful dialogue and faces. Those small, claustrophobic black and white images reveal the barest of sets. The location usually requires an act of the imagination: it contains just enough information to suggest a house, an apartment, an office. Within the symbolic sets of domestic situation comedies, very little actually happens, and yet volcanic emotional eruptions occur so frequently that, in essence, they become generic conventions: Jackie Gleason bellowing and pawing the floor of his tiny kitchen in *The Honeymooners;* Joan Davis or Lucille Ball literally climbing the walls of their dollhouse living rooms; Dwayne Hickman whining among the stacks of canned food in his father's Lilliputian grocery store; Danny Thomas exploding in his New York apartment; Robert Young's family circling frantically at the beginning of every episode. The energy is cataclysmic and constant. But don't be fooled; climb and pound as many walls as they like, chew as much scenery as they can, there is no way out. The set stays.

It should seem odd that the conventions of this unrealistic genre would be internalized by viewers as a yardstick for "life" itself. As Waters recalls, "When I was a kid, you were raised to believe that your family should be like *Leave It to Beaver* or *Father Knows Best* . . . I was raised to think that *Father Knows Best* was the Way It Was. Now even my parents can look back and see how ridiculous it was, but at the time, *it was reality*" (Edelstein 17). But as Waters knows all too well, this "looking back" can hardly be objective, for what we see in those snowy images is what we already know, what the sixties taught us to think about the American Dream, and what the reversals in the imitative scripts of our own lives have revealed of the underbelly of the Good Life. We criticize the mythology from within, analyze the subtext while living it—but the set stays, like a permanent part of our lives.

This sense of cultural and psychological confinement that surfaces in many of our cult works has led some critics to describe them as "bomb shelter" films, works reminiscent of "the fortress mentality of the fifties." While this description is particularly appropriate for films like *Night of the Living Dead* (1968) and *Eraserhead* (1978)—both intensely claustrophobic black and white films in which characters speak in sitcom clichés—it is just as fitting for any film that attempts to decimate Beaver Cleaver's Mayfield (or the Anderson family's Springfield, or David Lynch's Lumberton) with a parodic wit or satiric irony, for it is driven right back to the center, to an underground bunker well stocked with the mass-produced imperishables from above ground.

Of course, what links directors like Waters and Lynch (as well as performers like David Letterman and the "Saturday Night Live" comedy alumni Chevy Chase, Dan Aykroyd, and Eddie Murphy) is an ironic stance and the belief that their comic send-ups or, in Waters' case, extreme examples of "bad taste" not only reveal profound discrepancies between popular culture and personal truth, but actually pinpoint the repressed sources of our postwar mythology of nuclear family bliss and hometown fun. But the subtext of this mythology has become mythologized itself, for most artists today seem to agree that the dimensions of the American Dream are directly proportional to the measure of our own repressions. Waters thus describes his *Polyester* (1982) as "a ludicrous melodrama, like *Father Knows Best* gone totally berserk." The plot consists of "all the stuff we didn't see on television, when Robert Young's fucking his secretary and Betty's hooked on smack" (Chute 26).

This reading of the postwar Family as the comic facade of sexual repression and various psychoses has become so standard in the cult film (see *Rock 'n' Roll High School* [1979], *Eating Raoul* [1982], *Targets* [1968], *Eraserhead* [1978], *Blue Velvet* [1986], and *Parenthood* [1989], among others) that it begs its own reading. For the "truth" always assumed to lie beneath the surface of the fabricated American idyll is itself finally a kind of deranged sensibility influenced by or derived from popular media. The spectacle of the all-American family (as in Waters' beloved "Visit Our Concession Stand" drive-in ads of the fifties) "happily munching monstrous meatball sandwiches, overpriced tubs of popcorn, and disgusting warmed-up hamburgers" (*Shock Value* 92) might easily be the controlling metaphor of the cult vision, as if the culture had imploded at some point in mid-century, spilling its mass-produced banalities into consumers' hollowed-out psyches.[1]

Waters himself, the connoiseur of popular culture's detritus, has been the cult world's most flamboyant "demystifier." One of his earliest efforts, *The Diane Linkletter Story*, shows where his later works would head. The "film" was shot in one afternoon in 1970 and recounts a recent headline event—the LSD-influenced suicide of Art Linkletter's daughter. The dialogue is filled with sixties clichés ("I'm doing my own thing in my own time") and ends with the record made by Linkletter after his daughter's death ("That record Linkletter put out was in worse taste than anything I could ever think of," Waters says). But the distinguishing feature of this exercise in "bad taste" is the leading character, played by the late Divine, a three-hundred-pound transvestite, who starred in all but one of Waters' films. "We both idolized Jayne Mansfield," claims Waters, "and since Divine was getting quite heavy, we agreed she could play the perfect takeoff of a blond bombshell" (*Shock Value* 54). Divine's Mansfield impersonation later became the centerpiece of *Pink Flamingos,* which itself takes off on the 1956 Mansfield vehicle *The Girl Can't Help It*. As Waters says, "I *love* clichés. . . . I especially love a cliché with something wrong with it; that makes a joke" (MacDonald 59). The "joke" in *Pink Flamingos*, of course, is the casting of a gigantic transvestite in the blond bombshell role—a spectacle that mocks the monstrously exaggerated sexual stereotype of the fifties. But more than that, Waters has transformed Frank Tashlin's "sexiest woman alive" into the "filthiest woman alive," a happy-go-lucky murderess on the loose who literally stoops to anything (including, at film's end, real dog droppings). All of the smarmy, furtive, double-entendre lust usually projected onto the figure of the passive "knockout" is thus deflected right back at its source, at the viewer, by the brazenly lewd Divine.

Yet Waters' "trash vision" is not easily constructed. His efforts to reach the center, to exhume and display the "sleazy" subtexts of American life, are all vigorously "overtheatrical." If he had a million-dollar budget for a film, he claims, he would buy "fake trees, fake sky, fake everything . . . like a Sirk movie" (Chute 28). He would, in other words, imitate the intentional "fakeness" of a foreign director who, through artifice, tried to comment on the falsity of fifties American culture. Thus Divine's pink and gray trailer in *Pink Flamingos* was a "mere shell," Waters claims, purchased for one hundred dollars and decorated with "the ugliest items" from "every lousy thrift shop and white-trash furniture showroom"; the set of *Desperate Living* "was made almost entirely out of garbage" (*Shock Value* 4, 167); and Divine's suburban home in *Polyester* (1981) was arranged, as one critic put it, in "a blinding conglomeration of the tacky and the tasteless . . . from actual furniture stores all over Baltimore" and suffused with "Sirk-Fassbinder lighting" (Chute 32, 26). His makeup man "totally understands the look of 'inner rot'" he wants to achieve and carefully applies "pimples made out of eyelash glue," "blackheads," "age lines," "severe bags," ad nauseum, to the actors who people those fake sets (*Shock Value* 133).

Waters' vision of "inner rot" could hardly be captured in *cinema vérité* style. In fact, for someone who reveres "disgusting" images as much as he claims to, he is no fan of documentary: "I take pleasure in watching a *fake* operation. I have very little interest in hard-core porn . . . and I wouldn't want to see a real snuff film" (Chute 28). His concept of psychic decay is simply a self-conscious fabrication, the shadow cast by the postwar consumer dream, a "TV rerun." Lurking inside is the mirror image of the lie that bolsters the myth of Home and Family. Thus he aims for a castle that is a "cheesy version of Disneyland" and a film score that is a "cheesy *Dr. Zhivago*-type score."

In light of this obsession with sleaze, Waters' description of *Pink Flamingos*, the story of a feud between "the filthiest people in the world," as "a very American film" (*Shock Value* 173, 2) finds its proper context, for what constitutes "filth" in this film ultimately seems almost desperately banal. Beneath his characters' parodic sitcom behavior, few if any "sinister" impulses emerge. Peeling back layers of inhibition and repression, Waters finds only more mediation—no heart of darkness. What is probably most memorable about this film, in fact, is its revulsion at carnal pleasures, for it devises myriad substitutions to avoid "flesh handling." Our instincts, he seems to suggest, are no less acculturated than the ego, driving Divine, in her final exercise in bad taste, to lust after the casual droppings of a poodle (an appropriately self-conscious image to end on, since the poodle is one of those archetypal "posh" images of fifties status-mongering).

What Waters understands about the self-reflexive nature of "culture" in this country is something many critics do not. Albert Goldman, for example, in his biography of Elvis Presley, paints a picture of "the King" that seems perversely inspired by *Pink Flamingos*. Under his scrutiny, Elvis emerges as a mammoth white-trash transvestite with a penchant for trashy decor. Goldman's baroque, detailed descriptions of both the man and his home return repeatedly to one thesis: Elvis had "bad taste," the taste of a combination "hillbilly," "rich old queen," "Italian gangster," and "middle-aged woman"—in other words, a taste for Amerikitsch. "Elvis detests everything antique with the heartfelt disgust of a real forward-looking American of his generation" (10), sniffs Goldman, appalled by the King's failure to appreciate what everyone with money should. "Nothing," he says of Graceland's furnishings, is really "worth a dime" (8). Expensive, yes, but valuable, no—bad investments. Velour substitutes for velvet, relatives' trailers spoil the backyard view, and the den is decorated in "Polynesian Primitive." Clearly, Elvis Presley made several major mistakes: he didn't move to Hollywood or New York, and he didn't hire interior decorators. And clearly, if he had allowed his frightful tastes to be "corrected," he might have fared better in Goldman's postmortem evaluation.

Goldman's scandalized sensibility simply represents the strident defense of middle-class taste confronted by its own shadow. Already highly determined by the class-conscious aspirations of consumer culture, it cannot risk the appearance of "cheapness." But what else is that culture based on but the disposability, replaceability, and democratically affordable "cheapness" of industrial items? As the avatar of the postwar sacraments of vinyl, plastic, and celluloid, how else *should* Elvis Presley have furnished his home? One walks through Graceland to sense the "spirit" of someone whose image has been mass-produced millions of times, and what does one see? The tacky goods of mass production. His inner sanctum mirrors the culture, filled as it is with the refuse of its dream factories, the ultimate fifties bomb shelter.

This essentially postmodern sense of inner life as a repository of cultural detritus, however, could not be further from the spirit of avant-garde film-makers like Maya Deren, Stan Brakhage, or Kenneth Anger. Unlike the "structural" and "lyric" films of such underground modernists, whose "great unacknowledged aspiration," according to P. Adams Sitney, was "the cinematic reproduction of the human mind" (408), the cult films of the seventies and eighties have no interest—or belief—in an autonomous subjectivity. The alienated modernist stance itself seems a romantic relic to a later generation of filmmakers who have peered within and seen "TV re-runs." While the politics of modernism asserts the primacy and mystery of inner life, the politics of postmodernism that shows most nakedly in these cult films finds little or no difference between social superstructure and psychological substructure, and simply obliterates depth altogether.

If any director might bridge the postwar avant-garde and contemporary cult visions, it would probably be Andy Warhol. He broke and exposed (in the best modernist fashion) more "rules" of film structure than most audiences would stay awake for, and held his camera unblinkingly on what he found beneath the artifices of form: absolute banality—of behavior, of speech, of spirit. In countless improvised, unedited films off his Factory's assembly line, Warhol showed the poverty of the imagination long before the drug culture admitted defeat.

While Waters represents one branch of the Warholian sensibility—its "trash" aesthetic, an emphasis on the inherent commodification of all art in the postmodern era—David Lynch represents the other branch, one that attempts to revive avant-garde's aesthetic "seriousness" within a blatantly commodified form. Lynch's training as an artist is evident in the highly stylized mise-en-scène of all his films, yet his fascination with culture cliché constantly injects banality into these overwrought images. Thus in *Eraser-head*, sitcom dialogue echoes within surrealistically rendered sets. In *Blue Velvet*, however, Lynch launched a full-scale, big-budget effort to restore a sense of modernist alienation to postmodern "Amerikitsch." Like his cult colleagues, he ostensibly set about deconstructing the American Dream, showing middle-class sensibility as an elaborate, highly constructed *style*; but unlike other cult directors (and more like a psychoanalytically inclined modernist), he implied an authentic reality "behind" such constructions. "*Blue Velvet*," he says, "is about things that are hidden. . . . That's the horror of the world—so many things are hiding behind things that it's a frightening, sick place" (Edelstein 20). Yet despite some Hitchcockian voyeurism, it is hard to see what is really hidden in his film. His characters end up seeing no more or less than what their culture has prepared them for, the "dreams" woven not only by the songs of Roy Orbison but by the entire popular culture machine. Evil, in the character of Frank (played by cult hero Dennis Hopper), is simply the all-American Jeffrey's "worst nightmare" come true.

The title and title song reveal just how hermetically sealed Lynch's imagination remains. To anyone acquainted with avant-garde film (as Lynch certainly is), Bobby Vinton's song inevitably recalls its prior use in Kenneth Anger's *Scorpio Rising* (1966), where it ironically counterpoints the narcissistic, homoerotically charged costuming ritual of a motorcycle gang member (we hear "She wore blue velvet" as a macho biker zips his blue jeans). The song itself is about a romanticized moment in the past and functions (like the film's other "memory song," Orbison's "In Dreams") as a subconscious trigger of Frank's awesome destructiveness. Yet Frank's behavior holds little irony, for there is no critical perspective from which to view it, no culture extrinsic to the pop nightmare of the film itself (and in this sense it is quite similar to *Eraserhead*). Unlike the layers of taboo cultural and psychological ironies in *Scorpio Rising* (as obvious as they now seem), only a smooth continuum exists in *Blue Velvet;* each seeming layer simply parodies a different genre: melodrama—Sandy and Jeffrey's courtship; sitcom—Jeffrey's home life; crime—the absurdly gory shoot-out. Each is a different channel on the tube. The clichés of "Amerikitsch" easily exchange with the clichés of *film noir;* neither is more "true," and neither transcends the self-referential cosmos of popular culture. Robin Wood notes the film's "foregrounding of cliché," which he says might lead some to attribute Brechtian intentions to Lynch, but which to him "expresses a cynicism totally alien to Brecht." To Wood, the defining image of *Blue Velvet* is the mechanical robin seen at film's end, an image that leads us right back into the world of cliché. The film, he says, "parodies certain basic structures of classical Hollywood whilst remaining helplessly locked within them" (12). The set, in other words, stays.

Waters, moving into the big-budget mainstream himself, has attempted a similar project in *Hairspray* (1988). But unlike *Blue Velvet,* his film does not seem destined for cult status, and perhaps that might be attributed to Waters' more undisguised desire to assert a horizon beyond the postmodern mediascape. The character of Tracy Turnblad (who is, significantly, Divine's daughter in the film—cultism's "new generation"), possesses a kind of historical consciousness not previously seen in a Waters film. Her world seems to transcend her immediate early-sixties culture. In fact, she helps bring a civil rights demonstration onto the set of a live television broadcast in the final scene, dislodging the "sprayed and set" fifties dream images from both the TV and film screens. Yet the "new and improved" sixties spectacle takes place *on television,* and while earlier in the film a clear distinction exists between the television *set* (shown in color) and the televised *image* (a small black and white picture watched by home viewers), the televised image is, finally, inseparable from the film frame itself. No one is at home; everyone is absorbed in television's omnivorous set.

Whether it attempts to be terrifying or comic, the cult vision is essentially apocalyptic (hence its attraction to the conventions of science fiction and horror) and unwaveringly committed to the finality of its "readings" (hence too its inherent cynicism). It typically lays bare our psychological, sexual, and political mysteries and finds them all to be fictions. But this reading itself could very easily be the last defense of our crumbling cultural hegemony, a final shoulder-struggling in the face of exhausted questions and answers. It is the kind of ultimately postmodern response displayed in Dennis Hopper's *Colors* (1988), a film that cannot imagine a world after the collapse of heroism and villainy, masculine order and authority, and heterosexual romance. But as Terry Eagleton has noted, postmodernism typically "commits the apocalyptic error of believing that the discrediting of this particular representational epistemology is the death of truth itself" (144).

Maybe so. The cult vision has been one of the most reliable indicators of our addiction to what Baudrillard terms "the obscene delirium of communication" (132), a fascination with the closed circuitry of our own "information network." Our obsession with the banality of what some critics call "Americanarama" is, on the one hand, certainly a critique of one of this culture's most pervasive and futile myths: that of a definable national "essence," a core of "selfhood" ("the heartbeat of America," as advertisers call it). For "Americanism," "un-Americanism," "the American spirit," "the American experience" are all phrases that seem to appeal to a sense of context, but that are actually completely self-referential. And Americanarama, as J. Hoberman points out, ultimately aestheticizes this isolation, offering a wide-screen vision of "one nation—anesthetized, sealed in plastic, self-absorbed" (8). When the Coen brothers instructed the cinematographer on *Raising Arizona* (1987) to make all shots "look flat" in order to create the impression of "bad rear-screen projection" (Edelstein 20), they weren't simply striving for a campy juxtaposition of high and primitive "tech." They were creating an appropriate context for characters whose aspirations stretch no further than the images on the family television set. They were, as well, finding a wicked metaphor for the contemporary era: a flattened, artificial, nostalgically rendered background whose borders defined the dimensions of our culture's dreams for much longer than most television sets.

Like college students of the early eighties playing the fad game called "Hi, Bob!" (which consisted of watching *The Bob Newhart Show* and drinking from a passed bottle each time a character said, "Hi, Bob!"), we have all become expert decoders of Americana's motifs. Like them, we see a single structure housing these motifs: the Dream and its Double, the Text and its Subtext. But whether we choose to contemplate the facade of this decomposing tract dream through a soft-focus lens, in the best Reagan-era fashion, or to zoom in to the generic "glue" between its cracks and splinters, in the best cult fashion, our frame of reference never seems to extend beyond the walls of a backlot relic. We may climb the rafters or get high sniffing the glue between the seams when we become bored, but these are hard times for Hollywood. Even in the cult film, the set stays.

NOTES

1. Mainstream popular films in the 1980s have often offered the same reading of Home and Family. Think only of Dad in Kubrick's *The Shining* (1980), who invokes the spirits of Johnny Carson and Ward Cleaver before setting out to kill his family; or of another dad in *The Stepfather* (1982), who watches "Mister Ed" to get in the mood to do the same thing; or of the American soldiers in *Full Metal Jacket* (1988), who chant the Mickey Mouse Club anthem after decimating a Vietnamese town. Demystifying the American way of life, however, has been a central mission of the cult vision ever since George Romero graphically detailed the shattering of Home and Family in *Night of the Living Dead* (1968), and it is worth noting that the film only started to attract a cult following in the 1970s, when its spirit more closely matched that of its audience.

WORKS CITED

Baudrillard, Jean. "The Ecstasy of Communication." In *The Anti-Aesthetic*, ed. Hal Foster, 126–134. Port Townsend, Wash.: Bay Press, 1983.
Chute, David. "Still Waters." *Film Comment* 17, no. 3 (1981): 26–32.
Cremer, Robert. *Lugosi: The Man behind the Cape*. Chicago: Henry Regnery, 1976.
Eagleton, Terry. *Against the Grain*. London: Verso, 1986.
Edelstein, David. "Kitsch and Tell." *Village Voice Film Supplement*, June 30, 1987.
Goldman, Albert. *Elvis*. New York: McGraw-Hill, 1981.
Hebdige, Dick. *Subculture: The Meaning of Style*. London: Methuen, 1979.
Hoberman, J. "What's Stranger Than Paradise?" *Village Voice Film Supplement*, June 30, 1987.
———., and Jonathan Rosenbaum. *Midnight Movies*. New York: Harper, 1983.

Lilly, John. *The Center of the Cyclone: An Autobiography of Inner Space*. New York: Julian Press, 1972.
MacDonald, Scott. "John Waters' Divine Comedy." *Artforum* 20, no. 5 (1982): 52–60.
Medved, Harry, and Michael Medved. *The Golden Turkey Awards*. New York: Perigee, 1980.
Sitney, P. Adams. *Visionary Film*. New York: Oxford Univ. Press, 1974.
Waters, John. *Crackpot: The Obsessions of John Waters*. New York: Macmillan, 1983.
———. *Shock Value: A Tasteful Book about Bad Taste*. New York: Dell, 1981.
Wood, Robin. "Leavis, Marxism, and Film Culture." *CineAction!* 8 (1987): 3–13.

CHAPTER 10

Science Fiction Double Feature: Ideology in the Cult Film

Barry K. Grant

Before examining the cult film as a cinematic category, we must first ask, "What is a cult film?" Despite the phenomenon's popularity, critical work in this area has been sparse and tentative, so this question is somewhat more difficult to answer than it might at first appear. We all know, say, a western or musical when we see one. By definition, westerns are overdetermined by their physical and temporal settings. They must be set in the West, that is, between the Mississippi River and California, usually between 1865 and 1890. Less determined in this regard, musicals may be set in any time or place, from Ernst Lubitsch's mythical prewar Europe to the contemporary ghetto of *West Side Story*. Still, musicals remain relatively easy to identify generically, since if a movie contains several instances of song and dance *within* its diegetic world, it is by definition a musical.

In contrast, the cult film can come from any genre. It can modify classic generic forms, as Philippe de Broca's *King of Hearts* does to the war film, or it may defy generic category, like David Lynch's *Eraserhead*. While its disparate generic affinities make the cult film far more slippery to grasp than conventional genre works, we can find a number of underlying similarities shared by this otherwise varied group of movies. Indeed, although these movies might differ on the surface, in what Edward Buscombe terms their "outer forms," they are similar on a deeper, ideological level, what Buscombe calls a genre's "inner forms" (12).

In his *Theories of Film*, Andrew Tudor explains a major problem of all genre definition, which he terms "the empiricist dilemma":

To take a genre such as a western, analyze it, and list its principal characteristics is to beg the question that we must first isolate the body of films that are westerns. But they can only be isolated on the basis of the 'principal characteristics,' which can only be discovered *from the films themselves* after they have been isolated. (135)

Tudor's pragmatic solution to this problem of definition is to rely on what he calls a "common cultural consensus," to analyze works that almost everyone would agree belong to a particular genre and generalize from that point. But the problem is more acute for the cult film for two reasons: first, its disparate generic affinities make the category even more unwieldy than conventional genres; and, second, the lack of a substantial body of cult criticism provides little help in establishing a cultural consensus. Thus critical confusion over identifying particular cult movies inevitably arises. J. Hoberman and Jonathan Rosenbaum in *Midnight Movies*, for example, call *The Cabinet of Dr. Caligari* "the cult film *par excellence*" (23), while Danny Peary in *Cult Movies* nowhere even mentions it.

In the cinema the term "cult" tends to be used rather loosely, to describe a variety of films, old and new, that are extremely popular or have a particularly devoted audience. Cult films, most of us would agree, tend to construct a microcosmic community of admirers. But what exactly makes this different from phenomenally successful popular movies like *Star Wars* or *E.T.*, which might more accurately be described as examples of "mass cult"? Such movies perfectly fit Harold Wilensky's definition of mass culture as "cultural products manufactured solely for a mass market" (175). Indeed, the cuddly Ewoks of the last *Star Wars* episode seem designed expressly for their merchandising potential. A similar problem is raised by those movies that seem consciously calculated from the time of their production (or even before) to become instant cult films. Examples might include *Repo Man, Liquid Sky,* and *Blue Velvet,* movies that represent the fast food of cult rather than the slowly simmered fare like *Blade Runner,* which became cult when released on video after its theatrical run.

Despite the critical difficulties arising from the equivocal nature of the cult corpus, however, one useful idea that has been suggested about all cult movies is that in some way they involve a form of "transgression" and that this quality is central to their appeal. This transgression can manifest itself in terms of subject matter, as with the "difference" evoked by Tod Browning's *Freaks* (1931)[1]; or in terms of attitude, as in the cheerful embrace of an aesthetic of the ugly—or perhaps simply the tacky—in John Waters' *Pink Flamingos* (1975). Transgression can manifest itself as well in a film's style, as in the Artaudian cinema of cruelty approach of Alexandro Jodorowsky's *El Topo* (1973), or in the kinetic visual pyrotechnics of George Miller's *Mad Max* movies.

Thus the films of Edward D. Wood, Jr., widely acknowledged as the worst filmmaker of all time, are cult because they transgress basic technical competency, even as they affront the consumer who shells out the considerable cost of a ticket at the box office. Wood's lurid 1952 transvestite movie, *Glen or Glenda?* (a.k.a. *I Changed My Sex*), is cult partly because of its subject but, more important, because it is so ludicrously inept as a documentary. Similarly, his 1956 effort, *Plan 9 from Outer Space*, is a cult favorite because it is so *obviously* awful in the context of the well-made classical narrative.

This embrace of "badness" also accounts for the cult status of such unhorrifying horror films as *Attack of the Killer Tomatoes* and antidrug propaganda movies like *Reefer Madness* (1936), a film which claims that smoking marijuana leads to addiction, rape, murder, and insanity. By the same reasoning, Frank Capra's *Why We Fight* series of World War II films, which are just as sensationalist in their bellicose jingoism, are not cult, since they are slickly made and have proven their ability to persuade an audience.

It has also been suggested that the element of transgressive difference central to cult films may be due largely to an alternative method of distribution or exhibition. This certainly applies to some of the midnight movies, which went against the logic of traditional "prime-time" exhibition. Thus, if John Waters' recent *Hairspray* (1988) does not achieve the cult status of his other films, it may be because it was released as a mainstream movie with a PG rating. But this idea seems more problematic when applied to many classical cult films, such as *Citizen Kane* (1941), *Forbidden Planet* (1956), or *Black Sunday* (1975), movies originally both produced and marketed through conventional studio channels.

While it is true that cult films seem commonly to offer some form of transgression, what these movies more precisely have in common, what essentially makes these movies *cultish,* is their ability to be at once transgressive *and* recuperative, in other words, to reclaim that which they seem to violate. Further, they tend to achieve this ideological manipulation through a particular inflection of the figure of the Other. Common enough in genre movies generally, in the cult film the Other becomes a caricature that makes what it represents less threatening to the viewer. As in classic genre films, then, the viewer ultimately gains the double satisfaction of both rejecting dominant cultural values and remaining safely inscribed within them.

Because of this structural doublethink of cult movies, it is not surprising that they have also been defined in terms of "sameness" rather than difference. Peary, for example, while hypothesizing the cult film's difference, oddly claims that sometimes films become cult by offering "'definitive' performances by stars who have cult status" (xiii). Hence the cult appeal of almost any film with actors like Humphrey Bogart, Marlon Brando, James Dean, Mae West, Marilyn Monroe, and even Ronald Reagan. Presumably this is why Peary discusses in his book movies like *All About Eve, Top Hat,* and *A Hard Day's Night*—works that perfectly capture the appeal of Bette Davis, Astaire and Rogers, and the Beatles, respectively. Movies that fulfill this function of showcasing the iconographical significance of their stars are necessarily more conventional than different, since they must rely for their meaning on the culturally accepted values of the star. This is quite opposite the strategy of "casting against type," which is more a strategy of difference.[2]

In yet another approach, Umberto Eco suggests that cult movies work by a kind of collage effect. "In order to transform a work of art into a cult object," he says, "one must be able to break, dislocate, unhinge it so that one can remember only parts of it, irrespective of their original relationship with the whole." This seems yet another aspect of the cult film's transgressive nature, since this collage structure is at odds with the usual appreciation of a work of art as an aesthetic unity (in Cleanth Brooks' famous phrase, the "well-wrought urn") and Hollywood's ideal of seamless ("classical") construction. For Eco, a cult movie survives by becoming "a disconnected series of images, of peaks, of visual icebergs. It should display not one central idea but many. It should not reveal a coherent philosophy of composition" (3–4). While Eco considers only *Casablanca* specifically, the idea seems to apply to many other cult films as well. *The Rocky Horror Picture Show*, perhaps the most obvious example, loosely joins elements of the horror, science fiction, and musical genres, with plenty of self-conscious allusions peppered throughout the text; *Mad Max*, to take another example, combines science fiction, road movies, and westerns. These films would seem to demonstrate Eco's assertion that "a cult movie is the proof that . . . cinema comes from cinema" (4).

Clearly, though, mainstream films have manifested this quality for decades. Neoformalist critics have recently argued for a view of Hollywood cinema as "a unified mode of film practice" with its origins dating as early as 1917 (Bordwell, Staiger, and Thompson). Eco's notion of a collagelike assembly of interchangeable parts is, in fact, an essential element of genre films, the mainstay of classical Hollywood cinema, whether among works of a particular genre or across different genres. *Casablanca*, Eco claims, "became a cult movie because it is not *one* movie . . . [but] the movies" (12); yet this same generalization can easily be made about hundreds of other undistinguished and now forgotten Hollywood films.

And so we define cult movies by the seemingly contradictory qualities of sameness and difference. The reason for this is that they are, in fact, at once different and the same, transgressive and recuperative. However, in the context of the cult film, it is not enough simply to talk about such properties in terms of the text alone. To understand why, let us consider the term "cult" itself. The first definition of the word offered by the OED is "worship; reverential homage rendered to a divine being or beings." In the case of cult movies, the "divinity" is the shimmering series of images cast on the silver screen which our devoted attention lifts above the realm of the merely representational and the secular. So the viewer's relation to the work is a crucial element of cult in film. With cult movies like *The Rocky Horror Picture Show*, where audience participation was first accepted and then ritualized until it became at least as much an attraction as the film itself, the term fits the OED's other, complementary definitions: "A particular form or system of religious worship; esp. in reference to its external rites and ceremonies," and "Devotion or homage to a particular person or thing, now esp. as paid by a body of professed adherents or admirers." In the first case, the emphasis is on the *object* of worship; in the second, on the *act* or *nature* of the worship; and in the third, on those who *engage* in the worship.

J. P. Telotte has observed that the close relation between the cult film as a text and as an experience allows us to conceive of both aspects together as what he calls the cult "supertext." He sees this feature of the cult film as distinguishing it from more traditional, conventionally defined genres (see the essay "Beyond All Reason" in this volume). The rapt attention of Woody Allen's Allan Felix in *Play It Again, Sam*, his face bathed in the beatific light of the movie screen as he reverently mouths Bogie's final speech to Ingrid Bergman on the airport runway in *Casablanca*, is the perfect cinematic expression of this cult "supertext." Now, since a movie's cult appeal becomes manifest in a particular way of experiencing it (in its most extreme form, as ritualized response), it seems logical to focus on this heightened relationship between spectator and text, a more intimate one than in the usual viewing experience.

Let us begin our examination of specific cult films with *Night of the Living Dead* (1968), probably the first genuine midnight movie. Along with the earlier *Psycho*, it helped establish what many critics have identified as a trend toward a progressive sensibility in the contemporary horror film because of its critique of dominant ideology through its treatment of the monster. According to Robin Wood, the horror film is structured by the simple formula of "normality, the Monster, and, crucially, the relationship between the two" ("Introduction" 14). This equation is fundamentally ideological. In the classic horror film, the normal characters successfully resist the threat of the monster which, in Wood's reading, represents the desires of the id that challenge dominant ideological values and thus must be denied or repressed. This denial takes the form of a distorted Other, a projection outward of unacceptable desires by way of denying them within ourselves. One of Freud's examples is witches, which he explains as psychic projections of repressed desire onto a scapegoat group (72). In the horror film, the threatening appearance of the monster signifies, as Wood appropriates Freud, an inevitable "return of the repressed." The 1956 horror and science fiction classic *Forbidden Planet*, with its expressly identified "monster from the id," only makes explicit this genre's underlying thematic concern.

The figure of the Other, as Roland Barthes explains, is a major strategy by which a dominant ideology maintains its hegemony (151–152). In some progressive horror films, like *Night of the Living Dead*, the classic relationship between the normal and the monstrous is subverted, or at least reversed, so that the normal characters appear as morally or psychologically "monstrous" as the monster is physically. Thus the progressive text questions the classic horror film's assumed values of "normalcy."

Night of the Living Dead consistently reverses generic conventions: the military is inept, the hero is black—and he dies, religion fails to ward off the monsters, and so on. The film also locates the monstrous *within* the normal—in the family patriarch Harry Cooper, as well as in the sibling relationship of Johnny and Barbara. Elliott Stein suggests that the zombies are metaphorical of Nixon's "silent majority" (105). While I essentially agree with this reading, it does depend upon, first, an awareness of generic expectations and how they are thwarted and, second, the viewer's reflection upon these generic subversions and his or her reactions to them.[3]

In fact, most viewers of *Night of the Living Dead* probably think little about its thematic implications, particularly when it comes to acknowledging their own moral culpability. Instead, they respond to its visual power and graphic violence. This is also the explanation for the popularity of Hitchcock's thrillers, despite the textually convincing case for their "therapeutic" value and their similar implication of the audience in their narratives.

Horror films that emphasize violence at the expense of character, plot, and theme are sometimes called "splatter" movies. As John McCarty describes them, such films "aim not to scare their audiences, necessarily, nor to drive them to the edges of their seats in suspense, but to *mortify* them with scenes of explicit gore. In splatter movies, mutilation is indeed the message—many times the only one" (1). McCarty identifies *Night of the Living Dead* as "the first official splatter movie to gain a real reputation" (3). Of course, such films are in one sense transgressive, since they treat violence in a way that challenges conventional notions of good taste. However, one's experience of such movies is most often an unconstructive, unfocused visceral response that is more accurately described as a gut reaction rather than as a truly transgressive experience. It is perhaps no more transgressive than applauding a good body check in a hockey game. This point was emphatically demonstrated during Robin Wood's retrospective of horror films at the 1979 Toronto Film Festival. There, George Romero, director of *Night of the Living Dead*, was asked about the ideological implications of his work. The audience, however, was impatient with such talk, became rude, and shouted for him to leave the stage so they could enjoy the movie. The majority of the audience, even in this supposedly sophisticated context, clearly just wanted to have a good time and to see the "good parts." This film's reception thus brings into focus a critical problem shared by many horror films: the discrepancy between textual interpretation and actual viewer reception.[4] The fact that the film can be read as a biting critique of the American middle class accounts for little of its cult appeal, although for those who can perceive it, this theme lends a degree of respectability to what Alex in *A Clockwork Orange* would call "a real horrorshow."

The Rocky Horror Picture Show, like *Night of the Living Dead*, is an ambiguous text that can accommodate opposing readings. Like Romero's film, it reverses some of the genre's classic conventions in a manner demonstrating a conscious awareness of generic traditions. It is a generic pastiche with many elements of horror, science fiction, and the musical. And it signals this "collage" quality from the opening credit sequence, as a pair of lips sing "Science Fiction Double Feature," a song that alludes to many classic science fiction films.

Despite the sameness implied by its dense intertextuality, the film also seems to diverge significantly from the horror and science fiction genres, in part by reversing the conventional appearance and sexual significance of the monster in relation to the normal. The eponymous creature is a good-looking hunk of a guy, while the "normal" couple, Brad Majors and Janet Weiss, are depicted as heavily repressed. Dr. Frank-N-Furter (Tim Curry in black garterbelt, hose, and heavy, sensuous makeup) is at once the standard, overreaching scientist figure and alternate monster who, as his name crudely suggests, threatens to overwhelm the normalcy of the bland bourgeois couple with his unrestrained sexual appetite and pursuit of physical pleasure.

When Brad and Janet, played as wimpishly as possible by Barry Bostwick and Susan Sarandon, arrive at the doctor's castle after having a flat tire, their repressed nature is challenged. "Don't judge a book by its cover," sings Furter, as he proceeds to seduce first Brad and then Janet. The seduction scenes are photographed in the same manner and the dialogue is identical in each, suggesting the common nature of desire, whether hetero- or homosexual. Such an attitude is in direct opposition to the dominant heterosexual, monogamous values of Western culture. "Be it, don't dream it," croons Furter as he urges them to be honest and unrepressed. The flat tire thus becomes emblematic of the breakdown of Brad and Janet's bourgeois values, an idea reinforced by both a visual reference to Grant Wood's famous "American Gothic" painting during the opening wedding scene and by Nixon's resignation speech, heard on the car radio just before their tire deflates.

In the climax, Riff-Raff and Magenta, Furter's two alien assistants, burst into the lab, stating that the doctor must be terminated because of his excessive pursuit of pleasure. His death occurs in a scene marked with castration imagery (the falling RKO tower, the reference to King Kong's death on the Empire State Building) and, significantly, results from a laser blast from Riff-Raff's weapon, which resembles the pitchfork in Wood's painting. Thus the middle American empire strikes back to restore dominant sexual values. (It is no coincidence that Richard O'Brien, the actor who plays Riff-Raff, appears earlier as the priest performing the marriage ceremony.) The film seems in the end to call the stability of the heterosexual couple's relationship into question, since Brad has come out of the closet and Janet has revealed her hidden lust ("Touch-a, touch-a, touch me/I wanna be dirty," she sings). But narrative closure results, and dominant sexual values are restored as the couple survives and Furter is eviscerated.

In this context, the film's use of the musical genre becomes especially significant. The musical traditionally develops two central themes: constructing a sense of community and defining the parameters of sexual desire. These themes are, of course, intimately related, since unchanneled desire poses a threat to the dominant ideology of heterosexuality and monogamy so insistently represented in classical Hollywood cinema.[5] *Rocky Horror* shows just how close the musical and horror genres really are. And just as classical musicals inevitably end in the valorized union of the monogamous couple—*Seven Brides for Seven Brothers* is the ultimate example— so Brad and Janet, with the elimination of the Furter between them, can come together as promised at the beginning when Janet catches the bridal bouquet at the wedding.

Given this exmple, Hoberman and Rosenbaum seem right in identifying alternate sexuality as a pronounced motif in cult movies (263), but it is equally important to consider *how* the alternative is used or consumed by audiences. *Rocky Horror,* for example, develops a strong sense of community generated by individuals in the audience dressed similarly, in the manner of the characters. But the predetermined costumes, repetition of the characters' lines at specific times, and the ritualization of certain acts during the screening (throwing rice or toilet paper) ultimately reconstitutes *outside* the film a community not unlike the one lampooned *within* it. The rote quality of these rituals, which discouraged the spontaneous improvisation by newcomers,[6] suggests that this community is in its own way every bit as conformist and repressive as the middle class satirized on the screen.

The costuming and play-acting aspects of the *Rocky Horror* experience also foreground style over meaning, making it, in effect, an expression of the camp sensibility that Susan Sontag has described. According to Sontag, camp attacks the serious in a way that irony and satire, because of contemporary media saturation, can no longer do (288). Thus she says, "Camp asserts that good taste is not simply good taste; that there exists, indeed, a good taste of bad taste" (290). Certainly this helps explain the appeal of cult films like Edward Wood's, of *Eraserhead*, of *Killer Tomatoes,* of splatter movies, and of Russ Meyer's *Beyond the Valley of the Dolls.* Waters' *Pink Flamingos* ends with Divine eating dogshit in perhaps the ultimate image of the cult film as bad taste! Camp, then, partially accounts for one significant aspect of the cult film's transgression, for to like these movies is to embrace aesthetic—and, by extension, social—values in apparent opposition to the accepted norm. To like them, or to claim to, clearly sets one apart from the "decency" of the mainstream.

The celebration of sexual alternatives also seems to be at the root of the cult appeal of Edouard Molinaro's popular gay sex farce *La Cage Aux Folles* (1979). In his essay on horror films, Wood offers "deviations from ideological sexual norms" as one version of the Other ("Introduction" 10), and indeed, the film appears to be structured somewhat like a horror film. The normals are the Charrier family, the heterosexual parents of Andrea, who are contrasted to the gay couple, Renato and Albin. The gay couple may at first seem monstrous to the average viewer, but ultimately they appear to be like any normal—that is, heterosexual—couple.

The Charriers are made laughable by their strict conservative moral code, exaggerated to the point that M. Charrier works as the secretary for the Union of Moral Order. That his values are both silly and unrealistic is made clear by his ludicrously excessive response to what he considers moral turpitude and by the fact that the president has been found dead in the arms of a prostitute—a black, underage one at that!

The gay couple are clearly the sympathetic characters in the film, the heterosexual ones rather unlikable in varying degree. While the Charriers, for instance, are interested only in marrying their daughter to help restore M. Charrier's failing career, Renato and Albin would sacrifice their personal integrity by denying their gayness so that Laurent's marriage will be approved by his conservative in-laws-to-be. Their parental sacrifice is so noble that they even allow their apartment to be redecorated—and in a nice visual metaphor for this sacrifice, the erect penis of an erotic statue is accidentally snapped off by Renato as he moves it. Laurent himself is so eager to hide the truth of what he euphemistically terms his father's "special" quality that he begins to transform the apartment even *before* consulting Albin.

Aside from its generally sympathetic treatment of the gays, the film occasionally challenges the viewer in another way by suggesting a discrepancy between appearance and truth in sexual terms, and so periodically thwarting our probable response. The initial meeting early in the film between Renato and Laurent, for example, seems at first to be a clandestine sexual rendezvous between the two—a likely response for a straight viewer because of the popular stereotype of gays as sexually profligate. Similarly, the dominant macho image of masculinity is undermined by being revealed *as* an image, particularly in the scene where Renato tries to teach Albin to butter his toast like a man and to walk "like John Wayne." The scene culminates with Renato assuming this macho pose himself and, to Ennio Morricone's music (the composer who provided the distinctive music for Sergio Leone's cult westerns with Clint Eastwood), walking through the contemporary equivalent of the saloon doors to confront a gay basher—only to be pummeled himself. The Wayne tough-guy image is thus undercut by the incongruity of the person adopting it, and so, as a result, revealed as fantasy.

But again, while *La Cage Aux Folles* would seem to attack dominant sexual ideology, its challenges are not sustained to any significant degree. For example, the characters remain too simplistic to make the conflict really work. The gay characters hardly rise above the level of stereotype to become fully rounded figures. They are depicted in clearly defined male and female roles, although Albin, as the neurotic drag queen, is, as we might expect, more broadly played. The film mocks the prissy self-preoccupation typical of the role with Albin's first appearance, hiding petulantly beneath a bedsheet because he feels he is aging. His self-pitying monologue stops only when the doctor, summoned because he knows what is "important" to Albin, makes him forget his own problems to consider the pros and cons of cooking with a particular kind of pan. Renato, by contrast, is not nearly as comical a figure, since he remains in part "a man," capable of heterosexual experience and reproduction. So he is depicted with the conventional signifiers of masculinity: he is hairy (Simone, Laurent's mother, specifically admires his chest hair), more rational than Albin, and the one in charge of the family business.

The narrative itself is also quite conventional, seeming in fact much like a television sitcom. As in the typical situation comedy, most of the action takes place in one domestic space, the gay pair's apartment; and this space is treated circumspectly: we see neither the bedroom nor the bathroom—according to Horace Newcomb, a convention of the TV sitcom (29). Physicality is, in fact, deemphasized throughout the film. There is virtually no sexual or even intimate scene between the two gay men, and the only scene of this kind we do see is between Renato and Simone. Like many newer sitcoms (e.g., "Cheers," "Three's Company," "Bosom Buddies"), *La Cage Aux Folles* spices its situation with a twist of sexual difference while directly avoiding that difference itself.

The narrative conflict is never really resolved, or even concluded; rather, it simply stops. In the climax, Albin takes off his wig to reveal that he is actually a gay male and not Laurent's mother, which immediately precedes a larger "unmasking" as the transvestites from the adjacent La Cage Aux Folles Club come through an adjoining door. The alternative sexuality the Charriers had wished to repress here seems joyously to return. But then the plot conveniently arranges for Charrier to have to dress in drag (even his wife "lets down her hair") in order to escape the club undetected by reporters. Albin finds them a way out, the problem is solved, life goes on, and the film is over. With such disguises, confusions, complications, and a pat conclusion, the film's narrative neatly fits the conventional TV sitcom plot structure (Newcomb chap. 2). Charrier in drag is finally much like Lucy Ricardo trapped in one of her situations—and he has no explaining to do. So the specifics of the disguise become less important than the plot mechanics that end the story. In the end the viewer feels "progressive" by laughing at the film's representative "normal" characters for their uptight attitude, while at the same time remaining safely distant from gayness through the comforts of stereotype and popular narrative formula, as well as through the comic deflation of the sexual issues seemingly addressed. Such a strategy would seem to explain the enormous popularity of this film in North America at a time when gay bashing was rumored to be increasing dramatically.

Yet another form of the Other noted by Wood is a specific ethnic group or, more generally, another culture ("Introduction" 10). A good example of the cult treatment of this type occurs in *The Gods Must Be Crazy*, an enormously popular South African comedy directed by Jamie Uys. The film begins by unambiguously contrasting modern, technological (white) society with the pastoral simplicity of the (black) Kalahari bushmen. Their Rousseauesque simplicity, completely in harmony with nature, seems to give them an edge over the "civilized" whites trapped in the urban ratrace.

But despite this initial explicit comparison, clearly favorable to the bushmen, the white viewer's sense of cultural superiority is then systematically restored by a voice-of-god narrator who presumes to tell us everything that the bushman !Ky thinks—although he makes no such presumption for any of the white characters. The narrator emphasizes !Ky's naivete as either exotically charming or laughably simple. He tells us, for example, that !Ky perceives land rovers as strange animals with round legs. One might justify this narration as a parody of the typical voice-of-god narrator in the tradition of travelogue documentary (e.g., Buñuel's *Land without Bread*) and thus in keeping with the film's humorous spirit. But such an argument falls apart because the narrator's knowledge and authority are in no way undercut in the film.

Following the contrast between the two cultures, the first of three interwoven plots is introduced. A thoughtless airplane pilot drops an empty Coke bottle into a family of bushpeople, who begin to covet it and fight over it; so to resolve these disputes !Ky must trek to the end of the earth and toss the bottle off, returning it to the gods. Then begins a plot concerning black revolutionaries in a neighboring country, followed by the romantic narrative involving Andrew Styne, a white biologist, and Kate Thompson, a schoolteacher. The three plots merge, as the rising action builds to a climax: Styne's rescue of Kate and the black schoolchildren who had been taken hostage by the revolutionaries.

But as these plots come together, the black characters are displaced by the white. The threat posed by the revolutionaries is defeated by the white man, with his ingenuity and technology—supported by the cheerful, obedient black servant, his version of a faithful Indian companion. It is Styne who devises the rescue plan and gives the orders, who uses his telescope and animal tranquilizer as tools, while !Ky comically drives the jeep backwards and is given no opportunity to employ the bushmen's own natural tranquilizer said earlier to be so useful in hunting.

The whites are presented as ecologically concerned (Styne's job) and sincerely interested in the welfare of blacks, while the blacks are depicted as childlike (as seen in the simplicity of !Ky and the literal "innocent children" kidnapped by the political radicals), gratefully subservient, or bumblingly dangerous (the inept revolutionaries manage to trip on banana peels while fleeing from government troops; later they hit the helicopter with a bazooka purely by accident). The conventional romance between the two white characters is increasingly foregrounded at the expense of !Ky's story. Their union at the end provides a narrative closure, capped by an abrupt coda informing us that !Ky has successfully completed his quest. Ultimately, then, the film claims to envision blacks as morally noble, even socially superior people, but in its narrative structure inscribes them as inferior to the whites, who are seen as necessary for maintaining social order (read apartheid).

In this way the film works like *La Cage Aux Folles:* while that film makes homosexuality safe for straight audiences, *The Gods Must Be Crazy* makes blacks safe for whites. In fact, its vision of blacks is not much of an advance over Hollywood's traditional stereotyping of them. As Roland Barthes says, "How *can* one assimilate the Negro . . . ? There is here a figure for emergencies: exoticism. The Other becomes a pure object, a spectacle, a clown" (152).

Interestingly, all of the films discussed here share a strategy of presenting a conflict between the normal and the Other, and of making a clownish spectacle—of caricaturing—the normal while minimizing the threat of the Other. Even the least comic of these movies, *Night of the Living Dead*, lapses into this approach in its treatment of the sheriff, who, along with Harry Cooper, carries the metaphoric burden of equating the living dead with the normal. He gets the lines that always bring the laughs from the audience. When interviewed on TV, for example, he offers the opinion that the zombies are "dead; they're all messed up." In Romero's sequel, *Dawn of the Dead* (1978), the threat of the zombies is to a large extent reduced to a comic treatment. The film takes place almost entirely in a large suburban shopping mall, where the zombies tend to congregate. One of the living characters hypothesizes that they are drawn there by instinct, by a dim memory of their former existence; and indeed, except for their pallid skin, they look surprisingly like shoppers going about their business to the strains of the ubiquitous Muzak.

Because such characters emphasize the comic nature of normalcy or bourgeois life at the expense of any positive or redeeming features, they tend to flatten into caricature. This tendency toward caricature may be essential to the cult film, making an otherwise bitter pill somewhat easier to swallow.[7] While cult movies gain some appeal through this textual strategy, they lose much potential power. As Sontag remarks of camp, it is "art that proposes itself seriously, but cannot be taken altogether seriously because it is 'too much'" (284). Thus Leslie Fiedler, while championing Russ Meyer as the great American filmmaker of the seventies, notes that, for all the depiction of blood and death in *Beyond the Valley of the Dolls,* "one leaves the theatre feeling exhilarated, amused—assured at the level of absolute childlike credence that nowhere is blood or death real" ("Beyond" 5).

Like classic genre films, cult movies work in terms of clearly defined oppositions. Their conflicts invariably can be reduced to some version of white hats versus black hats. And, too, they provide satisfactions similar to those of generic entertainment. The difference is that the genre movie tends to deemphasize its potential transgression. In gangster movies, for instance, we identify with the kinetic charisma of Edward G. Robinson or James Cagney for virtually the entire film, until the climax, of course, when the gangster meets his inevitable fate and social order is restored. We may have been vicariously antisocial for ninety minutes, but we are emphatically reformed in the last five. In musicals we identify with the sexual sophistication of Fred Astaire or bravado of Gene Kelly, but we are always satisfied when in the end their desire focuses on one partner only, and they dance in harmony to valorize the monogamous couple. But cult movies, like splatter films, boast of their transgressive qualities through excesses of style or content, treating normally taboo subjects or violating commonly accepted standards of taste. Yet they too end, like genre films, recuperating that which initially has posed a threat to dominant ideology.

This is not to claim, however, that no cult films are genuinely disturbing, for clearly some are—*Freaks, Flaming Creatures*, and Kenneth Anger's films, for example. But *Freaks* was banned for decades; *Flaming Creatures* was withdrawn from exhibition in New York during a lengthy litigation; and Anger's films showed only in a few art cinemas in major cities. These movies exist at a far remove from the mainstream narrative tradition that dominates the cult marketplace. For in those cult movies, ideological transgression is consistently recuperated by textual strategies and the very level of reception.

Cult films encourage viewers not to take very seriously the threat of the Other. At the same time, they prod us to laugh at representations of the normal, usually our own surrogates on the screen. Thus viewers cheer when in *The Texas Chain Saw Massacre* and other, less interesting splatter movies like *I Spit on Your Grave* and the various *Friday the 13th* films, their figures of identification are killed off serially in ever more prolonged and gruesome ways. People become, in these films, objectified bodies submitted to the inevitable fate of special effects and dismemberment. We hardly think of these characters as people, but rather as excuses, or pretexts, for splatter. In short, in cult movies viewers laugh at the normal, tame the Other, but nowhere see themselves. Perhaps this is why cult audiences tend to be composed of teenagers, disenfranchised youths who are caught between childhood and adulthood, who have little sense of belonging. There are, of course, other reasons for the cult appeal of specific movies, but it would seem that this "double feature" of transgression and recuperation accounts for much of the appeal of these otherwise diverse films we have come to describe with the unwieldy term "cult."

NOTES

1. See Leslie Fiedler's discussion of "difference" in his *Freaks*.

2. On the ideological significance of stars, see Richard Dyer, *Stars* (London: BFI, 1979), and Maurice Yacowar, "An Aesthetic Defense of the Star System," *Quarterly Review of Film Studies* 4 (1979): 39–52.

3. See my "Experience and Meaning in Genre Films" for a detailed analysis of *Night of the Living Dead*.

4. Discussing the potentially subversive qualities of comedy, Wood parenthetically remarks, "I have argued elsewhere that the horror film—prior, that is, to its co-option into '80s reactionary revisionism—does also" work subversively. It is not clear, though, whether he is referring to the film texts or audience reception. See *"Rally 'Round the Flag, Boys,* or, Give It Back to the Indians," *CineAction!* 9 (1987): 8.

5. For more on the ideology of the musical, see Altman, Feuer, Telotte, and my own "The Classic Hollywood Musical and the 'Problem' of Rock 'n' Roll."

6. See the discussion of this film's cult following in *Midnight Movies* for further details about the ritual formed around it.

7. Wood recently made a similar point about Lynch's *Blue Velvet,* a film quickly becoming a cult favorite. He sees the film as catering to viewers by inviting them to adopt a position of superiority toward the normal characters, partly through a condescending laughter. This tone is invoked from the first images, the brilliant white domestic picket fence, followed by a shot of the town fire engine crossing the frame, the fireman with cheerful, Norman Rockwell–type countenance, waving to the viewer. Wood consequently judges the film to be relatively simplistic in its vision as compared with its obvious analogy, Hitchcock's *Shadow of a Doubt.* In Hitchcock's film, the bourgeois family is also related to the eruption of the monstrous, but for Wood the crucial difference is that its depiction of bourgeois life is not simply laughable. Through what he sees as its more ambiguous attitude, therefore, *Shadow of a Doubt* offers a more complex, disturbing experience ("Leavis").

WORKS CITED

Altman, Rick, ed. *Genre: The Musical.* London: Routledge, 1980.

Barthes, Roland. "Myth Today." In *Mythologies,* trans. Annette Lavers, 109–159. New York: Hill and Wang, 1977.

Bordwell, David, Janet Staiger, and Kristin Thompson. *The Classic Hollywood Cinema.* New York: Columbia Univ. Press, 1985.

Buscombe, Edward. "The Idea of Genre in the American Cinema." *Film Genre Reader.* Ed. Barry Keith Grant, 11–25. Austin: Univ. of Texas Press, 1986.

Eco, Umberto. *"Casablanca:* Cult Movies and Intertextual Collage." *SubStance* 47, no. 2 (1985): 3–12.

Feuer, Jane. *The Hollywood Musical.* Bloomington: Indiana Univ. Press, 1982.

Fiedler, Leslie. "Beyond *Beyond the Valley of the Dolls." American Journal* 1, no. 5 (1973): 5.

———. *Freaks*. New York: Touchstone, 1984.

Freud, Sigmund. "Introduction: A Seventeenth-Century Demonological Neurosis." In *New Introductory Lectures on Psycho-Analysis: The Complete Psychological Works of Sigmund Freud*, trans. James Strachey and Anna Freud, 19: 67–105. London: Hogarth, 1961.

Grant, Barry K. "The Classic Hollywood Musical and the 'Problem' of Rock 'n' Roll." *Journal of Popular Film and Television* 13, no. 4 (1986): 195–205.

———. "Experience and Meaning in Genre Films." In *Film Genre Reader*, ed. Barry Keith Grant, 114–128. Austin: Univ. of Texas Press, 1986.

Hoberman, J., and Jonathan Rosenbaum. *Midnight Movies*. New York: Harper, 1983.

McCarty, John. *Splatter Movies*. New York: St. Martin's, 1984.

Newcomb, Horace. *TV: The Most Popular Art*. Garden City: Anchor, 1974.

Peary, Danny. *Cult Movies*. New York: Delta, 1981.

Sontag, Susan. "Notes on 'Camp.'" In *Against Interpretation*, 277–293. New York: Dell, 1966.

Stein, Elliott. "*The Night of the Living Dead*." *Sight and Sound* 39, no. 2 (1970): 105.

Telotte, J. P. "Ideology and the Kelly-Donen Musicals." *Film Criticism* 8, no. 3 (1984): 36–46.

Tudor, Andrew. *Theories of Film*. New York: Viking, 1973.

Wilensky, Harold. "Mass Society and Mass Culture: Interdependence or Independence?" *American Sociological Review* 29 (1964): 173–197.

Wood, Robin. "Introduction." In *The American Nightmare*, ed. Robin Wood and Richard Lippe, 7–28. Toronto: Festival of Festivals, 1979.

———. "Leavis, Marxism and Film Culture." *CineAction!* 8 (1987): 3–13.

CHAPTER 11

Midnight S/Excess:
Cult Configurations of "Femininity" and the Perverse

Gaylyn Studlar

Excess defines the midnight movie, a cult phenomenon that seems to catalogue perverse acts with the same enthusiasm as nineteenth-century sexologists such as Richard von Krafft-Ebing, whose *Psychopathia Sexualis* offered detailed clinical descriptions of sadomasochism, fetishism, transvestism, homosexuality, voyeurism, exhibitionism, necrophilia, bestiality, and myriad other sexual "abnormalities" considered to be the essence of perversion. Midnight movies often present a comparable compendium of sexual acts, but their interest in perversion extends beyond clinical curiosity and cataloguing. Encompassing everything from the coprophagic antics of Divine in *Pink Flamingos* (1970) to the gender-bending generic pastiche of *The Rocky Horror Picture Show* (1975), these films often use perversion as a means of shocking their audience. However, this exploitation of sexual imagery should not lead us to dismiss automatically cult films such as *Rocky Horror, Pink Flamingos, The Texas Chain Saw Massacre* (1974), *Eraserhead* (1978), or *Liquid Sky* (1982), for the sexual excess of the midnight movie also marks its preoccupation with a culturally ubiquitous problem—that of defining the meaning of sexual difference.

Freud defined perversions as "sexual activities which either (a) extend, in an anatomical sense, beyond the regions of the body that are designed for sexual union, or (b) linger over the intermediate relations to the sexual object which should normally be traversed rapidly on the path towards the final sexual aim" (150). Consequently, perversion is not only a form of sex that takes a taboo aim or object (such as foot fetishism); it also includes "normal" acts (such as sexual looking as foreplay) that when taken to excess deflect sexuality from the aim of heterosexual genital intercourse. However, as post-Freudians such as Jean Laplanche assert, the meaning of perversion extends beyond the use of bodies in sexual practice or any implied deviation from a universal sexual instinct.[1] Perversion reflects on the meaning assigned to the gendered body within a given culture, on the precariousness of "normality," and on the construction of sexuality as a process taking place in the head rather than in the genes or genitalia.

Midnight movies typically crystallize this problem of sexual difference and the s/excess of perversity in a feminine though not always *female* figure. The three films that form the focus of this chapter—*Pink Flamingos, Rocky Horror,* and *Liquid Sky*—use varying textual strategies to represent sexual difference, but all construct a deeply ambivalent discourse that depends upon "femininity" as a vector point uniting revulsion and fascination, excess and lack, pleasure and the perverse. The precedent for this ambivalent linking of the excess of perversion with female sexuality can be found in many cultural discourses. One unexpected and important source is Freud's work on perversions, "Three Essays on Sexuality."

In the first of these essays, Freud defines perversity as an infantile form of eroticism that becomes abnormal in adulthood when it replaces rather than coexists with the "normal sexual aim and object," i.e., genitally focused heterosexuality. Children's "aptitude" for polymorphous perversity, remarks Freud, is "innately present in their disposition" (160–161). Therefore, perversity encounters "little resistance" in children because they have not yet developed the "mental dams against sexual excesses—shame, disgust and morality" (191) that properly control and channel their sexual desires.

Freud's remarks are a predictable part of his theory of childhood sexuality, but what is disconcerting is his comparison of children's lack of "mental dams against sexual excesses" with the sexuality of women. "In this respect," he continues, "children behave in the same kind of way as an average uncultivated woman in whom the same polymorphously perverse disposition persists" (191). In this easy comparison Freud presents us with a conceptual slippage that is not supported by his other studies on perversions.[2] Instead, these comments reveal a stubbornly persistent patriarchal myth, the same sexual ideology that Bram Dijkstra finds in academic painting of the late nineteenth century and Klaus Theweleit locates in the culturally pervasive fantasies of protofascists in twentieth-century Germany. "Uncultivated women," remarks Freud, are easily seduced into finding "every sort of perversion to [their] tastes." Therefore, "the immense number of women who are prostitutes or who must be supposed to have an aptitude for prostitution without becoming engaged in it" proves that "this same disposition to perversions of every kind is a general and fundamental human characteristic" (191). Although attributed to humanity as a whole, the deviance of perversion finds its specific example in women.

Even if we ignore the deployment of women's sexuality by and for a system privileging male sexual desires, Freud's remarks are consistent with the nineteenth-century belief that women do not have the same sense of sexual and social restraint as men. Freud confirmed this belief in his essay "On Some Consequences of the Anatomical Differences between the Sexes." He explains that the boy's fear of being castrated by the father teaches him the lesson of sexual prohibition. This "castration complex" proves to be crucial to the development of the superego in men, to their introjection of civilized values. But little girls are already "castrated," so that "the level of what is ethically normal is different [in women] from what it is in men" (193). With little superego constraints on their sexuality, women could be expected to behave like polymorphously perverse children. It was the logical result of their psychosexual development.

In light of this essay, Freud's citation of the "uncultivated woman" is significant, for it reveals the assumption that the "disposition" for perversion is actually class specific in women. In *Male Fantasies,* Theweleit finds this same association of perversity with lower-class women underlying the fantasies of the Freikorps, a post–World War I protofascist German military organization that became the core of Hitler's S.A. Freikorpsmen divided women into two groups. High-born women could be idealized as pure angels, asexual and nurturing, but lower-class women became the signifier of a dark and degenerate femininity. The body of the proletariat woman was a secret terrain containing "filthy floods." She embodied perverse sexual excess in all its frightful and fascinating possibilities. Theweleit argues that rather than being an anomaly in Western culture, these protofascist fantasies linking perversity with femininity constitute the "equivalent to the tip of the patriarchal iceberg" (407, 171).

That same "patriarchal iceberg" is also evident in midnight movies, but Freud's remarks and Theweleit's examples can serve only as the point of departure for considering the complex representations of femininity and perversion in these films. Some of them, such as *Eraserhead* (1983) and *Pink Floyd: The Wall* (1980), represent "normal" heterosexual desire in ways clearly analogous to the Freikorps fantasies. For example, the entire pattern of visual iconography in David Lynch's *Eraserhead* suggests the "filthy floods" of a menacing femininity, simultaneously a lack (female genitalia as orifice) and fluid (vaginal) too-much-ness. *Eraserhead*'s disturbing dream world is dominated by one man's hapless attempt to nurture a reptilean baby, the abhorrent product of his girlfriend's body. Henry, the film's protagonist, quietly asserts that it is "impossible" for him to be the father of Mary's offspring, but he is forced to marry her by her mother, a worn, working-class woman who is aroused into orgasm by the sight of Henry carving a "man-made" chicken that oozes an unidentifiable liquid from its empty body cavity as it rhythmically rocks back and forth on a dinner plate.

Through such scenes, *Eraserhead* suggests that the family is saturated by the very forms of sexuality it has deemed taboo; females become the primary representatives of this perverse sexuality, which ultimately victimizes the male. By mothering the baby when Mary abandons it, Henry usurps the only traditionally positive aspect of femininity allowed by the film.

While *Eraserhead* makes sex a loathesome and repellent thing, the midnight movie more frequently embraces perversion as an outlaw sexuality, a revolutionary excess of desire unhinged from accepted values and celebrated as social deviance. Although its depiction of sex often appears lewd or pornographic, the midnight movie's channeling of sexuality into perversion produces a kind of incoherence. This effect is particularly clear when we compare these films with pornography's structurally coherent use of the sexual iconography of the perverse. The de-eroticized visual treatment of varied sexual acts in midnight movies like *Pink Flamingos, Female Trouble,* and *Rocky Horror* displaces the porno film's predictable climax of/in genital coitus and its presumed spectatorial imperative of arousal. Instead, these films ritualize perversion into a subculture icon of rebellion against bourgeois norms by celebrating the possibilities of sex as ironic play and playacting.

Such an attitude is reminiscent of Herbert Marcuse's view of perversion expressed in *Eros and Civilization.* Marcuse argued that perversions challenge the very foundation of capitalistic society by upholding "sexuality as an end in itself," and by placing sexual practice outside the domination of society's structuring "performance principle" (45–46). That principle perpetuated surplus-repression in the interests of profit, the key to the capitalist socioeconomic system. Perversions were culturally inadmissible in the capitalist system because they did not fulfill the requirement that sex must be "socially useful and good" (45). For Marcuse, the common belief that perversions were immoral or unnatural was patriarchal capitalism's predictably repressive reaction to sexual practice focused exclusively on producing pleasure rather than babies.

From a Marcusean perspective, any appearance of perversion in the midnight movie might be regarded as a progressive movement toward subverting the dominant sexual practice sanctioned by the patriarchal bourgeois family, but analysis reveals that most of these films do little to subvert oppressive norms. This can be attributed to the failure to recognize that perversions are easily assimilated into and controlled by dominant culture.[3] However, such a failure can also be read as the result of the films' unwillingness to be perverse enough. Although midnight movies often revel in breaking sexual taboos through homosexuality and inverted sex roles or cross-dressing, these elements suggest a contemporary "sexual revolution" that does not necessarily question the hierarchical status of gender or the patriarchal power imbalance in sexual practice. Mike Brake notes this irony in so-called sexual freedom: "The more sexuality is brought into the open, into a 'liberated zone' freed from puritanism, the more women are open to exploitation by men, unless they too contribute to the sexual debate" (28). Despite its subcultural associations, the midnight movie's sexual politics, like those of other youth-oriented media such as rock videos, are full of the contradictions of patriarchal ideology, contradictions that foreground the difficult negotiation between our lived sexuality and cultural imperatives.

If she's a girl, then what is my sister?   —*The Girl Can't Help It*

John Waters' films are notorious. Among the first films to achieve cult status as midnight movies, they are archetypal examples of the contradictions of s/excess. Forthrightly described by its director as "the most disgusting film ever made" (Peary 263), *Pink Flamingos* typifies the midnight movie as aesthetic and sexual shock treatment. The Marquis de Sade once declared that "Art is the perpetual immoral subversion of the established order" (Carter 132). In *Pink Flamingos* Waters, who readily acknowledges a debt to de Sade, forges a transparent subcultural heterocosm where sexual perversity as social deviance shows up everywhere—especially in his hometown Baltimore.

As in most of Waters' other films, including *Mondo Trasho* (1969), *Female Trouble* (1974), *Polyester* (1981), and *Hairspray* (1988), Divine, a 300-pound transvestite, plays *Pink Flamingos'* heroine, Babs Johnson. Babs unites with her family to defend their mobile home and her reputation as the "Filthiest Person Alive." Her equally massive mother, Edy, sits all day, every day, in a baby crib. Clad in bra and girdle, she does nothing but eat eggs until she is carted off (literally) by the adoring egg man to lead a life of matrimonial bliss. Babs's son Crackers makes love to a woman while a live chicken struggles between them, to the voyeuristic satisfaction of Divine's female traveling companion, Cotton. All goes well for Babs's family until Connie and Raymond Mole challenge her filthiest-person title. Their claim is largely based on their cottage industry: they kidnap women hitchhikers to breed babies for lesbian couples. As a sideline to their greedy schemes, the Moles push heroin in elementary schools, and Raymond exposes himself in a purse-snatching scam. The Moles even send Babs a gift-wrapped turd on her birthday. Confident in her supreme filthiness, Babs accepts their challenge, and before the fight is over, she performs fellatio on her son, executes her rivals in a self-styled media event, and munches on dog excrement in the midnight movies' most notorious example of spatio-temporal integrity.

Characterized by one critic as a "sadistic, domineering female," Babs's character is actually as mercurial as a *film noir* femme fatale (Bell-Metereau 123). A pastiche of a personality, she first appears as a lovingly indulgent daughter to her senile mother. She becomes an enthusiastically incestuous mother, a heartless murderess, and finally the girl who, as the soundtrack tells us, "can't help it." Waters' disingenuous remark in his autobiography, that Divine is merely an actor who plays women characters, purposefully ignores the ambiguity and complex sexual implications of male trans-vestism here (108). By representing his "heroine" through Divine, he ex-tends cinema's dominant manipulation of the female image into "outlaw" filmmaking while also revealing, in a paradoxical way, the deeply problem-atic construction of femininity in patriarchal culture.

Angela Carter asserts that "a woman who pretends to be a man has also cancelled out her reproductive system, like the post-menopausal woman" (62). While she overstates both the force and predictability of cross-dressing as a signifier, her remark raises an interesting point here: does Divine dem-onstrate something of the reverse? Or is our awareness of Divine's male-ness, like that of any female impersonator, the unalterable difference that inevitably makes his/her sexual jokes and representation of female sexu-ality "a form of male aggression upon the women he personates"? (60).

Divine's presence relies on the notion that femininity is merely an act in which women and, therefore, anyone can successfully engage. This idea resembles one of the key concepts in modern feminist theory, the *masquer-ade,* explained by Michele Montrelay as the woman's use of "her own body to disguise herself." Femininity is created with "dotty objects, feathers, hat, strange baroque constructions," the purpose of which is "to say nothing" (93). However, Joan Riviere interprets the masquerade as having another function beyond masking the woman's lack. Women's masquerade of *excess femininity* works to disguise those attributes of masculinity that the pa-triarchy finds threatening in a female. Such feminine accoutrements are as-sumed in excess "to hide the possession of masculinity and to avert the reprisals expected if she was found to possess it" (131).

Divine's excess femininity is that of the bombshell whose undulating walk, "cha-cha heels," tight skirt, and clinging sweater define woman as walking sexual mine field. Divine's makeup is so extreme that her hairline is shaved back to accommodate her sweeping eyebrows, while her huge "breasts"—gigantic extensions into free space—are important twin signs of woman's mythical hyperbolized sexuality. Lest her appearance or actions leave any doubt, Babs confirms her polymorphously perverse nature in her declaration that she has "done everything."

Divine's excess femininity hides masculinity, but her possession of the masculine-sexed body alters the masquerade's meaning. While a woman who employs such a masquerade of excess may do so to camouflage qualities not believed rightfully hers because she lacks the patriarchal emblem of power (the penis), Divine's masquerade parodies a woman's *performance* of femininity. However, it fails to expose the masquerade's origins in patriarchal culture's demand for the construction of femininity. Thus, Divine's appropriation of the cultural signs of female subjectivity is a symbolic theft and transformation that leaves femininity to be interpreted as women's self-styled excess and men free to ridicule "the manners they have invented" (Carter 39).

Divine's wo/man, as an act of *bricolage*, parodies not only the assumption of femininity, but also the "natural" spectacle of women's corporeal excess—simultaneously too much and yet never enough. In effect, she is a parody of a parody, Marilyn Monroe's fifties bombshell ideal mediated through Jayne Mansfield's mind-boggling too-much-ness. Divine's too-much-ness is convincingly and yet uncomfortably feminine; as Rebecca Bell-Metereau observes, "We must often remind ourselves that 'She' isn't even really a woman . . . we find ourselves thinking of her as feminine" (122–123). So daring is her masquerade that in *Female Trouble*, Divine as Dawn Davenport walks to the altar in a transparent lace bridal dress that defies our ability to find the "visually ascertainable" difference that would reaffirm his/her phallic integrity (Mulvey 13).

But regardless of her fake *mons veneris* and gay deceivers, we believe Divine is a woman primarily because she is fat. As Noelle Caskey observes, fatness is "a direct consequence of her [woman's] sexuality . . . Fat and femininity cannot be separated physiologically" (176). The marker of the "natural" somatic excess of femininity, fatness is a sexual liability and social taboo in contemporary America. As Caskey notes, it is also condemned as disgusting and a sign of self-indulgence that is class specific (178). Divine confirms this notion as, clad in fake leopard skin, cheap lamé, and stretch polyester, she becomes the literal representation of Marx's notion of lumpen proletariat. She inevitably lives on the edges of a working-class world of hairdressers and waitresses, mobile homes and neighborhood saloons. Her obesity, her self-proclaimed filthiness, and her outrageously trashy outfits serve as signs of lower-class femininity reminiscent of the image of the shameless proletarian woman created by the German Freikorps as its most insistent symbol of perverse femininity: a physically monstrous and grotesque embodiment of woman as political and sexual outlaw (Theweleit 66–67).

If Divine parodies femininity, we can still find a minimally subversive function in the spectacle of "her" attempt to forge a perverse subjecthood. In *Pink Flamingos* as the Filthiest Person Alive, and in *Female Trouble* as a greedy juvenile delinquent turned into the world's worst mother, she re-invents herself as a Sadeian woman: lewd, orgiastic, aggressively pursuing self-gratification in defiance of feminine cultural norms of passivity. In *Pink Flamingos* Divine orders that Connie and Raymond Mole be tied to a tree. After they are tarred and feathered, she shoots them point-blank in the face as reporters from the tabloids watch. Her motto at their execu-tion, "Killing makes me come," also recalls the Sadeian woman who em-braces tyranny instead of martyrdom to challenge "her own socially condi-tioned role in the world" (Carter 133). Her execution of the Moles serves as a nihilistic act of aggression that is paradoxically paired with the coprophilic *coup de grace* that confirms Divine's right to be called, not only the fictive filthiest person alive, but also, as the voice-over narrator cheerfully informs us, "the filthiest actress alive." Femininity and perversity are thus doubly inscribed, in extrafilmic as well as filmic terms.

Although she finds sadistic satisfaction in killing, Divine's sexuality is expressed mainly as a narcissistic exhibitionism. Because her exhibitionism breaks free of female passivity and the aim of producing male pleasure, it becomes an autoerotic, perverse act that recalls the late nineteenth-century notion of narcissism as a distinctly feminine perversion. While painters and novelists of the time obsessively depicted scenes of female self-absorption, sexologists in the 1860s and 1870s eagerly confirmed the idea that the "weaker sex" was susceptible to an autoerotic fixation that perverted their natural altruism and threatened to destroy civilization by unleashing sexual impulses that only men could control (Dijkstra 154–159).

In *Pink Flamingos*, Divine fulfills this description to become a nineteenth-century sexologist's worst nightmare of the effects of female narcissism. She gets "all dressed up to fall in love" and leaves her trailer for an errand in town. Stealing from a meat counter, she walks off with a round steak stuffed between her legs, then defecates in front of a mansion. As she un-dulates down a crowded city sidewalk to the song "The Girl Can't Help It," the lyrics declare that "the girl can't help it if she was born to please." With her onanistic gestures aimed at no one and everyone, she makes cul-turally approved feminine exhibitionism perverse because she is so nar-cissistic that she no longer needs a fetishizing male subject to confirm her objectification. It is no surprise, however, that Divine's spectacle of female carnality elicits incredulity rather than desire from those who observe her on the street.

The uglier and fatter Divine gets, the more beautiful she believes herself to be and the more aggressively exhibitionist she becomes. Her desire to exhibit herself inevitably leads her to celebrate her notoriety. Waters' *Female Trouble* provides the most striking example of this. After being hideously scarred by acid, Divine takes to the stage in a nightclub act that juxtaposes trampoline tricks with shooting at her audience. By combining ugliness and aggressive female exhibitionism, Waters' films echo the Sadeian spectacle of the grotesque. Just as we venerate beauty as a spectacle of excess, in the Sadeian regime ugliness is venerated as an equally extraordinary excess that challenges rather than confirms a refined bourgeois sensibility (Carter 76). However, Divine's exhibition of her excess of ugliness also contributes to reinforcing the comic stereotypes of the ugly woman who unknowingly elicits ridicule (rather than desire) when she presumes to satisfy the male gaze.

The antierotic, parodic treatment of Divine guarantees that the position of the heterosexual male viewer will not be made problematic. Just as the homoerotic possibilities of looking are averted, so is the potential for overtly challenging the straight male spectator's sexuality. He can safely enjoy Divine's "feminine" outrages against social and sexual convention while using the figure of the grotesque wo/man to confirm his own perfection in masculine normality.

Paradoxically, in spite of this, Divine still represents a threat to patriarchal norms. The threat rests in the illogic of transforming "him" to "her." While Divine playfully demonstrates that sexual identity has no biological mandate and is not a condition of genitality, she may also suggest the truth in Janine Chasseguet-Smirgel's assertion that men denigrate women not because they fear difference defined as castration, but because they fear a helplessness first experienced in infancy, in the interaction with the controlling, powerful mother (275–286). Theweleit suggests that the Freikorpsmen's fantasies reflect a similar dread of the mother's power. As a result, women are split into the image of the asexual, powerless nurturer, and femininity represented as an overwhelming flood, an engulfing tide, the perverse Other that threatens to suck them into the disorder and dissolution of female sexuality. As a defensive reaction, the patriarchy must censor any male who appears effeminate and chooses to align himself with the "inferior" gender. Any "he" who appears as "she" risks becoming a perverse "feminine body," a soft, flowing, multiple-sited morass of dissolute, perverse sexuality that threatens to dismantle the patriarchy's tenuously maintained, phallically centered subjectivity.[4] Even if initially greeted with derisive laughter, Divine's acting out of such a sexual identity must ultimately be condemned as incoherent—"unhinged"—in a phallocratic order.

Such a perfect specimen of manhood, so dominant!
— *The Rocky Horror Picture Show*

In *Rocky Horror,* the transvestite alien Frank-N-Furter seduces males and females with equanimity, creates his own ideal sex object, and has everyone emulating his drag queen chic. Yet such androgyny has its ironies. Within the film's generic pastiche, drawing on horror, science fiction, and the musical, Frank-N-Furter represents a gender transformation that borrows from perverse possibilities but safely recuperates the revolutionary promise of a homoerotic hedonism through the sexual politics of masculine aggression.

Probably the most famous of midnight films, *Rocky Horror* follows the misadventures of Janet Weiss and her straight-laced fiancé, Brad Majors, as they journey from Denton, "The Home of Happiness," to visit Dr. Everett Scott, their ex-tutor. On a rainy night, they end up at the castle that is not, as Brad first surmises, "some kind of hunting lodge for rich weirdos," but the home of Dr. Frank-N-Furter and his "foreign" friends—all aliens from the planet of Transexual in the galaxy of Transylvania. Janet and Brad become reluctant witnesses to Frank-N-Furter's "biochemical research" and then rather more willing participants in some sexual research before they escape being beamed back with the castle to the galaxy of Transylvania.

While we might forget that Divine is a man, we cannot forget that Tim Curry, the "sweet transvestite from Transylvania," is male. A young fan thus explains why he cross-dresses as Frank: "There's no other role I could play. It's the one that's closest to me. Frank N. Furter is vicious and likes to be on top. The first time I walked down the stairs to show my mom my transvestite outfit, she was a little upset. . . . It's fun to see people freak out at something that's not that weird" (Bell-Metereau 17). When he first emerges to greet Janet and Brad, Frank appears in a satin vampire cape. He then sheds this apparel to appear in a black sequined corset and G-string. To escort his guests on a tour of his laboratory, he dons a green laboratory coat. These costumes may signify a transcendence of gender norms, but neither Frank-N-Furter nor his fan who models his "transvestite outfit" for his mom has transcended the cultural contradictions of masculinity. The surface confusion of masculinity and femininity in Frank's costuming and manner does not denote any confusion about the privileges of *being* masculine. Frank is "not that weird" because the perverse Otherness of transvestism and bisexuality are normalized by his comforting sameness—the very apparent masculine qualities that confirm his active, phallic power. When Brad aggressively attempts to remind Frank that his requests to telephone for help have been ignored, Frank ridicules Brad: "How forceful you are, Brad! So dominant. Do you have any tattoos?" Ironically, it is Frank who has the tattoos.

In spite of his feminine attire and "swishy" ways, Frank remains a transvestite figure with whom males can safely identify without endangering the power base of their prescribed masculinity. The "master" of his castle, Frank asserts his masculinity in destruction and seduction. When his servants get out of hand, he brings out the whip. When his former lover Eddie comes roaring out of an oversized deep freeze, Frank chops him into a dinner entrée. With dissension quelled and his ax put away for the night, Frank proceeds to seduce Brad and then Janet. By maintaining his status as the seducer, not the seducee, he escapes the real danger of gender transformation—by which the plurality of perversion might render the male passive, nonphallic, and truly "femininized." However, if, as Lawrence Kubie maintains, human beings are constantly engaged in denying and affirming their gender identities, then Frank-N-Furter may provide a safety valve for unconscious feelings that are normally repressed in straight males (202). Frank himself speaks of the possibility of male identification with and envy of culturally inscribed femininity in his song lyrics: "Whatever happened to Fay Wray," he sings, "that delicate satin-draped frame. / As it clung to her thigh, how I started to cry . . . 'cause I wanted to be dressed just the same!"

Paradoxically, Frank endangers his own power base because he feminizes the archetypal Hollywood image of the mad scientist. As a character remarks, "It was over when he had the plan / To start working on a muscle man." Frank creates a creature, but his mission is love, not science: He wants a new mate. When his creation, Rocky, prefers Janet to him, Frank cries out: "Oh, Rocky! How could you!" Frank's sexual rejection suggests the melodramatic dilemma of Joan Crawford in *Humoresque* or Gloria Swanson in *Sunset Boulevard,* films in which the powerful older woman fails in her attempt to forge her young male protégé into a sexually acquiescent partner. But Frank's ladylike disappointment quickly gives way to a vengeful spree in which he zaps Janet, Brad, and Rocky into stony immobility with his sonic transducer. Ultimately, Frank-N-Furter's sexual and scientific escapades are brought to an end by the new commander, Riff-Raff, who declares that Frank's "lifestyle's too extreme!" and shoots Frank with a laser. Imitating King Kong's skyscraper ascent with Fay Wray, a remorseful Rocky carries Frank's lifeless body up the radio tower of the RKO Pictures logo, which has served as the backdrop to Frank's final musical extravaganza celebrating sexual freedom.

Although Frank-N-Furter may provide a way of identifying with a sexually uninhibited and self-expressive character who ultimately evokes a measure of sympathy, the more vulnerable "feminized" side of Frank is not the image with which his fans, male and female, straight and gay, seem to consciously identify. A female fan who dresses up as Frank reaffirms the power politics of the character's sexuality and the appeal of identifying with him through costume: "As Frank, I have a chance to be on top of things, to be a faggot Clint Eastwood. Frank-N-Furter may wear Joan Crawford makeup and high heels, but he's still so masculine there's no way you could mistake him for a woman" (Henkin 23). Frank's fans identify with the Frank who, in juxtaposing the pearl necklace of a demure matron with a sequined lace-up corset, spiked heels, and gartered stockings, evokes Marlene Dietrich's erotic ambiguity in von Sternberg's *The Blue Angel,* while hinting at the tantalizingly taboo possibilities of sadomasochistic bondage.

The joke is that Frank would never be caught dead on the bottom—and his fans know it.

The desire to hide, to be camouflaged. To be elsewhere. Other . . . not a person; to be done with personhood.   —Susan Sontag

Liquid Sky, a science fiction entry into the midnight movie genre, conceptualizes the problem of sexual difference and desire in a radically different way than either *Pink Flamingos* or *Rocky Horror.* Directed by Russian émigré Slava Tsukerman, *Liquid Sky* clearly understands how sexuality has been invaded by patriarchal power politics. The possibility of a truly revolutionary expression of desire gives way to a dubious sexual "liberation" that produces, as Jeffrey Weeks offers, "a false sexuality, which palliates while leaving the real structures of power untouched" (297).

In *Liquid Sky* this false sexuality fails even temporarily to satisfy people, who turn to other forms of gratification. The film focuses on a group of New Wave performers and models who are unaware that an alien space craft (the size of a dinner plate) sits on the Soho rooftop of an apartment occupied by Margaret, a model, and her lesbian lover Adrian, who signs at a club and pushes drugs on the side. According to a German scientist studying aliens, they are attracted to subculture types and this particular site because they feed on substances created in the human brain during orgasm or heroin use.

In spite of the fact that she appears to have achieved freedom from arbitrary sex roles and gender stereotypes, Margaret is sexually and socially alienated. She and her gay male alter-ego Jimmy (Anne Carlisle plays both roles) are both fashion models whose sexual ambiguity represents androgyny as an undernourished, emaciated refusal of gender, as Dick Hebdige describes in his *Subculture: The Meaning of Style* (151). Looking like mirror reflections of each other, Margaret and Jimmy's visual sameness represents a personal and cultural paradox centering around the problem of sexual difference. Margaret recognizes one aspect of this paradox in the double standard of gender and aging. When Jimmy says that she is old and ugly, she retorts that Jimmy is "the most beautiful boy in the world." At a photo session, Jimmy sadistically taunts Margaret, and she counters Jimmy's sadistic game-playing with a masochistic act: "I know I'm ugly; you should punish me." When he hits her, the photographers encourage their hostilities and dare them, as the punk ideals of "Mr. and Miss America," to culminate their session with sex. It is clear that Jimmy does not wish to have sex with a woman. "I can't," he protests, but he is pressured by the group to demand that Margaret "beg for it." While she fellates him, he looks away, gazing at himself in a mirror. When he climaxes, he disappears: the alien has killed him.

Since Carlisle plays both Jimmy and Margaret in this disturbing scene, *Liquid Sky* extends both *Pink Flamingos'* tranvestism and Tim Curry's bisexuality in *Rocky Horror* into a radical statement on desire and sexual difference. Masculinity and femininity are culturally irreconcilable, even within an ethos of androgyny and bisexuality. Jimmy finds Margaret sexually repugnant and socially inferior, even though she bases her gender identity on the model of an adolescent male. Her refusal of traditional gender boundaries is marked by a refusal of the biological "excess" of the female. In that fashion ideal, the physical signs of female sexuality (breasts, hips) indicating the possibility of maternity—the extreme of female bodily excess—disappear. Yet Margaret knows she is following fashion: "I am androgynous not less than David Bowie himself," she comments in self-abasing irony. Thus *Liquid Sky* does not read the appropriation of punk androgyny into an eighties fashion statement as a liberating blend of male and female traits, but rather as another capitalist cannibalization of the signifiers of cultural rebellion (punk).

Margaret's attempt to refuse gender stereotyping is also linked to her personal loss of desire. Without desire, she is reduced to a commodity, a token of exchange in a game of exploitation. It is in this context that she rejects sexual puritanism and assumes the identity of the profane whore who will permit anyone to do anything to her. Owen, her college acting teacher and former lover, tells her she has become a "real mean bitch" who looks and acts like a prostitute. Margaret replies that at least hookers are independent; "I'm nobody's victim," she says. However, events belie that notion. When she lets a man pick her up at a nightclub to obtain cocaine, she is viciously beaten and raped; a junkie client of Adrian's rapes her, just to prove that junkies can "get it up"; Adrian makes her engage in necrophilia. These events show that while Margaret has increased her field of sexual choices and options for sexual identity, she has not changed the structures of power or oppression.

Within this milieu of sexual brutality masquerading as liberation, Margaret attempts to detach herself from her past and her middle-class Connecticut roots, which Adrian obsessively cites as the source of her being "an uptight WASP bitch." If, on the one hand, memory is presented in this context as cultural excess, the baggage of past identity that demands refusal, Margaret, on the other, fails to successfully reinvent herself within the punk ethos. She remains the victim of patriarchal goals for femininity that shift, but continue to place women in a powerless position. First, she was told to be a suburban housewife to her lawyer-prince; then she was told to be a successful ("free and equal") New York model with a male agent. But her new identity proves as empty as the old, her new "family" as repressive as the old, and her female lovers as willing, she says, to step on her as men.

Margaret has simply replaced one assigned identity with another, currently more fashionable one, but her "genderless" body remains irrefutably exploitable and thus defined as belonging to a specific class—female. Margaret discovers that one can cross boundaries of sexual difference but not undo them. The charade of androgyny only obfuscates ideology, as the dominance/submission agenda remains in all her relationships.

Owen tells Margaret that she should "try to be nice," but she says that her defensiveness warns men that "this pussy has teeth." Her figurative remark becomes fact. Before she can escape the burden of her gender, she becomes the ultimate representative of the myth of feminine perversity: the woman who kills with her sexuality. The rooftop alien kills everyone who has sex with her, so Margaret inadvertently becomes a kind of death hole—but that too can be fashionable. She wryly suggests that as a "killer cunt," she is suitable headline material for the *National Enquirer*. She then uses her hidden weapon as a means of revenge. Like the Sadeian woman, she willingly creates corpses, but finds she cannot control her new power. Adrian bets that she can fuck Margaret and live: Adrian dies, but Margaret's lack of desire saves her from death, as the blankness of androgyny transmutes into erotic blankness.

Rather than mourn Adrian, Margaret leads their friends to the club to dance. Her camouflage of punk regalia—painted face, wild hair, and feathered costume—temporarily transfigures her body into something verging on the nonhuman, but even this simultaneously exhibitionist and self-protective masquerade cannot provide comfort, intimacy, equality, or love. Ironically, Margaret's source for these scarce human qualities is the alien spaceship. When the bodies first begin to pile up, she goes to the apartment roof and instinctively asks for help. Immediately, the junkie's body dematerializes. Margaret's response is one of complete surprise: "Is that for me, Chief?" For the first time in the film someone—something—responds positively to her desires. However, the alien's gift is counterpointed by the burden it imposes on Margaret: killing her sexual partners. Nevertheless, by appearing to turn Margaret into a "killer cunt," the alien merely fulfills the already established myth of female sexuality as a perverse and dangerous mystery.

Although she finds temporary escape in drugs and sex, Margaret finally exhausts her earthly possibilities for escaping a culturally inscribed gender identity. She joins the alien, who becomes her prince, the husband she once dreamed of, and dons a traditional white wedding dress. Begging the departing ship to take her along, she mainlines heroin, known in its best forms as "liquid sky." Caught in a beam of light from the space craft, she dances a tormented dance of erotic self-destruction as she dematerializes. In a transfiguring act of "merging into the nonhuman" (Sontag 118), she finally finds erotic bliss, the "liquid sky" of orgasm.

Liquid Sky shows how sex and gender permutations can easily be signifiers of artificial change, meaningless in themselves, unable to alter woman's social status as victim. Margaret's known transgression of the bourgeois norms of her childhood does not make her free. In spite of her subculture efforts at "refusal," she finds no acceptable model for her being, only a negation that turns into self-destruction. Margaret's final act acknowledges that in a patriarchal culture women must always be aliens.

In attempting to define the cult movie, Umberto Eco links its generic and narrative excess to a postmodern impulse, "where the quotation of the topos is recognized as the only way to cope with the burden of our encyclopedic filmic competence" (11). As cult films, *Pink Flamingos, Rocky Horror,* and *Liquid Sky* obviously mix genre categories to create a narrative pastiche, but the image of gender they fashion is also a pastiche of sorts, an intertextual and intersexual burden in which cultural signs of a shift in masculinity and femininity are sometimes scrambled but never disarticulated. In films like *Rocky Horror* and *Pink Flamingos*, the gender-bending of androgyny and transvestism creates a visual disorientation that disorients but does not destroy patriarchal law (Hebdige 126).

Although the three films discussed here serve as typical examples of the midnight movie's association of femininity with perversion, there are many more cult films, such as *The Texas Chain Saw Massacre 2* and *Day of the Dead*, that mark a similar convergence—but to a different end. These films radically refuse to make s/excess pleasurable and therefore remain marginal, films for hardcore cultists rather than assimilable objects of the Saturday-night ritual of midnight-movie audiences. Frequently X-rated, these "sick" films, however, may be the most uncompromisingly subversive examples of sexual excess, for their violent fantasies often embrace at least one disturbing truth that the midnight movies discussed here generally avoid: the explicit emergence of perversion from within the patriarchal family unit and its conservative function in maintaining rather than exploding that structure (Stoller 214–217).

With the self-conscious exception of *Liquid Sky*, the sexual rebellion of midnight movies like *Pink Flamingos* and *Rocky Horror* shows that gender power relations are not necessarily subverted by a vision of perversely erotic freedom. On the contrary, femininity and perversity are bound together in a formula that provides the male with a rationale for denigrating "femininity" and female sexuality. What results, finally, in all these films' contradictions and ambivalences is a masculine vision of the mysteries and pleasures of s/excess. Desire unencumbered by difference and division remains a dangerous dream, a "liquid sky," perhaps too much, too overwhelming, too perverse—even for the midnight hour.

NOTES

A version of this essay appeared in *Journal of Popular Film and Television* 17, no. 1 (1989): 2–14. Reprinted with permission of the Helen Dwight Reid Educational Foundation. Published by Heldref Publications, 4000 Albemarle St., N.W., Washington, D.C. 20016. Copyright © 1989.

My thanks to Bruce Kawin and J. P. Telotte for their comments on earlier drafts of this essay.

1. Jean Laplanche argues that perversion, as the exception to a supposed normative "sexual instinct," ends up by "taking the rule along with it." The result is that "the whole of sexuality, or at least the whole of infantile sexuality, ends up by becoming perversion" (23).

2. Ironically, most of Freud's case studies confirm neurosis or repression as the primary feminine pathology and perversion as predominately a male syndrome.

The only perversion Freud associated consistently with women was masochism. Of course, Freud had no doctor/patient contact with those lower-class women he cited as so easily seduced into perversion.

3. Marcuse's views can be contrasted with those of Michel Foucault, who contends that modern society actually encourages the "implantation" of perversions and multiple discourses of sexuality. Perversions emerge as "the real product of the encroachment of a type of power on bodies and their pleasures" (48); they are managed, categorized, and controlled by modern society so that their subversive potential is neutralized. The subversive value of perversion was questioned by Marcuse himself in his 1966 preface to a new edition of *Eros and Civilization* (see Ober 82–107).

4. See Theweleit 367, 402–406. Felix Guattari argues for the subversive value of perversion in a controversial essay, "Becoming Woman," wherein he contends that perversion in general and homosexuality in particular have been made into illnesses by psychoanalysis when they should be considered as a revolutionary repudiation of a phallic power. While psychoanalysis reduces desire to a binary operation (feminine = passive, masculine = active), he suggests, "every 'dissident' organization of the libido" opposes this binary operation and "must therefore be directly linked to a becoming-feminine body; as an escape route from the repressive socius" (86–87). Chasseguet-Smirgel believes that the basis of all perversion is the denial of difference between the sexes and also between the generations. Also common to all perversions, she claims, is a disavowal of the father's genital capacities (79).

WORKS CITED

Bell-Metereau, Rebecca. *Hollywood Androgyny.* New York: Columbia Univ. Press, 1985.

Brake, Mike. "Sexuality as Praxis—A Consideration of the Contribution of Sexual Theory to the Process of Sexual Being." In *Human Sexual Relations,* ed. Mike Brake, 3–29. New York: Pantheon, 1982.

Carter, Angela. *The Sadeian Woman in the Ideology of Pornography.* New York: Harper, 1980.

Caskey, Noelle. "Interpreting Anorexia Nervosa." In *The Female Body in Western Culture,* ed. Susan Rubin Suleiman, 175–189. Cambridge: Harvard Univ. Press, 1986.

Chasseguet-Smirgel, Janine. *Creativity and Perversion.* New York: Norton, 1984.

Dijkstra, Bram. *Idols of Perversity.* New York: Oxford Univ. Press, 1986.

Eco, Umberto. "*Casablanca:* Cult Movies and Intertextual Collage." *SubStance* 47, no. 2 (1985): 3–12.

Foucault, Michel. *The History of Sexuality.* Trans. Robert Hurley. New York: Pantheon, 1978.

Freud, Sigmund. "On Some Consequences of the Anatomical Differences between the Sexes." In *Sexuality and the Psychology of Love,* ed. Phillip Rieff, 171–194. New York: Collier, 1963.

————. "Three Essays on the Theory of Sexuality." *Standard Edition of the Complete Psychological Works of Sigmund Freud*, ed. and trans. James Strachey, 7: 133–243. London: Hogarth, 1953.

Guattari, Felix. "Becoming Woman." *Semio-texte* 4 (1981): 86–88.

Hebdige, Dick. *Subculture: The Meaning of Style*. London: Methuen, 1979.

Henkin, Bill. *The Rocky Horror Picture Show Book*. New York: Hawthorn/Dutton, 1979.

Krafft-Ebing, Richard von. *Psychopathia Sexualis*. Trans. F. J. Rebman. New York: Special Books, 1965.

Kubie, Lawrence S. "The Drive to Become Both Sexes." In *Symbols and Neurosis: Selected Papers of L. S. Kubie*, ed. Herbert J. H. Schlesinger, 191–263. New York: International Univ. Press, 1978.

Laplanche, Jean. *Life and Death in Psychoanalysis*. Trans. Jeffrey Mehlman. Baltimore: Johns Hopkins Univ. Press, 1976.

Marcuse, Herbert. *Eros and Civilization*. New York: Vintage, 1962.

Montrelay, Michele. "Recherches sur la féminité." *Critique* 278 (1970). Quoted in *Sternberg*, ed. Peter Baxter, 90–103. London: BFI, 1980.

Mulvey, Laura. "Visual Pleasure and Narrative Cinema." *Screen* 16 (1975): 6–18.

Ober, John David. "On Sexuality and Politics in the Work of Herbert Marcuse." In *Human Sexual Relations*, ed. Mike Brake, 82–107. New York: Pantheon, 1982.

Peary, Danny. *Cult Films*. New York: Delta, 1981.

Riviere, Joan. "Womanliness as a Masquerade." In *Psychoanalysis and Female Sexuality*, ed. Hendrik M. Ruitenbeek, 112–133. New Haven: College and Univ. Press, 1966.

Sontag, Susan. "Fragments of an Esthetic of Melancholy." *Art in America* 74 (1986): 116–121.

Stoller, Robert. *Perversion: The Erotic Form of Hatred*. New York: Dell, 1975.

Theweleit, Klaus. *Male Fantasies. Vol. 1: Woman, Floods, Bodies, History*. Trans. Stephen Conway. Minneapolis: Univ. of Minnesota Press, 1987.

Waters, John. *Shock Value*. New York: Dell, 1981.

Weeks, Jeffrey. "The Development of Sexuality Theory and Sexual Politics." In *Human Sexual Relations*, ed. Mike Brake, 293–309. New York: Pantheon, 1982.

CHAPTER 12

Don't Dream It: Performance and The Rocky Horror Picture Show

Robert E. Wood

For all practical purposes, *The Rocky Horror Picture Show* (1975) has become a paradigmatic cult film. Its offbeat, irreverent humor and references to various popular genres—the musical, horror, science fiction films—fashion a nexus of memories and affections. While some of the cult behavior surrounding the film springs from these lures, they are clearly not its sole attractions—nor even its most important. In fact, its real impact seems almost incidentally linked to them; for its audience's behavior has arguably altered the norms of behavior of a whole generation of filmgoers. This effect is due to the fact that the film filled a need for both new rituals and new freedoms for moviegoers. And since the height of its popularity, no other film has induced a response that matches *Rocky Horror*'s ability to generate an audience *for* its audience.[1]

Of course, film criticism does not usually concern itself with audience behavior. While it may mention the anomaly, the naive violation of conventions of silence and isolation, it typically focuses on the text as a discrete phenomenon. But exploring audience behavior *is* central to stage theory and, in practice, to theatrical experiment. In fact, it was in a period when the theater was in the process of shattering certain conventions of audience passivity and exploring the limits of how a mass audience might interact with live performers that the *Rocky Horror* cult emerged. And as the spectators/performers of *Rocky Horror* have since shown, those theatrical limits are not quite binding on the movie audience.

Released in 1975, *Rocky Horror* had, within a year, begun attracting a loyal repeat audience. Some five months into its run at the Waverly in Greenwich Village, the audience—legend has it, at the instigation of one Louis Farese, Jr.—began a "counterpoint dialogue" with the film (Hoberman and Rosenbaum 176). Some weeks later, patrons began appearing in costume, which in turn led to physical performances of a kind that balanced the repetition of this dialogue with the innovation of new elements of an audience "performance." Through that play of repetition and innovation, these responses eventually took on an almost ritualistic character, the audience performance becoming a show with its own stars. In New York, Dori Hartley, a young fan, established a reputation by appearing as Frank-N-Furter, duplicating Tim Curry's costume and makeup in the film, while in the same group, former schoolteacher and off-Broadway actor Sal Piro built a following by playing numerous roles. With less national publicity, such informal "troupes" sprang up in movie theaters throughout the country (Hoberman and Rosenbaum 174–192).

Much of the audience participation that followed derives from those initial audience responses—responses reported and even promoted by the mass media. In 1979, Twentieth Century–Fox authorized a book documenting both the film *and* the varieties of cult activity that had sprung up around it. A sequence in the film *Fame* (1980) also depicts and even explains some of *Rocky Horror*'s rituals. Meanwhile, long after its initial run, the film continues to be distributed and promoted by its producers, and far more widely than was ever planned. However, the wide dissemination of the rituals, their appeal to a remarkable range of viewers, and attempts to copy the film and its peculiar attractions argue that the film's success depends not just on an effective publicity campaign, but on a ritualistic underpinning that responds to a deep-seated need felt by its audience.

In large measure, every film is conditioned by ritual, since it takes place as a communal act, partitioned from workaday life. Certainly, films that *depict* cultic activity, like *Scorpio Rising* or *The Harder They Come* (1973), are predisposed to attract a cult following, but the cult remains distinct from the behavior depicted in the films. In becoming a cult object itself, though, a film radically alters the normal experience of its exhibition. It intensifies the conditions of its showing and, in the process, solidifies its separation from ordinary life. In return, the viewing community enhances its own sense of communal identity and intensifies its synchronized action. In this respect, the cult film locates and reinvigorates something important that has largely been lost in the moviegoing experience—the cultic nature of film itself. By reclaiming this experience, the cult film counters a contemporary tendency—encouraged and accelerated by the video industry—for filmgoing to become less communal, less festive, and in many ways less significant.

The most visible sign of the *Rocky Horror* cult is its pattern of overt audience behavior. Tellingly, that behavior relies on those elements of film which directly relate to the human body—dialogue, gesture, makeup, costumes, props—in short, to the film's *theatrical* rather than specifically cinematic dimensions. Of those theatrical elements accessible to the audience, dialogue assumes the greatest weight. In fact, the most common act of veneration for any cult film is the quoting of its dialogue, or, more precisely, the *performance* of its dialogue (i.e., being true to the precise inflections, accents, etc.). Of course, when friends discuss a movie, such an activity is normal; but it reaches a ritual level in the context of a predictable frame in time and space—that is, when it occurs within a kind of sacralized space. So while a film cult can and does avail itself of private gatherings and conventions, it does not depend on them. For the central ritual of the film cult remains the repeated and formalized showing of the film, with its requirement of audience assistance or participation.

In that context, viewers anticipate—and even help evoke—a certain emotional response. For at the same time, viewers both *are* spectators and *play* at being spectators. Even if they take no action beyond this, they still ritualize their behavior, since the film corresponds to a psychic model fashioned by their previous viewings of it. To watch the film repeatedly is, in effect, to join memory and event. And to the extent that the repeated viewing constitutes any kind of new perception, that perception tilts toward a dramatic irony. Events are seen in terms of what will follow from them rather than of what they follow from. It is this ritualization of perception that lays the ground for those other activities which develop from our "playing the spectator."

The response to *Rocky Horror* demonstrates the range of ritualized activities that the film offers to the paying/playing spectators. While the film clearly defies passivity, little has been made of how it violates taboos about audience behavior or explores the parameters of the filmgoing experience through this violation. By encouraging viewers to acknowledge their presence and participation, *Rocky Horror* invites them not just to act out issues raised by its thematic focus on liberation from sexual and cultural taboos, but to explore the film-viewing environment in general. Consider, for example, an initial violation, its disruption of the customary experience of darkness in the auditorium. As one of the film's lyrics suggests, "there's a light in the darkness." That line usually provokes a display of cigarette-lighter flames from the audience, an act fraught with ceremonial significance in its own right. But this light also defines the darkness as a sign and the boundaries of the auditorium as an arena. A more sustained violation of darkness is the appropriation of the flashlight (the sacred wand of the usher, if you will) to spotlight performers wearing costumes and whose character imitations are revealed by the light. The violation of darkness, though, is ultimately a celebratory playing with the dark, even a playing at seeing in the dark. And the film's usual conditions of performance reenforce that attitude: since the film typically plays on Fridays and Saturdays at midnight, the audience's arrival, viewing, and departure constitute a kind of playful violation of the night.

A further violation of the spectator's normal limitations comes from the film's assault on the very process of narration. The audience periodically and vocally insists that "this movie has no plot." But it does, if an adroit compendium of B-movie narratives is a plot. At least, like all repeatedly viewed films, it is plotted *in memory*—outside the normal bounds of the cinematic experience. The film's opening sequence signals this unorthodox attitude toward narrative: a pair of red lips, set off by a black background, mouths the reflexive song, "Science Fiction Double Feature," a celebration of filmgoing that provides a brief plot summary as well. The song typifies the film's narrative overdetermination. The preannounced plot, the satire of familiar horror and science fiction film devices, the intrusive criminologist-narrator, and the underlining effect that results from using songs to help carry the narration collectively deemphasize both the linearity and conventional sense of realism usually associated with film narrative.

The audience's sense of a "plotless" narrative is reinforced by the film's refusal to settle into any one formula; rather, *Rocky Horror*'s plot rambles rapidly through several genres. The straight musical of young romance is dispatched with a single barb, as Brad and Janet, the film's naive young couple, are moved by a friend's wedding to express their undying affection for each other in a song marked by the off-rhymes of a desperate musical. Subsequently, on a dark and stormy night, the couple must seek help at a gothic "old dark house" when their car breaks down. There they encounter a stock horror-film butler, Riff-Raff, a hunchback in the Igor tradition, and his sister, a maid conceived in the same vein. At odds with these conventions, yet confirming their generic subtext, is the androgynous Frank-N-Furter, "a sweet transvestite from transsexual Transylvania"—both a proverbial mad doctor and an alien, a fugitive from a Transylvania not of this world. This Frankenstein figure has his own monster, a blond Adonis who is the object of his affections, and he casually murders intruders, such as the motorcycle thug Eddie. His primary threat, though, is one of sexual liberation, as we see when he successfully seduces both Janet and Brad. The authorities from Transylvania—who turn out to be Riff-Raff and his sister—have enough of his excesses and decide to transport Frank-N-Furter and his house back to his own galaxy. The science fiction plot thus suddenly departs, leaving Brad and Janet behind like lovers in the dawn following a midsummer night's dream.

A film dependent on our appreciation of so many plot conventions could be termed plotless for various reasons. Since *Rocky Horror* celebrates the usually formula-bound B-movie, it is subject to a semantic reversal in which bad becomes good: to undermine a predictable narrative is to celebrate it. Moreover, the performing segment of the audience struggles with the film for control of the narrative, although that struggle is ultimately a playful one. It reenacts in parodic form the dialectic of expectation and innovation that marks our normal experience of the genre film, as we expect certain conventions, but also take pleasure in the various ways that the film defies those expectations with its own innovations. Meanwhile, the film's narrator, Dr. Scott, becomes a focus of this tension, as he is linked to the narrative with cries of "This movie has no plot and you have no neck," salted with obscenities that vary with the venue.[2]

The characteristics of the audience's performance are generally well known. They typically throw rice at the wedding scene and toast at the banquet. They fire water pistols during the storm scene and ignite lights in the darkness. They dance the "Time Warp," which obligingly comes with dance instructions, and they touch the screen during Janet's solo, "Touch-a, Touch-a, Touch Me." In short, even beyond specific performances, the audience asserts its physical presence and surrenders its anonymity, as if in obedience to the refrain in Frank-N-Furter's lyric, "Don't dream it. Be it." That line exhorts the characters in the film to turn sexual fantasy into sexual liberty; however, this sexual liberty itself becomes a kind of acting out of film fantasy, as Frank becomes a version of *King Kong*'s Fay Wray. To be "it," apparently, is to be the film—or at least to be one with the film. The paradox of this crossover to the film world shows up most clearly in Janet's "Touch-a, Touch-a, Touch Me." A member of the audience who touches Janet's breast is, at that moment, perceived as performing a kind of sexual gesture.

Of course, a viewer touching Janet really only experiences the film image's insubstantiality, but in being observed by others, he ritualistically becomes part of it, partakes of the film's magic. And that is a key to the larger ritual character of *Rocky Horror,* for the participant in its ritual desires not simply to violate taboos or conventions, but to be *seen* violating them and to be *approved* for so doing. Because the audience members depend on this mutual approval, their freedom is substantially expended in the initial choice to participate. For as in every ritual, approval finally depends on the community's solidarity, which in turn derives from a common *subjective* response to the film that translates into a common *overt* response. The resulting audience performance is thus oriented to representation and dependent on a communal agreement over the signs employed in that representation.

For this reason, a playing with styles of representation is crucial to the audience response. The shadow world of the film image lines up with live stage representation, as when members of the audience reach in vain for the bouquet at the wedding scene, but then shower each other with real rice—rice which, like the image of rice, is present here as a sign. What results is a kind of dialogue with the screen that resembles the theatrical freedom of the live performer to improvise around a fixed text. However, that fixed text is also a basic ground of meaning, for the audience response is correct *because* it is synchronized with the film. And if the audience typically shows its knowledge of the film by anticipating the dialogue, it can also underscore that knowledge by ceding the punch line to the film dialogue rather than taking the last word for its own.[3]

The end product of this experience is a radical transformation of audience behavior that recalls various theatrical experiments contemporaneous with the film's release. It is worth exploring how the *Rocky Horror* experience proved more liberating for its audience than many of those experiments. Commonly, experimental theater of the early 1970s confronted audiences with a confusion about their roles, either as social beings or as spectators at a performance. Usually, it involved a political or sexual confrontation, and an ideological result of that confrontation was planned and expected. However improvisational a performance might seem to be, the performing troupe always had the advantage of experience and design over the audience—which actually had little real opportunity to express itself. Its only outlet was often pure aggression, directed at the performers or even other spectators. This aggression eventually led to the decline of such experimental theater experiences as *Dionysus in 69,* whose participants began to feel more victimized than liberated.

Another kind of dramatic experiment, the "happening," constructed a unique theatrical event designed to place audience and performer in the same category, as participants in something new to all. In this shared "new" experience, an attempt was made to keep the boundary between reality and representation fluid. One event staged by Richard Schechner involved interrogating an audience of members of the A.C.L.U. Individuals were labeled, asked to remove parts of their clothing, photographed, and questioned for about three hours. Such an event obviously required a rather specialized audience, one that knew of the psychological risks they were taking. But since the "happening" supposedly represented nothing other than itself, it could not work properly without that risk-taking participation. Such drama simply redefined the theater as bracketed experience, complete with the uncertainties and vulnerabilities common to most human experience (Schechner 60–64).

Through such experiments, the theater was reaching for greater audi-

ence involvement in the dramatic experience. It might thereby force the-
atergoers to reconsider the nature of art, to deepen their sensibilities, and,
in a return to drama's ritualistic roots, to undertake an emotional and spiritual passage. As Joseph Chaikin put it, such theater ideally hoped to help
us escape society's efforts at culturally stylizing the self, by offering "a way
of making oneself visible, recognizable, and comprehensible to the other"
(69). However, only in the most limited sense did the audience truly participate in these new alternatives. For, finally, the avant-garde theater of the
1960s and 1970s, with all its promise of self-fulfillment, emphasized the
actor's experience over and above the audience's.[4]

For film to follow this lead and reach for similar involvement, it would
have to move in a rather different direction. Film is, after all, an anomaly
among the arts in the way it assembles a large audience for a "performed"
event without a performer being present. Therefore, if a cult activity is to
center on film, or if the sort of cultural therapeutics aimed at by experimental drama is to surface, it must evolve from the behavior of the audience. And this development marks a radical leap in narrative and exhibition practices. For it has been a long-standing convention for film narrative
to efface all trace of the spectator's presence. Thus it typically avoids the
look of outward regard. At the same time, conventions limit audience
behavior, although they are largely collectively agreed on and designed
to prevent any problems in viewing the film (and most audience self-
expression can create such barriers). What distinguishes *Rocky Horror* is
the way it evolved new norms of behavior—a behavior that points in the
direction of experimental theater and the effects for which it strove.

The initial size of a cult film's audience is not crucial to its cult status: a
film may succeed, fail, or even be designed from the start to address a small
audience. As is well known by now, *Rocky Horror* began as a play, one that
succeeded in England but not in America. It has been suggested that
something of the play's spirit was lost as it acquired polish. Turned into a
film, it was intended for wide distribution, but the theatrical pattern repeated itself. The film succeeded in just a few theaters in major cities, and
then only on the basis of repeat business. Gradually it found a special
niche, a cult status, but almost despite distributors' expectations. Several
qualities contributed to this different sort of success. Particularly, its irreverent sense of humor and playful satire on sexuality appealed to a broad
counterculture audience. Also, the Frank-N-Furter figure drew heavily on
a preexisting rock music cult surrounding Mick Jagger's androgynous image.[5] But perhaps most important, the film was unusually mindful of its
audience and incorporated an implicit program for group response that
transformed spectatorship into a ritual activity.

This development is specifically rooted in the film text's theatricality. Adapting a play to film is always difficult. At the very least, the two forms conceive of space and balance sight and sound differently. But the stage version of *Rocky Horror* already included a homage to the movies, and the films to which tribute was being paid, horror films in particular, are rather compatible with stage techniques. Even apart from a generally melo-dramatic plot line, the horror film establishes a mythic structure verbally and then makes the myth visible. In fact, its visual climax usually depends on a sort of formulaic verbal prologue. Furthermore, the space of the horror film shows a special kinship to theatrical space, since both emphasize the audience's sense of "being there." A frequent concern of horror is con-finement, being in the proximity of some terror. What spatial freedom the characters have exists only to be lost by entering the domain of the mon-strous. A psychological equivalence results, as the movie audience, like the characters in the film, seem confined in the presence of something fright-ening and beyond their control.

Of course, *Rocky Horror* is not just a hybrid of horror and science fiction but also a musical satire, foregrounding both the plot and the conventions of the genre. Because satire distances an audience from the narrative and the musical employs radically different conventions from horror, these ele-ments would seem to dissipate the horror film's energies. But the satire here does point up the sexual undercurrents at work in most horror nar-ratives, and thus translates rather than reduces psychological risk. Music also serves to express rather than to conventionalize desire. For example, the song "Dammit, Janet" satirizes a desexualized courtship, while later lyrics explicitly celebrate a more erotic tradition. The rendition of "What-ever Happened to Saturday Night," with its equation of a saxophone "blowing on a/Rock and roll show" with "a chick who'd go," then links the sexual impulse to rock and roll's subversive energies—energies with which the film's audience could be expected to sympathize.

In the process, *Rocky Horror* recaptures the Dionysian elements of mu-sic and dance, drawing from them a unifying power of a sort often found in another ritualized, popular venue, the rock concert. "The Time Warp," the dance for which the narrator offers instructions ("For virgins," shouts the crowd), features a pelvic thrust and hip swivel which celebrates the sex-ual bump and grind that emerges thinly disguised in much modern dance. The later "Floor Show" number alternates male and female characters in lingerie in a chorus line. These and other songs are clearly accessible to audience performance: through choric refrain, through interpolation in the pauses, through an acting out, or through the common response to recorded music—singing along and faking the hard notes. A repeat audience automatically gains familiarity with the music and then shows its familiarity by joining in the performance. In a sense, through its music, the *Rocky Horror* ritual taps a familiar model of behavior: for a generation brought up on the rock concert, accustomed to its active audience response, self-abandonment, and even costumed self-display, the film only extends and encourages a familiar pattern of reactions.

To equal effect, the film celebrates the moviegoing experience and even the movie theater itself as an arena for pleasure. The movie theater has always combined a sense of opportunity with certain restraints. For example, the Saturday matinee, evoked in *Rocky Horror*'s song lyrics, provided children a chance for public mischief under the cover of darkness and for feasting on the forbidden fruits of American nutrition with some sense of parental sanction. The drive-in theater, similarly evoked by song and the types of films referred to here, has played an important role in American courting customs. In its celebration of moviegoing, just as in its use of established responses to rock music, *Rocky Horror* thus assimilates various familiar sorts of privileged behavior, rooted in popular ritual. In fact, the behavior at *Rocky Horror* may seem so comfortable to its audience because it renews several basic pleasures traditionally contained in the filmgoing experience, pleasures not limited to looking alone.

Theater, the cultural repository of the Dionysian in Western art, has puzzled over how to do just this: how to regain access to its own fundamental pleasures, to the primitive energies that have ebbed from much of mainstream theater. Peter Brook has outlined two alternative strategies, what he terms holy theater and rough theater. The holy, he suggests, makes visible the invisible by reestablishing links between art and prophecy. Its attitude toward the audience is simple: "one look at the average audience gives us an irresistible urge to assault it," to confront it with truth. Rough theater, on the other hand, celebrates "the vivid relationship between people . . . audiences standing, drinking, sitting round tables, audiences joining in, answering back" (42, 55, 65). In part, what the rituals of *Rocky Horror* accomplish is a combination of the two; they fashion a ceremony in honor of the rough audience, yet one that creates a kind of holy theater without the contempt of the priestly actor.

Rocky Horror has survived several shifts in audience makeup and response, but linking them all is a common theatrical denominator, the overt response—or performance—of a "rough" audience. For an initial audience, many of the film's references evoked nostalgia. Fay Wray, Charles Atlas, and Lili St. Cyr lived in the memory—or at least in popular culture. Tim Curry's evocation of Mick Jagger and Meatloaf's Elvis/Brando motorcycle rocker drew on slightly more contemporary contexts. While earlier audiences may have had a larger gay component, recent audiences seem younger and more conservative, in their rebellion more geared to beating the system than destroying it. As a result, response to Tim Curry's Frank-N-Furter seems more guarded,[6] while specific ironies, like those of the film's climactic moments with pale, blond Rocky playing Kong to dark Frank-N-Furter's furry Fay Wray, often seem lost. The comic permutation of these film icons apparently weighs less heavily with this audience than does the comparison of film conventions with reality.[7]

Despite these shifts, the ritual of filmgoing still sustains the *Rocky Horror* cult. If a change in the makeup of the film's audience points to a diminished appreciation of certain icons or even of film as art, we can still see the film's significance as a new kind of performance text, one that appropriates theater's oldest commitments to ritual. Locating and imitating images of the self that resist dominant cultural norms remains a liberating, even holy experience. Speaking out to or back at the narratives that promise to narrate us is indeed a "rough" pleasure. What *Rocky Horror* thus suggests is the emergence of a simultaneously holy and rough cinema, one that, in the best *theatrical* way, finds a kind of truthful experience in the presence and participation of its spectators.

NOTES

1. *Rocky Horror* has been analyzed from various vantages. Henkin presents promotional material and is a valuable source of data and song lyrics. Samuels places the cult in the context of 1970s entertainment, wherein the audience becomes spectacle. Hoberman and Rosenbaum explore the New York version of the phenomenon and its role as a cultural reference point for later films. Bell-Metereau views the film as having a liberating effect by adding the drag queen to the "repertoire of movie personalities." Twitchell sees it as a most explicit Frankenstein film, celebrating the triumph of procreation over unnatural creation. Siegel uses Van Gennep's *Rites of Passage* as a model for the film narrative but overlooks the ritual of audience participation. He sees the film as responding to a crisis in American attitudes toward homosexuality and bisexuality.

2. The attack on the narrator has been moderated in only one instance. Sal Piro announced for a time at the 8th Street Playhouse in New York that the local practice was not to make fun of the criminologist-narrator. Although responsible for initiating so many of the cult practices surrounding this film, the 8th Street group could not delete this one (Hoberman and Rosenbaum 207).

3. When the audience does get the last word, it is more often a coda than punch line. Calling for a rope, for example, the audience cedes a climax to the dropping of the rope in the film and adds its own anticlimactic "Thank you."

4. Peter Brook, Charles Marowitz, and Richard Schechner, for example, were

all known for the way they regarded the acting troupe as a kind of priesthood. In the background were Artaud's theories, concerned with the audience as receivers of an irresistible mystery emanating from the stage. From an academic perspective, critics like Michael Goldman celebrated those plays that revealed the power of the actor over the audience.

5. Hoberman and Rosenbaum trace the influence of Jagger's screen appearance back to *Performance* (1970).

6. Austin's examination of Rochester audiences in 1979 revealed a predominantly white, politically middle-of-the-road group with a mean age of nineteen.

7. The larger-than-life quality of film iconography remains important. In 1981 Richard O'Brien combined again with director Jim Sharman to create *Shock Treatment*, a vapid sequel to *Rocky Horror* that satirizes small towns and television. The satire is, however, ultimately a loveless one, showing how television diminishes rather than enhances the human image and sanctifies the banal.

WORKS CITED

Artaud, Antonin. *The Theater and Its Double*. Trans. Mary Caroline Richards. New York: Grove, 1958.

Austin, Bruce A. "Portrait of a Cult Film Audience: *The Rocky Horror Picture Show*." *Journal of Communication* 31 (1981): 43–54.

Bell-Metereau, Rebecca. *Hollywood Androgyny*. New York: Columbia Univ. Press, 1985.

Brook, Peter. *The Empty Space*. New York: Atheneum, 1968.

Chaikin, Joseph. *The Presence of the Actor*. New York: Atheneum, 1972.

Goldman, Michael. *The Actor's Freedom: Toward a Theory of Drama*. New York: Viking, 1975.

Grotowski, Jerzy. *Towards a Poor Theatre*. New York: Simon and Schuster, 1968.

Henkin, Bill. *The Rocky Horror Picture Show Book*. New York: Hawthorn/Dutton, 1979.

Hoberman, J., and Jonathan Rosenbaum. *Midnight Movies*. New York: Harper, 1983.

Marowitz, Charles. *The Act of Being: Towards a Theory of Acting*. New York: Taplinger, 1978.

Samuels, Stuart. *Midnight Movies*. New York: Macmillan, 1983.

Schechner, Richard. *Environmental Theater*. New York: Hawthorn, 1973.

Siegel, Mark. "*The Rocky Horror Picture Show*: More Than a Lip Service." *Science Fiction Studies* 7 (1980): 305–318.

Twitchell, James B. *Dreadful Pleasures: An Anatomy of Modern Horror*. New York: Oxford Univ. Press, 1985.

CHAPTER 13

Midnight Movies, 1980–1985: A Market Study

Gregory A. Waller

Because *Night of the Living Dead*, *Rocky Horror Picture Show*, *Pink Flamingos*, and *Eraserhead* all achieved cult status after hours, during weekend upon weekend of midnight screenings in the 1970s, there is a common tendency to link—or treat as synonymous—the post-1960s cult movie (a particular film or the phenomenon as a whole) and the midnight movie (a particular film exhibition practice or the product exhibited in this manner). While we may wax nostalgic over the special moviegoing experience offered by the picture palace, the drive-in, or the Saturday matinee, we do not usually associate classic cult films like *Casablanca* and *The Searchers* or cult stars like Rudolph Valentino, James Dean, and Marilyn Monroe with a specific film exhibition policy. Whether we identify a cult film through its ritualistic, cultural resonance and enthralled fans, its capacity to transgress taboos and articulate "a potent, new fantasy" (Hoberman and Rosenbaum 301), or the way its audience, like postmodern tourists, discover and appropriate a cult film's "unfamiliar style, frame and imagistic texture" (Corrigan 91), not all midnight movies qualify as cult films. And as several essays in this collection indicate, the phenomenon of the cult film extends well beyond *Rocky Horror* and other popular midnight movies of the 1970s.

However, it is the midnight movie as practice and product that I am concerned with here. More precisely, it is the midnight movie *after* what we may be tempted to take as its Golden Age in the 1970s. Governing my inquiry are two basic questions about the postlapsarian situation that emerged once an idiosyncratic, ghettoized, alternative form of exhibition became a commonplace, national, industrywide trend: what exhibition practices characterized the midnight movie market at its peak and what sort of product was offered to (and selected by) the midnight moviegoer in this period?

To answer these questions, I have examined the midnight movie venues, booking policies, and range of movies shown after hours in one locale,

Lexington, Kentucky, from 1980 through 1985. During these years Lexington was a growing city with a population of 200,000 (including over 20,000 students at the University of Kentucky), a healthy economy, a fairly high concentration of professionals, five high schools, a substantial gay community, a lively local music scene, a modest commitment to high culture, and nine movie theaters with a total of twenty-four screens. I focused on Lexington because it is the market I am most familiar with. This thriving market, I would argue, was rather typical, especially for Middle America during this period. The concluding section of this essay briefly puts the Lexington midnight movie market in the context of what was probably the major market for such films, New York City.

During the six-year period under study, Lexington had a total of 1,216 midnight movie playdates, that is, film screenings in commercial theaters on Friday or Saturday night at twelve o'clock, advertised in local newspapers and on rock radio stations as "midnight movies." To keep this seemingly large number of playdates in perspective, we should consider that a major hit like *Beverly Hills Cop* (showing at two theaters five times a day, seven days a week) probably had 1,000 or more screenings during its first run. These midnight movie playdates can be broken down as follows:

1. One hundred and eighty playdates at a small twin cinema (the Chevy Chase Twin Cinema) in an older, residential neighborhood. Part of the Mid-States Theatres chain of twin cinemas and multicinemas in Kentucky and Ohio, this theater was converted into a twin cinema in October 1981, and it offered *Rocky Horror* on both screens as a midnight attraction until closing in 1983. It reopened briefly in 1985, again with *Rocky Horror* as its midnight movie, before closing permanently.

2. Three hundred and ninety-six playdates at five different twin cinemas or multicinemas that otherwise almost exclusively screen first-run mainstream releases. (Only one of the city's mall cinemas did not book midnight movies at some point in the 1980s.) These theaters are all in shopping areas several miles from downtown and within easy access of suburban subdivisions: two twin cinemas (Fayette Mall Cinema and Turfland Cinema) located in shopping malls and operated by the General Cinema Corporation (among the largest national circuits in this period, with theaters in every area of the country); a twin cinema (Crossroads Cinema) located in a small shopping center and operated by Associated Theatres of Kentucky (a small corporation with theaters mainly in the Lexington and Louisville areas); and two multicinemas (North Park Cinema 6 and South Park Cinema 6) operated by Mid-States Theatres and located in large shopping centers on opposite sides of town. (All of these later became part

of the extensive USA Cinema chain, which now monopolizes the first-run theaters in the area.)

At various times in 1980–1982, each of these theaters tried to establish itself as a prime midnight movie venue, and on occasion two or three featured midnight movies on the same weekend. With few exceptions, the multicinema and mall cinema playdates were between October and April (roughly coinciding with the school year and the change in seasons). These playdates reached a high of ninety-eight in 1981 and ninety-six in 1982, then fell off to seventy-four in 1983, forty-six in 1984, and twenty in 1985. After January 1983 only one mall cinema continued to book midnight movies, and during 1985 this theater presented midnight movies on just four weekends.

3. Six hundred and forty playdates at a 1,100-seat theater (Kentucky Theatre) in downtown Lexington, within a mile of the university campus. Owned by Associated Theatres of Kentucky, this theater—built in 1922 as a "picture palace" and renovated in 1980—operated since the mid-1970s as a repertory cinema, specializing in a mixture of classic Hollywood and foreign films, second-run releases of major American productions, and first-run foreign films and "independent" features that had attracted attention in the New York market. Midnight movies have consistently been part of its repertory strategy of appealing to different kinds of filmgoers in order to establish a regular clientele. Between 1980 and 1985, the Kentucky Theatre showed midnight movies every weekend, usually scheduling different films on Friday and Saturday. Although it featured *Rocky Horror* for an extended continuous midnight run in the late 1970s, in the period under discussion it did not hold any single film for several consecutive weeks.

In Lexington, the mall cinemas and multicinemas appear to have certain advantages as midnight movie venues. They are closer to middle-class, predominantly white residential areas (only one of the multicinemas mentioned earlier is located in a less affluent, racially mixed area, and that theater made only a cursory attempt to capture the midnight audience). They are familiar leisure-time sites; teenagers shop, play video games, and hang out at malls and have grown up going to see first-run films there. (It is all the more ironic, therefore, to watch the cultish *Dawn of the Dead* there, a film in which zombies gather at a mall because it was "the most important place in their lives.") A theater like the Kentucky, however, has a certain cachet that makes it particularly well suited for midnight movies: it is farther from home and apart from everyday haunts; in this respect it is comparable to the drive-in theaters, which also geared much of their programming toward a teenage market. Yet unlike the drive-ins, the Kentucky is as unique in its repertory scheduling as in its architecture, and it is located in an older area of downtown, one not yet gentrified or redeveloped. While hardly situated in the spectacular, perilous, and exciting ultraurban environment depicted in such popular midnight movies as *The Warriors* or *Blade Runner*, the Kentucky was in the early to mid-1980s next to an X-rated adult cinema and a gay bar; so as an afterhours site it was obviously less mundane and "legitimate"—and thus by certain standards far more appealing—than any mall or shopping center.

Unlike the mall cinemas and multicinemas, which attempted rather haphazardly to exploit a preexisting trend, the Kentucky entered the 1980s with an established tradition of midnight screenings. It had cornered—if not actually created—this market by allying itself with the area's most "progressive" FM rock music station, which targeted a similar audience of teenagers and college students. In fact, in exchange for free advertising, the station was billed as copromoter of the midnight movies and split whatever profits remained after the theater recouped its operating expenses and rental costs. In the 1980s the midnight movie was an important part of the Kentucky's programming strategy. The theater booked midnight movies year round—suggesting that it did not cater simply to college students— and thus always offered its regular customers a reliable, inexpensive option for late-night entertainment, even if this only meant providing a site for relatively unsupervised partying.

Although the mall cinemas and multicinemas offered a different type of filmgoing experience from the Kentucky, these theaters sought to attract the same basic audience for midnight movies. (Thus when *Rocky Horror* became available for rental in October 1983, a mall cinema booked it seventeen times in five months.) They primarily played films that had appeared or would appear at the Kentucky, especially favoring rock music films like *Quadrophenia, AC/DC: Let There Be Rock,* and *The Kids Are Alright;* comedies like *The Kentucky Fried Movie* and *Richard Pryor Live in Concert;* horror films like *Dawn of the Dead;* and feature-length animated films like *Wizards.* Their midnight programming also featured an odd assortment of films that apparently did not do enough business to warrant a return engagement (including some marginally likely candidates—*Roadie, Carrie, Young Frankenstein, Don't Look in the Basement, Rollerball,* and *Nosferatu, the Vampyre*—and some highly unlikely candidates—*The Godfather, Pretty Baby, The Main Event, What Do You Say to a Naked Lady?,* and *Enter the Dragon*). Only rarely did these theaters introduce a film that had been a successful midnight movie elsewhere, such as *Attack of the Killer Tomatoes.*

Such premieres occurred much more often at the Kentucky, which introduced a diverse collection of atypical, independently produced or distributed films like *Rockers, Polyester, Koyaanisqatsi, Cafe Flesh, Liquid Sky, Taxi zum Klo,* and *Repo Man.* While the Kentucky, as noted earlier, did not in the 1980s hold any of these films over for an extended midnight run, it did bring back successful films. For example, *Mad Max* played in October 1983, in December 1983, and again in July 1985; *An American Werewolf in London* showed twice in February 1982, again in June, July, and August of that year, in April and October 1983, in March, June, October, and November 1984, and in July 1985; and *Monty Python and the Holy Grail*—the midnight movie shown most often at the Kentucky—played twice in 1980, three times in 1981, five times in 1982, five times in 1983, six times in 1984, and ten times in 1985. All told, the Kentucky filled its 640 midnight play-dates with 219 different movies; 82 of these played only once, while *Monty Python and the Holy Grail, Pink Floyd: The Wall, Up in Smoke, Alien,* Led Zeppelin's *The Song Remains the Same,* and five other movies accounted for 166 playdates, or over 25 percent of the theater's total of midnight screenings.

Of those films booked into the Kentucky only once as midnight movies, the majority were a diverse array of recently released Hollywood comedies, horror films, "teenpix," and action/adventure films that also played in the theater's regular repertory schedule. These included *D.C. Cab, Knight-riders, Octopussy, The Dark Crystal, 16 Candles, Ghostbusters, The Jerk, Revenge of the Nerds, Trading Places, Spring Break, Christine, Night School, Beat Street,* and *Outland.* We might also note that among the Kentucky's one-time midnight movies were a number of revivals (*Dr. No, Golden Age of Looney Tunes, Yellow Submarine, Love and Death, M*A*S*H, Where's Poppa?, King of Hearts, Midnight Cowboy, Halloween, A Hard Day's Night, Woodstock,* and *Vixen*), as well as recent films that garnered some midnight movie success elsewhere in the nation (*Eating Raoul, Suburbia, Rockers, Slumber Party Massacre,* and *Rust Never Sleeps*).

The Kentucky maintained its policy of booking midnight movies every Friday and Saturday night, even after attendance at midnight screenings waned considerably in 1984–1985, causing the mall cinemas and multi-cinemas to abandon such programming. This shrinking market may be symptomatic of a conservative consensus in the mid-1980s; perhaps it simply shows that the relative novelty of the midnight movie experience had worn off, much in the fashion of the video arcade. According to the theater managers and booking agents I interviewed, the market shrunk because so many once-popular midnight movies—and movies that might have become successful at midnight—became available on videocassette. From this view, the commercial viability of such an exhibition policy is a matter of supply and demand, with the success of midnight screenings dependent on the product offered rather than on what has been termed the midnight movie's unique status as the "most social form of filmgoing" (Hoberman and Rosenbaum 301). (Another example of VCR's effect on film exhibition is the precipitous decline of adult cinemas following the availability of X-rated films at neighborhood video stores.)

We might also surmise that the introduction of cable television in the Lexington area in the early 1980s affected the after-hours movie market, if only because basic cable service soon included MTV (the music channel pitched at the same target audience as most midnight movies), which from eleven o'clock at night through dawn on Friday and Saturday offered its own version of midnight programming, combining music videos, "rocku-mentaries," camp classics (e.g., *Reefer Madness*), comedies, and horror films. In addition, the "premium" cable channels—HBO, Cinemax, Show-time, the Movie Channel—provided a steady diet of recently released comedies, teenpix, and horror films, as well as a range of movies that had been or were potential midnight movie hits. By the end of 1983, for ex-ample, *The Kids Are Alright, Woodstock, Gimme Shelter, Let It Be, Rude Boy, The Last Waltz, No Nukes, King of Hearts, Outrageous, Barbarella, Perfor-mance, Rock 'n' Roll High School, The Man Who Fell to Earth, Smithereens, The Groove Tube, The Kentucky Fried Movie,* and *Eating Raoul* had all ap-peared on one or more of the national pay cable channels; the films of Cheech and Chong and Monty Python were repeatedly scheduled, as were *National Lampoon's Animal House, A Clockwork Orange, Heavy Metal,* and *Alien,* all of which, we shall see, were among the most often booked mid-night movies during this period.[1]

The films cited so far suggest the range of midnight movies shown in Lexington between 1980 and 1985. Any category that includes both *Koyaanisqatsi* and *Cujo, The Warriors* and *Yellow Submarine,* or *Dawn of the Dead* and *D.C. Cab* is broad and heterogeneous indeed. But if we take into account the frequency with which individual films were booked and the principal genres that contributed to the "super genre" of the midnight movie, we can draw certain conclusions about the 1,216 playdates under consideration. The theater managers, film booking agents, and corporate executives I queried assumed without question that midnight movies form a special class of films, as well as a unique exhibition strategy. These ex-hibitors and distributors readily cited representative titles (*Rocky Horror, Monty Python and the Holy Grail, Dawn of the Dead, Tommy,* and *Stop Making Sense*) and genres ("crazy comedy," horror, rock movies, adven-ture films), and their comments sketch a preliminary framework within which to discuss the varieties of midnight movies. (The opinions of regular midnight moviegoers during the period would also be very useful in this regard, but as far as I know, there are no surveys of this information.) *The Rocky Horror Picture Show* was by far the most often shown midnight movie during this period. Out of 624 possible weekend playdates between 1980 and 1985, it was booked 251 times. It ran for twenty-one consecutive weeks at a small twin cinema, played at the Kentucky 25 times, and at a mall cinema 18 times. (Yet even *Rocky Horror* was not quite as ubiquitous as it seems, since it did not appear at any Lexington theater during seven months of 1981 and nine months of 1984.) Obviously, *Rocky Horror* cannot be discounted, but it does, I think, constitute a special case because of its astounding commercial longevity and vitality as an after-hours attraction, its reputation as a unique performance event, and its devoted, costumed fans. Whether *Rocky Horror* differs in kind or in degree from other successful midnight movies is the subject of another essay; *Rocky Horror* could be taken as both the supreme embodiment of or the anomalous exception to the mass of midnight movies in that it is a comedy, rock movie, and horror film, combining the three genres that have proved to be midnight programming's mainstays. (Perhaps this degree of hybridization is what led Gene Siskel and Roger Ebert in a recent "At the Movies" telecast to predict culthood for 1986's similarly recombinant *Little Shop of Horrors*.)

As further proof of its special status, *Rocky Horror* had by the mid-1980s been singled out and accorded the status of cultic and cultural phenomenon by the American media and analyzed by academic scholars in a way that *Monty Python and the Holy Grail* and *Up in Smoke,* for example, had not.[2] Even if we assume that *Rocky Horror,* culturally and formally, merits so much critical attention, what of those other films that make up the remaining 80 percent of the midnight playdates during this period? Using, with some modification and elaboration, certain commonly understood generic categories, we can begin to sort out the 965 non-*Rocky Horror* playdates under consideration.

Comedy: Eighty-seven different comedies filled 317 (or over 25 percent) of the midnight playdates between 1980 and 1985. Those comedies booked more than 10 times were *Monty Python and the Holy Grail* (37 screenings), *Up in Smoke* (21 screenings), *National Lampoon's Animal House* (18 screenings), *The Kentucky Fried Movie* (17 screenings), *Flesh Gordon* (12 screenings), and *Richard Pryor Live in Concert* (12 screenings).

These six films share little, if anything, with romantic comedies filled with misprision and repartee or with family-based television sit-coms structured around varied punchlines, likable character types, and mild-mannered homilies. By and large the most successful midnight movie comedies favor a loose, episodic structure with self-contained (and quotable, memorable) set pieces rather than intricate plotting. Their methods are the farcical gross-out, parody and overstatement, and the stand-up routine—precisely the battery of techniques popularized by late-night (quasi-midnight) television programs such as *Saturday Night Live, SCTV,* and *Fridays.* (*Monty Python and the Holy Grail* and *The Kentucky Fried Movie,* obvious precursors of this TV genre, gained new life on the midnight circuit.) They challenge or ridicule "good" taste, though never to the degree of, say, John Waters' films. But these films do offer very different versions of comically bad taste—a toga party is not the same as a "live" Richard Pryor monologue. Perhaps *Up in Smoke, Richard Pryor Live in Concert, The Kentucky Fried Movie,* and *Flesh Gordon* had their greatest midnight popularity in the ealy 1980s because their topical jokes about sex and drugs were less suited for the age of Reagan than were *Animal House'*s celebration of partying in the harmless early 1960s and *Monty Python and the Holy Grail'*s more absurd and timeless parodic intertextuality and antiromance.

Many of the other midnight movie offerings have readily apparent affinities with the top-ranking comedies listed above: *Cheech and Chong's Next Movie* was screened ten times (though *Still Smokin'* played only once); Monty Python's feature films after *Holy Grail* together appeared eleven times; *Caddyshack* (nine screenings), *The Blues Brothers* (seven screenings), and *Bachelor Party* (seven screenings) are in different ways linked to *Animal House; Airplane!* (ten screenings) combines parody with a string of comic vignettes; and *The Groove Tube* (seven screenings) is an obvious companion to *The Kentucky Fried Movie.* With this overall emphasis, it is hardly surprising that the only Woody Allen and Mel Brooks films to be shown more than once were *Everything You Always Wanted to Know about Sex* (five screenings) and *Blazing Saddles* (seven screenings).

The fact that comedy was deemed a particularly suitable genre for midnight movies is also demonstrated by the frequency with which bookers for Lexington theaters looked to comedies released in the 1980s as potential after-hours fare. Thus high-grossing films like *Ghostbusters, Trading Places, Stripes, Police Academy, National Lampoon's Vacation,* and even *Cannonball Run* appeared as midnight movies, though of these films only *Stripes* had as many as three screenings. Similarly, of the 1980s teenpix/coming-of-age comedies shown at midnight (including *16 Candles, Fast Times at Ridgemont High, Revenge of the Nerds,* and *Spring Break*), the only one moderately successful was *Risky Business* with five screenings. First-generation midnight movie comedies like *Fritz the Cat* and *Harold and Maude* did not fare much better (neither did camp "golden turkeys" like

Reefer Madness), and the three John Waters films brought to Lexington played a total of nine times. The most notable failure, though, may have been *Eating Raoul,* one of the few 1980s films to score big in the New York midnight market; it was booked just once in Lexington—fewer even than *Caveman* or *Top Secret.*

Rock movies: While there is some consensus among producers, distributors, exhibitors, critics, and consumers about which films fit into the genre of film comedy, "rock movies" constitute a less readily understood category. To discuss such a genre is to define it (even if only by enumerating its members) and to propose a heuristic construct that brings together a range of often very different films, linked by their common emphasis on or ties to rock music. For my purpose, rock movies include documentaries of rock concerts, usually complete with *vérité* backstage or hotel-room footage (the so-called "rockumentary"); what Scott Forsyth terms the "teen musical" (like *Fame* or *Footloose*); and a range of dramatic narratives based on rock music albums (*Tommy, Quadrophenia, Pink Floyd: The Wall*), on star rock performers playing themselves or some facsimile thereof (*A Hard Day's Night, Rock 'n' Roll High School, Purple Rain*), or on the adventures of a fictional rock performer (*The Rose, American Pop, Streets of Fire*). Fifty-one such films played 246 midnight dates from 1980 through 1985, and the most frequently shown were *Pink Floyd: The Wall* (30 screenings), *The Song Remains the Same* (24 screenings), *The Kids Are Alright* (20 screenings), *Tommy* (18 screenings), *Ladies and Gentlemen: The Rolling Stones* (12 screenings), and *AC/DC: Let There Be Rock* (10 screenings).

By far the most popular type of midnight rock movie was the "rockumentary," which accounted for 144 playdates. This predominance underscores the obvious parallels between the rock concert and the midnight movie; although it is a canned experience, the rockumentary shown after hours at least has the benefit of being an inexpensive, accessible, repeatable simulacrum of the real thing. Whether the performers are Jimi Hendrix, the Grateful Dead, Genesis, or Bette Midler, these films seldom display any of the stylistic flashiness that marks even run-of-the-mill performance music videos (not to mention the more overtly "experimental" or "conceptual" videos) that emerged in the 1980s as a cable television staple. That *AC/DC: Let There Be Rock* generated more bookings than any other rockumentary released during the 1980s begins to suggest that the dominant chord in this sort of midnight movie was guitar-oriented hard rock, particularly what might be called the "canonical" British tradition: the Rolling Stones, the Who, and Led Zeppelin. This hegemony has only recently been challenged by *Stop Making Sense,* the Talking Heads concert film, which played six times when it was released in 1985 and has since become a consistent midnight attraction.

Films featuring Jimi Hendrix, the Grateful Dead, and Yes appeared only three times each, as did Neil Young's *Rust Never Sleeps*. Three different documentaries about the Beatles, including *Let It Be*, were booked a total of five times (and *Yellow Submarine* and *A Hard Day's Night* each screened but once). The Band's *The Last Waltz*, which played twice, and *No Nukes* (featuring Bruce Springsteen), which played three times, proved to be no more popular than *Woodstock* and *Gimme Shelter*, two seminal accounts of the rock concert cum cultural happening in the Age of Aquarius. Yet more recent concert films about the Rolling Stones—and less critically praised ones—played fourteen times (and, interestingly, by far the most successful of them was *Ladies and Gentlemen*, a 1975 film of a 1972 concert). And the Who, outside the confines of *Woodstock*, were something of a midnight movie mainstay with forty-four bookings between their greatest hits compilation, *The Kids Are Alright*, and the film versions of their concept albums, *Tommy* and *Quadrophenia*. However, the number one rockumentary was Led Zeppelin's *The Song Remains the Same* (released in 1976), which blended concert footage from a 1973 performance and floridly dramatic, ostensibly dreamlike narrative interludes set in exotic locations. No doubt the popularity of *The Song Remains the Same* came in part from the almost legendary status granted the disbanded Led Zeppelin by album-oriented FM rock stations (thus their songs *did* remain the same, like the classic songs featured in the Who and Rolling Stones rockumentaries) and possibly from the fact that the film—like a proto–music video—surrounds and illustrates its concert footage with liberal doses of latter-day psychedelia.

The only rock movie booked more often than *The Song Remains the Same* and *The Kids Are Alright* was *Pink Floyd: The Wall*, whose thirty bookings are especially significant since it did not become available for midnight screenings until the end of 1982. As its title indicates, *Pink Floyd: The Wall* is the legacy of a 1970s supergroup, and the film is intended to tap an audience that had made Pink Floyd albums among the most successful releases of the 1970s. It is surely the most ambitious and pretentious midnight rock movie; its portrait of the rock star as a young man includes echoes of *Metropolis* and *Triumph of the Will*, animated interludes, and highly stylized nightmare/fantasy sequences. Presumably, *The Wall* appealed to midnight audiences because it elaborately visualizes a well-known concept album (like *Tommy* in this regard) and offers a potentially relevant (though hardly ground-breaking or revolutionary) critique of adult authoritarianism, schools, militarism, and the perils of life in the fast lane.

No other rock movies came close to matching the popularity of *The Wall*, *Tommy*, and the top rockumentaries. *Hair* (seven screenings), *Purple Rain* (six screenings), and even *Jesus Christ, Superstar* (five screenings, coinciding with Christmas and Easter) were shown more often than films obviously produced for the youth market, like *Footloose* and *Rock 'n' Roll High School*, or than supposedly more "realistic" films like *Fame* and *The Rose*. As with the midnight comedies, these and other rock movies that failed to establish themselves in the midnight marketplace form a revealing group, including, besides the films mentioned earlier (*Woodstock, Gimme Shelter, A Hard Day's Night, The Last Waltz*), *Rude Boy*, featuring the Clash, the reggae film *Rockers*, and the rap music/breakdancing film *Beat Street*, all of which were screened only once. Furthermore, the most famous of all reggae films, *The Harder They Come*, and the hard-core punk music film, *D.O.A.*, never made it to the Lexington midnight circuit between 1980 and 1985.

Horror: Of the forty-two different horror films that accounted for 142 midnight movie playdates in 1980–1985, only *Dawn of the Dead* (28 screenings) and *An American Werewolf in London* (15 screenings) emerged as consistently successful.[3] These are two very different films, though both mix black comedy with horror: *American Werewolf* prominently features well-known rock songs, tongue-in-cheek dialogue, and state-of-the-art special effects, particularly in its man-into-wolf transformation scenes; whereas *Dawn of the Dead*—far more a satiric social fable—depicts a violent struggle for survival and shows off its special effects in scenes of cannibalism, dismemberment, and extermination.

If *Dawn of the Dead* and *American Werewolf* dominate the horror film entries in the midnight movie marketplace, it is not because Lexington theater bookers ignored other examples of the genre. On the contrary, twenty-eight different horror films released in the late 1970s and 1980s were screened at midnight, including *Halloween, Friday the 13th, Phantasm, Psycho II, Christine, Videodrome, Humanoids from the Deep, A Nightmare on Elm Street, Tourist Trap, The Shining*, and *Slumber Party Massacre*. But none of these was shown more than twice. Besides *American Werewolf*, the only 1980s examples of the genre to perform even moderately well as midnight movies were *Poltergeist* (four screenings) and *The Hunger* (five screenings). Once again, certain failures are noteworthy. *Basket Case*, like *Eating Raoul*, had an extended midnight run in New York, but was booked only twice in Lexington.

As for the low-budget, taboo-shattering, notoriously gore-filled horror films that proved so popular on the 1970s midnight circuit, *Night of the Living Dead, The Texas Chain Saw Massacre*, and *Last House on the Left* were each booked about as many times as *The Hunger* and fewer than *The Exorcist* (eight screenings), while none of Herschell Gordon Lewis's splatter movies made it to Lexington. Local theater owners looked even less frequently to classic horror, playing *Freaks* but once and *The Creature from the Black Lagoon* three times; and *Creature* was apparently booked not as a horror film but as a 3-D revival, along with *The Mask, 13 Ghosts,* and *It Came from Outer Space.*

Science fiction: Accounting for 150 midnight playdates were twenty-nine science fiction films (which in this case means simply any film set in the future or involving time travel or an encounter with extraterrestrials). Fewer different examples of this genre were screened than comedies, rock movies, and horror films, partly because programmers had fewer recently released science fiction films to choose from. Top-grossing, heavily merchandised, PG-rated, special-effects blockbusters have almost no place in the after-hours market; thus the *Star Wars* films and *Close Encounters of the Third Kind* never played midnight dates, and three *Star Trek* films together played nine times. *2001* and *Barbarella,* which after their initial release in the late 1960s achieved some measure of cult renown, each appeared but twice, no more often than 1980s releases like *Altered States, Escape from New York,* and the "new" *Metropolis.* And, more surprising, of the new wave of quirky and stylistically ingenious science fiction, only *Liquid Sky* had as many as six screenings, while *Repo Man,* the X-rated *Cafe Flesh,* and *The Adventures of Buckaroo Banzai* were booked at midnight three times each. Even *Eraserhead* (more surrealistic than science fictional) was booked only three times, a far cry from the popularity it achieved elsewhere as a midnight movie.

The science fiction films that appeared repeatedly as midnight movies form a diverse group: *Wizards* (twenty-six screenings), *A Clockwork Orange* (fifteen screenings), *Alien* (thirteen screenings), *Heavy Metal* (thirteen screenings), and *The Road Warrior* (nine screenings). *Alien,* for example, could just as well be termed a horror film, for it principally concerns a suspenseful, violent, life-or-death battle against a malevolent, monstrous Other. A good case can be made that *A Clockwork Orange,* for all its connections to a literary tradition of satiric, dystopian science fiction, gained success on the midnight circuit as what Hoberman and Rosenbaum call the prototypical "punxploitation" movie (287). The iconography of punk also figures prominently in *Blade Runner* (seven screenings), which did not approach the degree of midnight success that it achieved in New York, and in *The Road Warrior* (and the two other *Mad Max* films, which together played a total of five times). *The Road Warrior* contains the potentially disruptive, antisocial, subcultural power of punk within a narrative of a postholocaust struggle for survival, complete with the reconstruction of a mythical hero and the reaffirmation of communal values.

The after-hours popularity of *Heavy Metal* and *Wizards* was due, at least in part, to the fact that they are animated films, for animated features and anthologies found a home on the midnight movie circuit, following in the wake of 1970s midnight movies like *Fritz the Cat* (five screenings) and *Heavy Traffic* (two screenings). The fourteen animated films shown in Lexington accounted for fifty-three playdates (and, we might note, both *Monty Python and the Holy Grail* and *Pink Floyd: The Wall* include animated sequences). *Heavy Metal*, like *Rocky Horror* and *The Wall*, is a hybrid text; it combines R-rated vignettes—futuristic sex, violence, and dark comedy— with a rock music soundtrack. *Wizards* is a quite different case, though it too is something of a tour de force in its variety of animation techniques and incorporation of live-action film footage. Like *The Road Warrior*, *Wizards* begins with the premise that a nuclear holocaust is our inescapable fate; like *A Clockwork Orange*, it satirizes traditional religion and the machinations of the State; like *The Wall*, which equates frenzied spectators at rock concerts with hero-worshipping neofascists, *Wizards* is something of a critique of midnight moviegoing, for its villain's supreme weapon is a motion-picture projector that screens mesmerizing fragments of Nazi propaganda films. In the end, however, *Wizards* opts for neither unending struggle nor punk nihilism; magic, irreverent but morally correct, happily wins the day over technology.

Action-Adventure, drama, sexploitation: It is tempting to dismiss those midnight movies that are not comedies, rock movies, horror, or science fiction as simply "miscellaneous," but there are some important distinctions among the other types that occupy the remaining playdates. Of the forty-eight playdates filled, twenty-two were devoted to what the industry terms action-adventure films, a category encompassing 1980s releases like *Beverly Hills Cop* and *Conan the Barbarian*, two Indiana Jones films, and several James Bond films. Besides *48 Hours* (five screenings), the only film of this type to have more than three playdates was *The Warriors* (twelve screenings), which has less in common with *Raiders of the Lost Ark* and *The Spy Who Loved Me* than with the ultraviolence and stylized tribalism of *A Clockwork Orange* and *The Road Warrior*. Another handful of films shown once or twice after hours might rather loosely be called "realistic" dramas, ranging from *Midnight Cowboy* and *One Flew Over the Cuckoo's Nest* to *A Small Circle of Friends* and *The Breakfast Club*. Finally, ten playdates were filled by soft-core sexploitation movies like *Emmanuelle*, *Story of O*, and the

New York Erotic Film Festival. (Note, in contrast, that R-rated sexploitation triple features were standard drive-in theater fare during the 1970s and early 1980s, suggesting that the partying carried on at a midnight movie screening required a different sort of cinematic catalyst and accompaniment than the partying done at the drive-in.)

Do midnight movies constitute a genre? Or put in more general terms, should a group of films that share no obvious iconographic code, narrative structure, thematic preoccupations, or "inventory of options" (to use Todorov's phrase) be considered a genre simply because they all have been exhibited in a manner quite distinct from the motion-picture industry's standard mode of exhibition in any given period of film history? Have any groups of films been understood in this way by audiences, producers, exhibitors, or critics? The Saturday matinee could be taken as an example of genre-by-exhibition, for its array of products included cartoons, serials, B-westerns, and low-budget comedy series like the Bowery Boys or Abbott and Costello films. So could the "foreign art film" of the 1950s and early 1960s when, say, *La Strada* and *The Seventh Seal* were thought of together partly because of how they were exhibited to American audiences (see Tudor).

Midnight moviegoers, like other filmgoers and consumers, are free to choose where to spend their money, but their options are limited from the outset and from the outside. They are offered a limited selection (in Lexington between 1980 and 1985 this meant, for example, no *Performance, D.O.A., Myra Breckinridge, Fellini Satyricon,* or *The Harder They Come*). Yet they become a directly determining factor, since the films they patronize will be booked—revived—again and again, so long as 35 millimeter prints are available and the films turn a profit. (The paying customers at a first-run multicinema can in part determine how many weeks a particular film might be booked, but not whether the film will be repeatedly revived after its first run.) Thus while any movie screened after hours Friday or Saturday and advertised as a "midnight show" thereby becomes a "midnight movie," it is probably more accurate—and surely more useful—to say that those movies shown frequently at midnight constitute the ever-alterable genre of midnight movies as created (and understood) jointly by exhibitors and audiences. This genre, as the preceding market analysis indicates, includes horror films, comedies, rock movies, and science fiction, and like these "traditional" genres, the midnight movie is marked by variation as well as repetition, diversity as well as uniformity.

While I do not propose to analyze the ideological workings or formal characteristics of such a genre, I would like to suggest some parameters for such analysis. A formal analysis of the midnight movie might begin by pursuing the following topics:

1. The number of these films that operate reflexively to address the conditions of midnight moviegoing, including images of what it means to participate in the "social experience" of a collective audience (the fans and groupies in rockumentaries or *The Wall*) and to be partygoers (*Animal House*), manipulated movie viewers (*Wizards*, *A Clockwork Orange*), and "virginal" or experienced spectators (*Rocky Horror*).

2. The extent to which midnight movies offer teenagers or college students as protagonists and directly treat late-adolescent preoccupations and problems (*Quadrophenia*, *The Warriors*, *American Werewolf*, *Animal House*, and, of course, many of the songs in the rockumentaries), usually with the important proviso that in the end "the kids are alright."

3. The foregrounding of all manner of excess, from the structure of comic vignettes in *Monty Python and the Holy Grail* or extended monologues in *Richard Pryor Live in Concert*, the costumes and choreographed ultraviolence in *A Clockwork Orange* and *The Warriors*, the voracious undead masses and unrestrained mayhem in *Dawn of the Dead*, and the stylistic flamboyance of *Tommy*, *Wizards*, and *The Wall*, to the protean monster in *Alien*, the guitar solos in *AC/DC: Let There Be Rock*, the sexual escapades of *Flesh Gordon*, the mise-en-scene of *Heavy Metal*, and the drug subculture of Cheech and Chong.

4. The relation between excess and bad taste; the varieties of tastelessness, impropriety, and dirtiness and the concomitant assumptions about what constitutes good taste and thus "adult" conduct, values, and goals.

5. The oppositional spirit expressed in these films, whether in the form of parody (*Flesh Gordon*, *The Kentucky Fried Movie*, *Airplane!*, *Monty Python and the Holy Grail*), overt criticism of social institutions and cultural priorities (*Dawn of the Dead*, *Alien*, *Wizards*, *The Wall*), or the ridiculing of adult authority figures (*Up in Smoke*, *Animal House*); as a corollary, the relationship between these films and 1960s countercultural aspirations and fears.

6. The midnight movies as alternatives to coherent, plausible (and, again, by implication "adult") narrative, especially in its commitment to episodic fragmentation, comic or satiric exaggeration, and the primacy of the detachable set piece or "number" (even within goal-directed narratives like *American Werewolf*, *Alien*, and *Dawn of the Dead*).

Ideally, a description of the midnight movie phenomenon between 1980 and 1985 and an interpretation of the midnight movie as a genre would be based on a comprehensive examination of this exhibition practice and the audiences it attracted throughout the United States during this period.[4] Such an ambitious project is well beyond the scope of this essay, though a brief survey of the midnight movie booking patterns in a major market like New York City can begin to put my preceding regional analysis into a somewhat broader context.

With several Manhattan theaters committed to midnight programming and an obviously much larger and more cosmopolitan market, the midnight movie exhibition strategies in New York during 1980–1985 differ in certain important ways from those in Lexington.[5] Two theaters owned by the Walter Reade Organization, the New Yorker (with two screens) and the Waverly (which by 1983 had become a two-screen theater) were committed almost exclusively to booking extended consecutive runs of a single film, with the model, of course, being *Rocky Horror*, which had played at the New Yorker throughout the later 1970s and continued through 1984. (It premiered as a midnight movie at the Waverly in 1976.) Both of these theaters consistently looked to recently released films from outside the mainstream of commercial filmmaking in search of what Hoberman and Rosenbaum call "the fashionable must-see" midnight attraction (314). During this period the New Yorker featured, for example, *Rock 'n' Roll High School*, *D.O.A.*, and *Basket Case*. Continuing a run begun in 1979, the Waverly's midnight movie for 1980 and much of 1981 was *Eraserhead*; then between 1981 and 1985 its longest-running movies were *Basket Case*, *Eating Raoul*, and *Liquid Sky*, while it also offered for briefer engagements *Forbidden Zone*, *Slumber Party Massacre*, *The Alternative Miss World* (featuring Divine), *The 4th Man*, *The Adventures of Buckaroo Banzai*, and *Stop Making Sense*. As I have noted, several of these films were booked by Lexington theaters, but only *Stop Making Sense* proved to be successful enough to warrant repeat engagements at the regional level.

The other distinctive characteristic of the New York market was that two primary midnight movie venues—both independently owned and operated—initiated a policy of booking midnight movies in repertory fashion seven days a week. (This policy in itself is revealing since it targets an audience which doesn't assume that the weekend, as countless rock songs insist, is the privileged time for partying.) The 8th Street Playhouse went from weekend screenings of *Rocky Horror*, which had played there since 1978, to a repertory-style, full-week midnight schedule in July 1980 and continued it throughout the period. The St. Mark's Cinema adopted a similar strategy between February 1983 and September 1985. The 8th Street's weekly midnight schedule always included *Rocky Horror* and, after March 1983, *Pink Floyd: The Wall* as well. This theater also consistently booked *A Clockwork Orange*, *The Song Remains the Same*, and *Pink Flamingos*, featured *Cafe Flesh* for nine straight months in 1983–1984, and at different times regularly ran *Performance, The Texas Chain Saw Massacre, The Hunger, Head* (featuring the Monkees), William Blatty's *Twinkle, Twinkle, Killer Kane,* and a few X-rated features (*Roommates, Blonde Ambition*). The St. Mark's midnight schedule was anchored by *Blade Runner,* which ran for 139 consecutive weeks, but otherwise it was decidedly eclectic (and often inspired), mixing revivals, rockumentaries, older Hollywood films (like *Taxi Driver*), recent commercial releases, independent productions, and even foreign films from directors like Fellini and Herzog. In one week, the St. Marks midnight offerings could include Fellini's *Amarcord, Blade Runner, A Boy and His Dog, Paris, Texas, The Terminator,* and *The Tenant* (May 1985), or *D.O.A., Videodrome, Blade Runner, The Road Warrior, Nosferatu, the Vampyre, Lightning over Water* (a Wim Wenders documentary), and *Rock 'n' Roll High School* (June 1983).

This brief look at the booking patterns of the major New York midnight movie theaters between 1980 and 1985 reveals by way of contrast the more conservative nature of the Lexington midnight market. Aside from *A Clockwork Orange* and the Mad Max films, movies that in different ways embody what advertisers and reviewers call a "punk" or "new wave" sensibility and style (e.g., *D.O.A., Cafe Flesh,* and *Liquid Sky*) did not attract a large Lexington after-hours audience in that period. Neither did *Basket Case, Eating Raoul,* and *Eraserhead,* or holdovers from the previous decade like *Performance* and *Pink Flamingos. Rocky Horror, A Clockwork Orange, Pink Floyd: The Wall, The Song Remains the Same,* and to a lesser degree *Blade Runner* scored well in both markets. Yet comedies and horror films figured much more prominently in Lexington midnight movie programming than in New York, as witnessed by the fact that for the 8th Street Playhouse or the St. Mark's Cinema, *Monty Python and the Holy Grail,* Cheech and Chong's films, *Animal House, Dawn of the Dead,* and *American Werewolf* were at best occasional midnight features rather than repeatedly booked mainstays.

While it is important to note these differences in midnight programming from city to city and region to region, the data presented here begin to suggest the broad characteristics of this exhibition strategy in a period when independently owned repertory cinemas and theater chains specializing in multicinema venues were beginning to confront the VCR/cable TV "revolution." Though certain transgressive, subversive cult movies did find a home in the 1980s on the midnight circuit—particularly in the New York market—it is important to distinguish between such cult films and the midnight movie. And—pace *Rocky Horror*—it is also essential to note the distinctions between the most successful midnight movies of the 1970s and those of the 1980s. These distinctions can be seen when we consider midnight movies as a subcultural (or even, on occasion, a countercultural) genre. A necessary next step is to contextualize this genre by analyzing midnight movies against the backdrop of the transformation of popular film genres—particularly horror, comedy, and coming-of-age movies—in the 1980s, and by examining the relation between midnight movies as practice and product and the commercial breakthrough of a new wave of independent American feature films from *Eraserhead* to *Repo Man* and *Stranger Than Paradise*. These are movies that challenge our older, conventional distinctions and, in the process, our established ways of marketing—and seeing—films.

APPENDIX
▬▬

The following is a list of films booked ten or more times as midnight movies in Lexington from 1980 through 1985. The films are listed according to frequency of bookings.

The Rocky Horror Picture Show (1975). R-rated. 20th Century-Fox. Dir.: Jim Sharman. 251 screenings.
Monty Python and the Holy Grail (1974). PG-rated. Cinema 5. Dir.: Terry Gilliam. 37 screenings.
Pink Floyd: The Wall (1982). R-rated. MGM/United Artists. Dir.: Alan Parker. 30 screenings.
Dawn of the Dead (1979). Unrated. Laurel/United Film. Dir.: George Romero. 28 screenings.
Wizards (1977). PG-rated. 20th Century-Fox. Dir.: Ralph Bakshi. 26 screenings.
The Song Remains the Same (1976). PG-rated. Warner Brothers. Dir.: Peter Clifton, Joe Massot. 24 screenings.
Up in Smoke (1978). R-rated. Paramount. Dir.: Lou Adler. 21 screenings.
The Kids Are Alright (1979). PG-rated. Dir.: Jeff Stein. 20 screenings.
Tommy (1975). PG-rated. Columbia. Dir.: Ken Russell. 18 screenings.
National Lampoon's Animal House (1978). R-rated. Universal. Dir.: John Landis. 18 screenings.
The Kentucky Fried Movie (1977). R-rated. United Film. Dir.: John Landis. 17 screenings.
A Clockwork Orange (1971). R-rated. Warner Brothers. Dir.: Stanley Kubrick. 15 screenings.
An American Werewolf in London (1981). R-rated. Universal. Dir.: John Landis. 15 screenings.
Heavy Metal (1981). R-rated. Columbia. Dir.: Gerald Potterton. 13 screenings.
Alien (1979). R-rated. 20th Century-Fox. Dir.: Ridley Scott. 13 screenings.
The Warriors (1979). R-rated. Paramount. Dir.: Walter Hill. 12 screenings.

Ladies and Gentlemen: The Rolling Stones (1975). Unrated. Dragon Aire. Dir.: Rollin Binzer. 12 screenings.
Flesh Gordon (1974). X-rated. Mammoth. Dir.: Michael Benveniste and Howard Ziehm. 12 screenings.
Richard Pryor Live in Concert (1979). R-rated. Universal. Dir.: Jeff Margolis. 12 screenings.
AC/DC: Let There Be Rock (1982). PG-rated. Warner Brothers. Dir.: Eric Dionysius and Eric Mistler. 10 screenings.
Cheech and Chong's Next Movie (1980). R-rated. Universal. Dir.: Thomas Chong. 10 screenings.
Airplane! (1980). PG-rated. Paramount. Dir.: Jim Abrahams, David Zucker, and Jerry Zucker. 10 screenings.
Quadrophenia (1979). R-rated. World Northal. Dir.: Franc Roddam. 10 screenings.

NOTES

1. The Movie Channel even reserved the Friday midnight slot for what it advertised as "Friday Movie Madness," a series that in February 1984, for example, featured *The Rutles, 200 Motels, Alice's Restaurant,* and *The Man Who Fell to Earth.*
2. See, for example, Twitchell and Austin.
3. In weighing these figures, we should note that the independently produced and distributed *Dawn of the Dead,* originally released in 1979, did not appear on videocassette until 1984 and never played on pay cable television, while Universal's heavily promoted *American Werewolf*—released in August 1981—became available for midnight screenings in January 1982 and soon thereafter appeared on pay cable and in video stores.
4. The handful of articles on midnight movies in trade magazines provide only general suggestions of the characteristics of this national phenomenon. See Ginsburg, Robbins, and Cohn.
5. For background on the midnight movie market in New York, see Cohn, and especially Hoberman and Rosenbaum, who also bemoan the "poverty" of the New York after-hours movie scene in comparison with that of Paris and London.

WORKS CITED

Austin, Bruce A. "Portrait of a Cult Film Audience: *The Rocky Horror Picture Show.*" *Journal of Communications* 31 (1981): 45–56.
Cohn, Lawrence. "10 Years of U.S. Offbeat 'Midnight Movies' Phenom." *Variety,* Nov. 5, 1980.
Corrigan, Timothy. "Film and the Culture of Cult." *Wide Angle* 8, nos. 3–4 (1986): 91–99. (Revised version is reprinted in this volume.)
Forsyth, Scott. "Fathers, Feminism, and Domination: Marxist Theory on Ideology in Popular Film." *CineAction!* 2 (1985): 28–37.
Ginsberg, Steven. "Midnight Shows Worth $1,000,000 Per Wk., $3 Top." *Variety,* Jan. 28, 1981.

Hoberman, J., and Jonathan Rosenbaum. *Midnight Movies.* New York: Harper & Row, 1983.

Robbins, Jim. "Midnight Movies." *Box Office,* Jan. 14, 1980.

Tudor, Andrew. "Genre." In *Film Genre Reader,* ed. Barry Keith Grant, 3–10. Austin: Univ. of Texas Press, 1986.

Twitchell, James B. "*Frankenstein* and the Anatomy of Horror." *Georgia Review* 37 (1983): 41–78.

CHAPTER 14

Gnosticism and the Cult Film

David Lavery

Beam me up, Scotty. There's no intelligent life down here.

Just visiting this planet.   —1980s bumper stickers

[Modern nihilism is] infinitely more radical and more desperate than gnostic nihilism ever could be for all its panic terror of the world and its defiant contempt of its laws. That nature does not care, one way or the other, is the true abyss. That only man cares, in his finitude facing nothing but death, alone with his contingency and the objective meaninglessness of his projected meanings, is a truly unprecedented situation.

—Hans Jonas, The Gnostic Religion

The real horror of our present condition," Peter Marin has suggested, is "not merely the absence of community or the isolation of the self—those, after all, have been part of the American condition for a long time." Rather, he insists, it is "the loss of the ability to remember what is missing, the diminishment of our vision of what is humanly possible or desirable." What afflicts us is a kind of spiritual amnesia:

In our new myths we begin to deny once and for all the existence of what we once believed both possible and good. We proclaim our grief-stricken narcissism to be a form of liberation; we define as enlightenment our broken faith with the world. Already forgetful of what it means to be fully human, we sip still again from Lethe, the river of forgetfulness, hoping to erase the memory of pain. Lethe, lethal, lethargy—all those words suggest a kind of death, one that in religious usage is sometimes called accidie. It is a condition one can find in many places and in many ages, but only in

America and only recently, have we begun to confuse it with a state of grace. (48, my italics)

The particular form of contemporary myth we now call the "cult film" seems an especially adept medium for recording this confusion. Indeed, in this era in which it has become possible to believe that we are "just visiting this planet," we might say that "our broken faith with the world" is one of this inherently "spacy" genre's natural themes, a theme which its very sociology seems to sanction.

In his essay on the subject, Umberto Eco insists that it is now worse than useless to search for Jungian archetypes in contemporary film—so self-conscious are today's "semiotically nourished authors working for a culture of instinctive semioticians." Thus Eco declares his semiotic faith that all "works are created by works" and "texts . . . created by texts," that "all together they speak to each other independently of the intention of their authors." And the cult movie in particular he takes to be definitive proof that, "as literature comes from literature, cinema comes from cinema" (11).

But this essay springs from a different faith: that in tracing the intellectual roots of the ideas inherited and displayed in the cult film, we perform a worthy piece of intellectual detective work, one equal in value to the often bankrupt, ahistorical, apolitical, aesthetic solipsism of our contemporary obsession with signs and signifiers.

Eco speaks of a cult film like *Casablanca* as "a palimpsest for future students of twentieth-century religiosity" (3). Following Eco's hint, I would like to imagine—as a thought experiment—such a latter-day student of the cult film, not, however, with the postmodernist intent advocated by Eco of merely conducting "semiotic research into textual strategies" but of pursuing what might be called a "memeotic" investigation into the possible premodernist cultural origins of the cult film.[1] Eco would have us believe that in the "cosmic result" of the cult film we can sometimes miraculously overhear the "clichés" (that is, the "archetypal" signs) "talking among themselves, celebrating a reunion." We are struck by the impression that "Nature has spoken in place of men" (10). I would argue that the voices we sometimes hear in the cult film are not the work of some "cosmic" ventriloquist but have identifiable human and historical origins.

Bud. There's going to be some bad shit coming down one of these days.
Otto. Yeah, and where are you going to be then? On the moon?
Bud. No, I'm going to be right here, doing 110 flat out.　　—*Repo Man*

Imagine you are a cultural anthropologist from a future century (the late twenty-second) who has just participated in the excavation of a site believed to have once been a late twentieth-century public place known as a shopping mall. Inside one of the stores, a nearly destroyed building, you unearth four small, plastic black boxes containing some kind of tightly wound tape. Thanks to your knowledge of the material culture of that era, you know that these boxes are videocassettes, containing films (as the labels indicate) from the late 1970s and 1980s—twenty years into that period which history has come to call "The Space Age." Excited by this find, you secret them away from the dig, anxious to study them in private. Reputations, you know, are made from such discoveries, and anthropologists and historians have long sought a better understanding of the mad, paradoxical, decadent, spacy period to which the artifacts you now hold may provide a key.

The display case housing them, you recall, had been marked "Cult Film," though nothing in your reference books enables you to understand precisely what such a designation might mean. Other shelves in the store likewise bore the names of the kinds of films housed there—for example, "Children's," "Science Fiction," "Horror," "Action-Adventure," "Drama"— all categories the basic nature of which are clear enough, familiar as you are with the concept of "genre films" in the latter half of the twentieth century. A "genre," you recall, refers to a particular grouping of movies sharing a common set of conventions and expectations, either as the result of a film's authorship or because of its audience's anticipation of certain recognizable meanings which result from its close relationship to other films of its type.

"Cult Film," however, is a classification unknown to you. A computer bibliographical search discloses that several books and articles were in fact published on cult films in the 1980s, including at least one scholarly anthology, but none, it seems, survives. In the absence of more precise knowledge, you therefore conclude that (1) "cult film" is also the name of some genre or recognizable (in its day) type of film; (2) this genre, whatever its form and content, must have been an ephemeral one and did not endure long enough to "go down in history"; (3) such films may have been intended for special audiences, made to appeal to one or more of the many cults—religious, psychological, and scientific/technological—known to have proliferated in the 1970s and 1980s, a period famous for its efforts at producing a counterculture.

Fortunately, you know where to find an ancient but still operative "videocassette recorder" on which to play them back. With utter fascination, you watch the four "videos," studying them carefully with an anthropologist's eye, hoping to learn about that period's culture. For next to garbage dumps, the received wisdom of your discipline teaches, films, even inferior films (often labeled "trash" in the twentieth century), are thought to be the best mirrors of the popular attitudes and "life-styles" of the time and place of their making. A popular art like the movies can in fact be a fascinating revelation of the often unconscious controlling metaphors of a culture, of its mythological self-understanding. As you watch, you especially note the following points.

In the first film, a man appears mysteriously in the American Southwest. In one early scene, he slides down a long hill, battling the scree unsuccessfully as if being pulled toward the valley below. You learn that this stranger, Thomas Newton, is actually an alien who has journeyed to Earth from a drought-ridden planet in search of water. Using his own advanced technology, he succeeds in making hundreds of millions of dollars in worldly business ventures, money he hopes to use to finance a rescue mission for his native planet. His attempts to do so are, however, constantly frustrated by human avarice, government interference, personal betrayal, and his own loss of motivation.

In flashbacks, Newton dimly recalls his apparently happy life with his family on his desert-covered home world.

At one point, he decides to reveal his true form to his girl friend, Mary Lou. Removing his disguise—contact lenses, fake nails, artificial nipples, a wig—he finally stands before her as he truly is, naked, no longer masquerading as an earthling. Though fabulously wealthy, Newton more and more becomes an eccentric recluse. Seduced by the world, he turns to alcohol, sex, and television to numb his guilt over his failed mission.

In the second film, a mad scientist, a colleague of the man who developed the neutron bomb and himself the victim of a frontal lobotomy, drives all over the American Southwest in a Chevy Malibu with kidnapped dead aliens in its trunk. His motives are obscure, but he seems intent on making their existence public against the government's wishes. When the car's trunk is opened, the radiation emanating from the aliens causes anyone looking on to immediately disintegrate.

The main character, a young man named Otto, takes a job stealing cars professionally for "The Helping Hand Acceptance Corporation," a company which engages in an inexplicable activity (from which the film gets its name) known as "automobile repossession."

Before joining this new group, and occasionally thereafter, Otto "hangs out" with a crowd whom (thanks to your knowledge of the period) you readily identify as belonging to a cult known as "punk rockers."

A veteran car thief (Bud) takes Otto under his wing and teaches him the ethics and mores of his new profession. He also initiates him into some of the secret knowledge of the group—for example, when to take a drug known as amphetamines (all the time) and the meaninglessness of day and night. Bud and Otto, along with many other car-stealers, search for the Malibu, on which a $20,000 award (roughly equivalent at the time to a year's living wage) has been offered. Their search—and an unnamed government agency's equally energetic efforts to secure the vehicle—constitute the basic "plot" of the video.

Throughout, you note that labels on goods sold in stores and consumed in people's homes are singularly nondescript (for example, "Food," "Good," and "Drink") while—oddly enough—the characters themselves have taken on the names of what you know to be actual commercial products of the period (all of them types of an alcoholic beverage known as "beer"): "Bud," "Miller," "Oly," and "Lite."

A janitor named Miller—rumored to have taken too many hallucinogenic drugs in the 1960s and convinced that "Everybody's into weirdness"—explains his faith in the "lattice of coincidence" that unites all events. He proselytizes Otto on behalf of his theory that all missing persons have been abducted and carried away to the future by flying saucers, which are in reality time machines. He also refuses (presciently) to learn to drive a car because "The more you drive, the less intelligent you are" (a hypothesis which, of course, you now know to be absolutely true).

When the Malibu, turned white hot and nearly translucent from radiation, becomes unapproachable by interested scientists, this philosopher is, for some reason, the only one able to enter it. ("Just going for a little spin," he explains.) When Otto boards it upon Miller's invitation, the Malibu ascends into the heavens, levitating straight upward, cruises over the Los Angeles skyline ("This is intense!" Otto observes, as he looks down upon the city of confusion below), and then—in classic *Star Wars* fashion—attains warp speed and disappears from the screen in a flash of light in the film's last image.

In the third film, a tiny flying saucer, less than two feet in diameter, lands on a ledge overlooking the New York apartment of a fashion model (Margaret). (In one frame—a kind of "still life"—we see the saucer settled unobtrusively beside a plastic crate and empty, discarded bottles of something called "Perrier.") The saucer contains a tiny alien (who looks something like an eyeball) who has come to Earth hoping to fuel its heroin habit. A German scientist, who has come to the United States to study UFOs, explains to a friend that aliens have been discovered in specific subcultures—among punk rockers, for example. The fashion model and her lesbian roommate (a musician and drug dealer) you tentatively identify (by their shockingly unorthodox clothes, apartment decor, music, drugs, and hairstyles) as belonging to a cult known as New Wave—a sect about whose actual beliefs almost nothing is known.

The alien soon discovers that its heroin need can be satisfied through acquisition of an endorphin produced in the human brain at the moment of sexual climax. In securing its fix, however, the alien kills the individual involved. Unaware of what is going on, the fashion model kills several lovers. "I can't have all these bodies," she complains. "Please, no more bodies." From then on her victims (six all told)—including her former college professor and a man who had previously raped her—instantaneously and conveniently disappear. Since each dies with a tiny arrow in the back of the head, Margaret calls her invisible, admired collaborator "Indian" and comes to think of him as living on the Empire State Building (visible outside her apartment window). When Margaret finally discovers the alien on her roof, she pleads, "You can't leave without me!" and injects herself with heroin as a gift. Transformed into a beam of light, she too disappears, united in a moment of mystical transcendence with her alien savior/lover.

And in the fourth film (a Spanish-language film with subtitles), a strange man named Rantes appears at a hospital for the insane. Though he seems to have no identifiable past, the man claims to be an emissary from another world, one of many sent to Earth and placed in mental hospitals in order to study human beings.

The stranger spends many hours standing, facing southeast, in an almost catatonic trance. To his fellow patients, he becomes a saintly, ascetic figure, capable of a terrible empathy for the human condition.

A sympathetic but personally troubled psychiatrist (Dr. Dennis) engages the stranger in a movie-long dialogue about his past, the doctor's own life, and human beings.

Finally, Dennis's inability to either believe Rantes' story or cure him of his delusion causes him to resort to psychopharmacological treatment. The drugs which he forces upon Rantes destroy his spirit, and he dies a broken man. Whether Rantes was, in fact, an alien or a schizophrenic remains a mystery.

You look again at the titles of the four films: *The Man Who Fell to Earth* (1977), *Repo Man* (1984), *Liquid Sky* (1983), and *Man Facing Southeast* (1987). All four, you recognize, could be classified as "science fiction" films, concerned as they are with alien beings visiting our world—a staple of the genre. And yet they were categorized in the video store as cult films. Why?

For film audiences and other cult groups, cult action is radical bricolage, the play with and reassembly of signifiers from strikingly different cultures and contexts.   —Timothy Corrigan, "Film and the Culture of Cult"

Working on the assumption that even such bizarre cultural phenomena as these films—each, it would seem, completely eccentric—must nevertheless have identifiable historical sources and be part of the intellectual traditions of the civilization that produced them, you use your knowledge of the sister discipline memeotics in order to trace their genealogy.

A special data base in your computer enables you to identify a given cluster of memes exhibited by a religion, a philosophy, a social trend, or, for that matter, a movie, and then to ask that such a configuration's likely historical genesis be identified as specifically as possible. Since *The Man Who Fell to Earth, Repo Man, Liquid Sky,* and *Man Facing Southeast* are "cult films," you naturally seek, as one of your parameters, to identify their cultic origin. You attempt to track down the memes—extreme self-indulgence, world-weariness, alienation (all of which you know to be symptomatic of a troubled period in human history)—espoused in their secret, vatic, almost idiolectic language.

Familiar with the hypothesis of Elias Canetti that any "sudden suppression" of a cult results invariably in the "revenge" of secularization, and conversant with the theory of Max Weber that the triumph of capitalism represents the transformation (and routinization) of the Protestant conception of man's salvation into the "worldly asceticism" of a new economic and social order, and aware too of A. O. Lovejoy's characterization of the common memes of "otherworldly" thinking, whatever its particular manifestation, you begin to wonder what hidden cultural streams, what dormant memes, might have given rise to the strange belief systems—radical alienation, the reenactment of an age-old longing for escape from Earth and eternal union with the heavenly powers, the "otherworldly hedonism," the psychically numb, "far out," unearthly narcissism—portrayed in such cult films.

Along with general observations on the governing ideas that appear to inform both the films and the essential historical facts of their making, you input basic descriptions of the key incidents of each, asking the computer to search its "meme index" for the particular configuration present in the three specimens. And the computer's response is unequivocal. PROBABLE ORIGIN: EARLY CHRISTIAN GNOSTICISM.

What liberates is the knowledge of who we were, what we became; where we were, whereinto we have been thrown; whereto we speed, wherefrom we are redeemed; what birth is, and what rebirth.
—Valentinus the Gnostic, quoted in Jonas, *The Gnostic Religion*

Subsequent research into the early Christian heresy known as Gnosticism supports the validity of the computer's hypothesis. Though seemingly strange bedfellows, their memeotic similarities are unmistakable. The cult films in question, you conclude, can unequivocally be described as gnostic.

The dominant ideas of a culture, Marx taught, are always the ideas of the ruling class. And what the period from circa A.D. 300 to the end of the twentieth century came to think of as Christianity was, of course, only the particular version of the faith, the dominant memes, that survived the competition of the early Christian era to become accepted dogma.[2]

Gnosticism, a "transmundane" religion with a dualistic and transcendental conception of salvation (Jonas 31–32), taught that "the world is a stupendous mistake, created by a foolish or vicious creator-god . . . [a] Demiurge . . . of a very low grade on the celestial hierarchy, himself the result of an error, who thinks that he is supreme" (Godwin 84). "The gnostic God," Hans Jonas writes, "is not merely extra-mundane and supra-mundane, but in his ultimate meaning contra-mundane" (251). In the "mutant thought" (Lacarriere 10) of gnosticism, human beings thus came to seem "planetary detainees," "waging war against the very nature of our presence here on earth" (20, 28).

"The fundamental difference that separated the Gnostics from their contemporaries," Jacques Lacarriere writes, "is that, for them, their native 'soil' is not the earth, but that lost heaven which they keep vividly alive in their memories." They thus believed themselves to be *"autochthons of another world"*:

Hence their feeling of having fallen onto our earth like inhabitants from a distant planet, of having strayed into the wrong galaxy, and their longing to regain their true cosmic homeland. . . . Their uprooting is not merely geographical but planetary. And to treat them as aliens in the political or civic sense—which is what happened—could be nothing but an absurd misunderstanding, like giving a Martian a temporary residence visa. For the Gnostics, all men were in the same condition, although they were the only ones who knew it, and the human community as a whole is implicated in this universal exile, this galactic dispersion that has caused us to be dumped on the mud of planet earth. (29–30)

Despite this radically alienated state, the gnostic was sustained by the faith that above the tyrannical, monstrous demiurge there exists another, truly divine being, and that "humanity is not totally without hope of reaching this true God whom the Demiurge does his best to hide, both from himself and his subjects" (Godwin 84). Without the beyond, Jonas notes, gnosticism would have lapsed into "a hopeless worldly pessimism" (261), surrendering itself to that "universal shipwreck which is the history of matter and of man" (Lacarriere 20).

Thus the great "gnostic drama," enacted on a worldly stage which had become the equivalent of the underworld, came to seem "the metaphysical history of the light exiled from Light, of the life exiled from Life and involved in the world—the history of its alienation and recovery, its 'way' down and through the nether world and up again" (Jonas 50). Motivated by "the conviction that there exists in man something which escapes the curse of this world, a fire, a spark, a light," the gnostics believed that "man's task is to regain his lost homeland by wrenching himself free of the snares and illusions of the real" (Lacarriere 10).

In the midst of this world's "noise," worldly interference prevents the individual from hearing what the gnostics thought of as "the call": that which breaks the spell of the world, awakens the gnostic from sleep, from "intoxication" (Jonas 70–71). Alienation, you learn, was therefore taken to be a mark of excellence, a gnostic sign of grace, though it made the alien "incomprehensible to the creatures of this world" (Jonas 49–50).

And yet the gnostic contempt for the world did not inevitably lead to asceticism. Some gnostics, it is true, preached and practiced the avoidance of "further contamination by the world" (Jonas 46). But others believed that libertinism was the proper response: that the "privilege of absolute freedom" could lead to transcendence. For these "the first task was therefore to use up the substance of evil by combatting it with its own weapons, by practicing what might be called a homeopathic asceticism": "Since we are surrounded and pulverized by evil [these gnostics would say], let us exhaust it by committing it; let us stoke up the forbidden fires in order to burn them out and reduce them to ashes; let us consummate by consuming (and there is only one step, or three letters, between 'consuming' and 'consummating') the inherent corruption of the material world" (Lacarriere 76). For a time, you read with interest, these two seemingly incompatible strains existed side by side.

[Otherworldliness is] the belief that both the genuinely "real" and the truly good are radically antithetic in their essential characteristics to anything to be found in man's natural life, in the ordinary course of human experience, however normal, however intelligent, and however fortunate. The world we now and here know—various, mutable, a perpetual flux of states and relations of things, or an ever-shifting phantasmagoria of thoughts and sensations, each of them lapsing into nonentity in the very next moment of its birth—seems to the otherworldly mind to have no substance in it; the objects of sense and even of empirical scientific knowledge are unstable, contingent, forever breaking down logically into mere relations to other things which when scrutinized prove equally relative and elusive.

—A. O. Lovejoy, *The Great Chain of Being*

For reasons unclear to you, the dormant memes of gnosticism experienced a resurgence in the later twentieth century. According to Oswald Spengler's morphology of historical eras in *The Decline of the West*, the early Christian era and the twentieth century were, after all, strikingly similar. And truly many of its scholars appear to have felt a strong resonance with the movement. Elaine Pagels concludes, "The concerns of gnostic Christians survived only as a suppressed current, like a river driven underground" (179). Similarly, Jonas observes that gnosticism, considered in historical perspective, must be judged "a profoundly new attitude whose heirs at a far remove we are still today" (264–265). Revealingly, all the significant existent scholarship on the sect dates from that time. Judging from your data, gnosticism must have manifested itself as well in the forms of expression of the period. The enigmatic nature of these films must certainly have been decipherable only by those who possessed the necessary "gnosis" to read their hidden messages. Only twentieth-century followers of the cult could have understood *The Man Who Fell to Earth* and *Man Facing Southeast* as gnostic allegories of the entrapment of an "autochthon of another world" by the snares of Earth; only a fellow gnostic would have recognized the tragic poignancy of the plight of each film's "planetary detainee." Only those in the know could have grasped that *Repo Man* and *Liquid Sky* are really stories of the liberating grace of alienation, of the realization of the "divine spark" within, and the heeding of "the call" to surmount the "stupendous mistake" of this world.

Only fellow gnostics would have understood the omnipresence of the ersatz—in food, dress, religion—in the four films as a symbolic description of the world's immersion in illusion, or would have accepted the libertine immersion in drugs and sex of Newton, Otto, and Margaret as legitimate responses (though unsuccessful in Newton's case) to the falsity of the world. Only the insight granted by membership would have made it possible to see that Otto's and Margaret's pursuit of absolute experience has prepared them to detach themselves from "the real." And only a gnostic would have recognized that the dissonant, absurd, illogical, spacy form of the films is in fact intended as a faithful, indeed realistic record of the world's "noise."

What cultural forces brought the memes of gnosticism back to cultural life in the 1970s and 1980s, you cannot say with real validity; the era is too obscure, too much a historical conundrum.

The rational Jeffersonian pursuit of happiness embarked upon in the American Revolution translates into the flaky euphoria of the late twentieth century. Every advance in an objective understanding of the Cosmos and in its technological control further distances the self from the Cosmos precisely in the degree of advance—so that in the end the self becomes a space-bound ghost which roams the very Cosmos it understands perfectly.
—Walker Percy, *Lost in the Cosmos*

Those who have actually lived during the years which witnessed the creation of the cult films which so puzzle this imaginary anthropologist recognize that the mystery of their origin is not so esoteric as he or she might think. For we know what the anthropologist does not: that these films are more mimetic and less symbolic than he or she could imagine. We know that they are films worthy of being put in a time capsule as records of the contemporary psyche. We know that if they are gnostic, it is because we have become, in our spaciness, in "our broken faith with the world," increasingly gnostic ourselves.

In "The New Narcissism," Peter Marin records the following dialogue: "I kept thinking about a conversation I had recently with a man much taken with mysticism and spirituality. He was telling me about his sense of another reality. 'I know there is something outside of me,' he said. 'I can feel it. I know it is there. But what is it?' 'It may not be a mystery,' I said. 'Perhaps it is the world.'" Marin's response surprised his listener, for "he had meant something more magical than that, more exotic and grand, something 'above' rather than all around him"; as Marin concludes,

It had never occurred to him that what might be calling to him from beyond the self were the worlds of community and value, the worlds of history and action—all of them waiting to be entered not as a saint or a mystic, but in a way more difficult still: as a moral man or woman among other persons, with a person's real and complex nature and needs. Those worlds had been closed to him, had receded from consciousness as he had ceased to inhabit them fully or responsibly or lovingly, and so he felt their ghostly presence as something distant and mysterious, as a dream in which he had no actual existence. (49–50)

Such a man is not just an "instinctive semiotician" but, more significant, a gnostic without portfolio, governed by an "otherworldly" mentality yet seemingly without self-knowledge. Is it not this man who rents those black boxes marked "cult films" in the video store?

NOTES

1. "Memeotics" is—or rather will be—the study of the genesis and propagation of ideas, "memes," over time and within and between cultures: the equivalent in intellectual history of genetics in biology. As a future discipline, memeotics will trace back to *The Selfish Gene,* a 1976 book by this field's Gregor Mendel, British sociobiologist Richard Dawkins, who first proposed the existence of "memes"— units of "cultural transmission" or "imitation." While genes "have propagated themselves in the *gene pool* by leaping from body to body via sperm or eggs"— a process going on since the primeval soup, memes (from the Greek root for imitation—"mimesis"—but altered by Dawkins to resonate with "gene" and suggest as well "memory") "propagate themselves in the *meme pool*"—that is, in cultures, "by leaping from brain to brain via a process which, in the broad sense, can be called imitation" (206). Thus the genes of, say, a Socrates or even a Dawkins may have had no recognizable effect on the evolution of the species, while the influence—the "infectivity," as it is sometimes called—of their memes may be pervasive and capable of delineation through memeotic analysis.

2. The severity of the competition, as well as the harshness with which the victors silenced spokesmen for the defeated memes, is recorded in the intellectual fossil record we call etymology. As Owen Barfield observes in *History in English Words,* "The stigma which still attached to the ordinary Greek word for 'choosing' (*heresy*) is a fair indication of the zeal with which the early Popes and Bishops set about expunging from the consciousness of Christendom all memory of its history and all understanding of its external connections" (117).

WORKS CITED

Barfield, Owen. *History in English Words.* London: Faber, 1926.
Canetti, Elias. *Crowds and Power.* Trans. Carol Stewart. New York: Continuum, 1960.
Corrigan, Timothy. "Film and the Culture of Cult." *Wide Angle* 8, nos. 3–4 (1986): 91–99.
Dawkins, Richard. *The Selfish Gene.* New York: Oxford Univ. Press, 1976.
Eco, Umberto. "*Casablanca:* Cult Movies and Intertextual Collage." *SubStance* 47, no. 2 (1985): 3–12.

Eliade, Mircea. *Myth and Reality*. New York: Harper, 1963.

Godwin, Jocelyn. *Mystery Religions in the Ancient World*. New York: Harper, 1981.

Jonas, Hans. *The Gnostic Religion: The Message of the Alien God and the Beginning of Christianity*. Boston: Beacon, 1963.

Knee, Adam. "*Liquid Sky, Repo Man,* and Genre," *Wide Angle* 8, nos. 3–4 (1986): 1–13.

Lacarriere, Jacques. *The Gnostics*. Trans. Nina Rootes. New York: Dutton, 1973.

Lavery, David. "Departure of the Body Snatchers, or the Confessions of a Carbon Chauvinist." *Hudson Review* 39 (1986): 383–404.

———. "Space Boosters: Reflections on the Marketing of Unearthliness." *ETC: A Journal of General Semantics* 41 (1984): 389–397.

Lovejoy, A. O. *The Great Chain of Being: A Study of the History of an Idea*. Cambridge: Harvard Univ. Press, 1964.

Marin, Peter. "The New Narcissism." *Harper's,* October 1975, 45–56.

Pagels, Elaine. *The Gnostic Gospels*. New York: Vintage, 1979.

Percy, Walker. *Lost in the Cosmos: The Last Self-Help Book*. New York: Washington Square, 1983.

Spengler, Oswald. *The Decline of the West*. Ed. Helmut Werner and Arthur Helps. Trans. Charles Francis Atkinson. New York: Knopf, 1962.

Weber, Max. *The Protestant Ethic and the Spirit of Capitalism*. Trans. Talcott Parsons. New York: Scribner's, 1958.

A Selective Cult Film Bibliography

What follows is by no means a comprehensive listing of books and articles on the subject of the cult film. I have, for example, omitted numerous studies of individual film stars, many books that offer a behind-the-scenes look at the making of a particular film, and a great number of fan-oriented pieces offering background comments on the *Star Trek* films and TV series, *The Rocky Horror Picture Show,* and so forth, mainly because they are too numerous to list and would make this particular bibliography more cumbersome to consult. It does, however, include the major commentaries on the subject, and it is a highly representative list of the sorts of examinations the cult phenomenon has inspired.

Affron, Charles. *Star Acting: Gish, Garbo, and Davis.* New York: Dutton, 1977.

Anobile, Richard J., ed. *Casablanca.* New York: Avon, 1974.

Aufderheide, Pat. "The Domestication of John Waters." *American Film* 15, no. 7 (1990): 32–37.

Austin, Bruce A. "Portrait of a Cult Film Audience: *The Rocky Horror Picture Show.*" *Journal of Communications* 31 (1981): 450–465.

Barker, Martin, ed. *The Video Nasties: Freedom and Censorship in the Media.* London: Pluto Press, 1984.

Behlmer, Rudy. *America's Favorite Movies: Behind the Scenes.* New York: Ungar, 1982.

———. *Inside Warner Bros.: 1935–1951.* New York: Viking, 1985.

Biskind, Peter. *Seeing Is Believing: How Hollywood Taught Us to Stop Worrying and Love the Fifties.* New York: Pantheon, 1983.

Braudy, Leo. *The Frenzy of Renown: Fame and Its History.* New York: Oxford Univ. Press, 1986.

Burchill, Julie. *Girls on Film.* New York: Pantheon, 1986.

Cagin, Seth, and Philip Dray. *Hollywood Films of the Seventies: Sex, Drugs, Violence, Rock 'n' Roll, and Politics.* New York: Harper, 1984.

Cawelti, John G. *Adventure, Mystery, and Romance: Formula Stories as Art and Popular Culture.* Chicago: Univ. of Chicago Press, 1976.

————. "The Question of Popular Genres." *Journal of Popular Film and Television* 13, no. 2 (1985): 55–61.

Chase, Donald. "The Cult Movie Comes of Age: An Interview with George A. Romero and Richard P. Rubinstein." *Millimeter* 7, no. 10 (1979): 200–211.

Chute, David. "Outlaw Cinema: Its Rise and Fall." *Film Comment* 19, no. 5 (1983): 9–11, 13, 15.

————. "Still Waters." *Film Comment* 17, no. 3 (1981): 26–32.

Corrigan, Timothy. "Film and the Culture of Cult." *Wide Angle* 8, nos. 3–4 (1986): 91–99. (Revised version is reprinted in this volume.)

Costello, John. *Virtue under Fire: How World War II Changed Our Social and Sexual Attitudes*. Boston: Little, Brown, 1985.

Dick, Bernard F. *The Star Spangled Screen: The American World War II Film*. Lexington: Univ. of Kentucky Press, 1985.

Doherty, Thomas. "The Exploitation Film as History: *Wild in the Streets*." *Literature/Film Quarterly* 12, no. 3 (1984): 186–194.

Donnelly, William. "Love and Death in *Casablanca*." In *Persistence of Vision*, ed. Joseph McBride, 103–107. Madison: Wisconsin Film Society Press, 1968.

Dowdy, Andrew. *The Films of the Fifties: The American State of Mind*. New York: William Morrow, 1973.

Dyer, Richard. *Stars*. London: British Film Institute, 1979.

Eco, Umberto. "*Casablanca*: Cult Movies and Intertextual Collage." *SubStance* 47, no. 2 (1985): 3–12.

Francisco, Charles. *You Must Remember This: The Filming of "Casablanca."* Englewood Cliffs: Prentice-Hall, 1980.

Goldberg, Joe. "The Death of Sam Spade." *Evergreen Review* 7 (1963): 107–116.

Grant, Barry, ed. *Film Genre Reader*. Austin: Univ. of Texas Press, 1986.

————, ed. *Planks of Reason: Essays on the Horror Film*. Metuchen: Scarecrow, 1984.

Gray, Tony. "Those Lovely Ladies." *American Classic Screen* 7, no. 1 (1983): 19–22, 34.

Green, Gary. "'The Happiest of Happy Accidents'? A Reevaluation of *Casablanca*." *Smithsonian Studies in American Art* 1, no. 2 (1987): 3–14.

Greenberg, Harvey R. *The Movies on Your Mind*. New York: Dutton, 1975.

Greenspun, Roger. "Carrie, and Sally and Leatherface among the Film Buffs." *Film Comment* 13, no. 1 (1977): 14–17.

Haas, Charlie. "Headsploitation." *Film Comment* 19, no. 3 (1983): 67–71.

Haver, Ronald. "Finally, the Truth about *Casablanca*." *American Film* 1, no. 8 (1976): 11–16.

Hebdige, Dick. *Subculture: The Meaning of Style*. London: Methuen, 1979.

Henkin, Bill. *The Rocky Horror Picture Show Book*. New York: Hawthorn/Dutton, 1979.

Hoberman, J., and Jonathan Rosenbaum. *Midnight Movies*. New York: Harper, 1983.

Javna, John. *Cult TV*. New York: St. Martin's, 1985.

Jenkins, Henry, III. "*Star Trek* Rerun, Reread, Rewritten: Fan Fantasy as Textual Poaching." *Critical Studies in Mass Communications* 5, no. 2 (1988): 85–107.

Kellman, Steven G. "Everybody Comes to Roquentin's: *La Nausée* and *Casablanca*." *Mosaic* 16, nos. 1–2 (1983): 103–112.

Kennedy, X. J. "Who Killed King Kong?" In *Focus on the Horror Film*, ed. Roy Huss and T. J. Ross, 106–109. Englewood Cliffs: Prentice-Hall, 1972.

Knee, Adam. "*Liquid Sky, Repo Man*, and Genre." *Wide Angle* 8, nos. 3–4 (1986): 101–113.

Koch, Howard. *As Time Goes By*. New York: Harcourt, Brace, 1979.

———. *"Casablanca": Script and Legend*. Woodstock: Overlook Press, 1973.

———. "Notes on the Production of *Casablanca*" and "Excerpts from the Original Treatment." In *Persistence of Vision*, ed. Joseph McBride, 93–100. Madison: Wisconsin Film Society Press, 1968.

Loud, Lance. "'The Virgin Mary is a Chicken . . .' and Other Thoughts of Surrealist Director Alejandro Jodorowsky." *American Film* 15, no. 6 (1990): 80.

Mackey, Mary. "The Meat Hook Mama, the Nice Girl, and Butch Cassidy in Drag." *Jump Cut* 14 (1977): 12–14.

Marsden, Michael T., John G. Nachbar, and Sam L. Grogg, eds. *Movies as Artifacts: Cultural Criticism of Popular Film*. Chicago: Nelson-Hall, 1982.

McCarthy, Todd, and Charles Flynn, eds. *Kings of the B's: Working within the Hollywood System*. New York: Dutton, 1975.

McCarty, John. *Splatter Movies*. New York: St. Martin's, 1984.

Michael, Paul, ed. *The Great American Movie Book*. Englewood Cliffs: Prentice-Hall, 1980.

Middleton, David. "*Casablanca:* The Function of Myth in a Popular Classic." *New Orleans Review* 13, no. 1 (1986): 11–18.

Modleski, Tania. *Loving with a Vengeance: Mass-Produced Fantasies for Women*. London: Methuen, 1985.

Morris, George. "Just Folks: John Waters." *Take One* 6, no. 4 (1978): 21–23.

Morton, Jim, ed. *Incredibly Strange Movies*. San Francisco: Re/Search Press, 1986.

Nichols, Bill. *Ideology and the Image*. Bloomington: Indiana Univ. Press, 1981.

Palmer, William J. *The Films of the Seventies: A Social History*. Metuchen: Scarecrow, 1987.

Peary, Danny. *Cult Movies*. New York: Delta, 1981.

———. *Cult Movies 2*. New York: Delta, 1983.

Rapping, Elayne. "Hollywood's Youth Cult Films." *Cineaste* 16, nos. 1–2 (1987): 14–19.

Ray, Robert B. *A Certain Tendency of the Hollywood Cinema, 1930–1980*. Princeton: Princeton Univ. Press, 1985.

Rosenzweig, Sidney. *"Casablanca" and Other Major Films of Michael Curtiz*. Ann Arbor: UMI Research Press, 1982.

Samuels, Stuart. *Midnight Movies*. New York: Macmillan, 1983.

Sarris, Andrew. *Confessions of a Cultist: On the Cinema, 1955–1969*. New York: Simon & Schuster, 1970.

Schickel, Richard. "Bogart." *Film Comment* 22, no. 3 (1986): 33–44, 46.

Schiff, Stephen. "The Repeatable Experience." *Film Comment* 18, no. 2 (1982): 34–36.

Scott, Tony. "Romero: An Interview with the Director of *Night of the Living Dead*." *Cinefantastique* 2, no. 3 (1973): 8–15.

Shales, Tom. *Legends: Remembering America's Greatest Stars*. New York: Random House, 1989.

Siegel, Mark. "*The Rocky Horror Picture Show:* More Than a Lip Service." *Science Fiction Studies* 7 (1980): 305–318.

Sitney, P. Adams, ed. *Film Culture Reader*. New York: Praeger, 1970.

Skorman, Richard. *Off-Hollywood Movies: A Film Lover's Guide*. New York: Harmony Books, 1989.

Sontag, Susan. "Notes on 'Camp.'" In *Against Interpretation*, 277–293. New York: Dell, 1966.

Spoto, Donald. *Camerado: Hollywood and the American Man*. New York: New American Library, 1978.

Springer, Alice. "Sell It Again, Sam." *American Film* 8, no. 5 (1983): 50–52, 54–55.

Strout, Andrea. "In the Midnight Hour." *Film Comment* 6, no. 4 (1981): 34–37, 72, 74.

Telotte, J. P. "*Badlands* and the Souvenir Drive." *Western Humanities Review* 40, no. 2 (1986): 101–115.

———. "*Casablanca* and the Larcenous Cult Film." *Michigan Quarterly Review* 26, no. 2 (1987): 357–368. (Revised version is reprinted in this volume.)

Thomson, David. *America in the Dark: Hollywood and the Gift of Unreality*. New York: William Morrow, 1977.

Waldman, Diane. "From Midnight Shows to Marriage Vows: Women, Exploitation, and Exhibition." *Wide Angle* 6, no. 2 (1984): 40–48.

Waller, Gregory A., ed. *American Horrors: Essays on the Modern American Horror Film*. Urbana: Univ. of Illinois Press, 1987.

———. *The Living and the Undead: From Stoker's* Dracula *to Romero's* Dawn of the Dead. Urbana: Univ. of Illinois Press, 1986.

Waters, John. *Crackpot: The Obsessions of John Waters*. New York: Macmillan, 1983.

———. *Shock Value: A Tasteful Book about Bad Taste*. New York: Dell, 1981.

Williams, Carol Traynor. *The Dream beside Me: The Movies and the Children of the Forties*. Rutherford: Associated Univ. Press, 1980.

Williams, Tony. "American Cinema in the '70s: Family Horror." *Movie* 27/28 (1981): 117–126.

———. "Cohen on Cohen." *Sight and Sound* 53, no. 1 (1983–1984): 21–25.

———. "Horror in the Family." *Focus on Film* 36 (1980): 14–20.

Wood, Robin, ed. *The American Nightmare*. Toronto: Festival of Festivals Press, 1979.

———. *Hollywood from Vietnam to Reagan*. New York: Columbia Univ. Press, 1986.

———. "Leavis, Marxism and Film Culture." *CineAction!* 8 (1987): 3–13.

———. "Neglected Nightmares." *Film Comment* 16, no. 2 (1980): 24–32.

Yakir, Dan. "Morning Becomes Romero." *Film Comment* 15, no. 3 (1979): 60–65.

Notes on Contributors

James Card, professor of English at Old Dominion University, is the author of *An Anatomy of "Penelope"* and of several articles on film appearing in *Literature/Film Quarterly*.

Timothy Corrigan is associate professor of English at Temple University. His publications on film and literature include the seminal study of contemporary German film, *New German Cinema*.

Allison Graham is associate professor of communications and director of the Women's Studies Program at Memphis State University. The author of *Lindsay Anderson*, she has edited an issue of *Film Criticism* and is currently working on a book about nostalgia in film.

Barry K. Grant is associate professor of film and popular culture and head of fine arts at Brock University. He has edited several volumes of film criticism, including *Film Genre Reader* and *Planks of Reason: Essays on the Horror Film*, and has published articles in such journals as *Persistence of Vision*, *Journal of Popular Film and Television*, and *Literature/Film Quarterly*.

Wade Jennings, professor of English at Ball State University, is the author of various articles on film and literature and of a forthcoming volume on Judy Garland.

Bruce Kawin is professor of English and film studies at the University of Colorado at Boulder. His first book, *Telling It Again and Again: Repetition in Literature and Film*, has been reissued by the University Press of Colorado. His other books include *Faulkner and Film*, *Mindscreen*, *The Mind of the Novel*, and the introductory textbook *How Movies Work*.

David Lavery, associate professor of communication at Memphis State University, has written essays for such journals as *Georgia Review, Hudson Review, Film Criticism,* and *Literature/Film Quarterly.* His study of American culture's fascination with space, *Late for the Sky: Earth, Space, and the Destiny of Man,* is forthcoming.

T. J. Ross is professor of English at Fairleigh Dickinson University, where he teaches courses in modern literature and film genres. The editor of *Film and the Liberal Arts* and *Focus on the Horror Film,* he has published articles on film and popular culture in *New Republic, Film Quarterly, Quarterly Review of Film Studies,* and elsewhere, and he is a film reviewer for New Jersey Cablevision.

Gaylyn Studlar is assistant professor of film and theater studies at Emory University. The author of *In the Realm of Pleasure: Von Sternberg, Dietrich, and the Masochistic Aesthetic,* she has also written on feminist and psychoanalytic film theory for *Movies and Methods II, Film Quarterly,* and *Quarterly Review of Film Studies.* She is currently working on a book about feminist reception theory and the representation of gender in contemporary American cinema.

J. P. Telotte, associate professor of English at Georgia Tech, has written *Dreams of Darkness: Fantasy and the Films of Val Lewton* and *Voices in the Dark: The Narrative Patterns of Film Noir.* Coeditor of *Post Script,* he also serves on the editorial boards of *Literature/Film Quarterly* and *Film Criticism.*

Larry Vonalt is associate professor of English at the University of Missouri—Rolla. His articles on modern literature have appeared in such journals as *Sewanee Review, Parnassus,* and *Critique: Studies in Contemporary Fiction.*

Gregory A. Waller, author of *The Living and the Undead* and editor of *American Horrors,* is associate professor of English at the University of Kentucky. His articles on film and popular culture have appeared in such journals as *Film Criticism* and *Journal of Popular Film and Television.*

Robert Wood is associate professor of English at Georgia Tech. He has published on drama and film in *South Atlantic Review, Shakespeare Quarterly, Literature/Film Quarterly, Post Script,* and elsewhere. He is currently completing a book on *Hamlet.*

Index